Task-Based English Language Teaching in the Digital Age

Advances in Digital Language Learning and Teaching

Series Editors: Michael Thomas, Liverpool John Moores University, UK; Mark Peterson, Kyoto University, Japan; Mark Warschauer, University of California – Irvine, USA

Today's language educators need support to understand how their learners are changing and the ways technology can be used to aid their teaching and learning strategies. The movement toward different modes of language learning – from presence-based to autonomous as well as blended and fully online modes – requires different skill sets such as e-moderation and new ways of designing and developing language learning tasks in the digital age. Theoretical studies that include practical case studies and high quality empirical studies incorporating critical perspectives are necessary to move the field further. This series is committed to providing such an outlet for high quality work on digital language learning and teaching. Volumes in the series focus on a number of areas including but not limited to:

- task-based learning and teaching approaches utilizing technology
- language-learner creativity
- e-moderation and teaching languages online
- blended language learning
- designing courses for online and distance language learning
- mobile-assisted language learning
- autonomous language learning, both in and outside of formal educational contexts
- the use of web 2.0/social media technologies
- immersive and virtual language-learning environments
- digital game-based language learning
- language educator professional development with digital technologies
- teaching language skills with technologies

Enquiries about the series can be made by contacting the series editors: Michael Thomas (m.thomas@ljmu.ac.uk), Mark Peterson (tufsmp@yahoo.com) and Mark Warschauer (markw@uci.edu).

Also available in the series:

Autonomous Language Learning with Technology: Beyond the Classroom,
Chun Lai
Autonomy and Foreign Language Learning in a Virtual Learning Environment,
Miranda Hamilton
Digital Games and Language Learning: Theory, Development and Implementation, edited by Mark Peterson, Kasumi Yamazaki and Michael Thomas
Language Teacher Education and Technology: Approaches and Practices,
edited by Jeong-Bae Son and Scott Windeatt
Online Teaching and Learning: Sociocultural Perspectives,
edited by Carla Meskill
Task-Based Language Learning in a Real-World Digital Environment: The European Digital Kitchen, edited by Paul Seedhouse
Teacher Education in Computer-Assisted Language Learning: A Sociocultural and Linguistic Perspective, Euline Cutrim Schmid
Teaching Languages with Screen Media: Pedagogical Reflections,
edited by Carmen Herrero and Marta F. Suarez
Teaching Languages with Technology: Communicative Approaches to Interactive Whiteboard Use, edited by Euline Cutrim Schmid and Shona Whyte
Technology-Enhanced Language Teaching and Learning: Lessons from the Covid-19 Pandemic, edited by Karim Sadeghi, Michael Thomas and Farah Ghaderi
Video Enhanced Observation for Language Teaching: Reflection and Professional Development, edited by Paul Seedhouse
WorldCALL: Sustainability and Computer-Assisted Language Learning,
edited by Ana María Gimeno Sanz, Mike Levy, Françoise Blin and David Barr

Task-Based English Language Teaching in the Digital Age

Perspectives from Secondary Education

Valentina Morgana

BLOOMSBURY ACADEMIC
LONDON • NEW YORK • OXFORD • NEW DELHI • SYDNEY

BLOOMSBURY ACADEMIC
Bloomsbury Publishing Plc
50 Bedford Square, London, WC1B 3DP, UK
1385 Broadway, New York, NY 10018, USA
29 Earlsfort Terrace, Dublin 2, Ireland

BLOOMSBURY, BLOOMSBURY ACADEMIC and the Diana logo are trademarks of
Bloomsbury Publishing Plc

First published in Great Britain 2023
This paperback edition published 2025

Copyright © Valentina Morgana, 2023

Valentina Morgana has asserted her right under the Copyright, Designs and
Patents Act, 1988, to be identified as Author of this work.

For legal purposes the Acknowledgements on p. xiii constitute
an extension of this copyright page.

Cover design by James Watson
Cover image © shutterstock.com

All rights reserved. No part of this publication may be reproduced or
transmitted in any form or by any means, electronic or mechanical, including
photocopying, recording, or any information storage or retrieval system,
without prior permission in writing from the publishers.

Bloomsbury Publishing Plc does not have any control over, or responsibility for,
any third-party websites referred to or in this book. All internet addresses given in
this book were correct at the time of going to press. The author and publisher regret
any inconvenience caused if addresses have changed or sites have ceased to
exist, but can accept no responsibility for any such changes.

A catalogue record for this book is available from the British Library.

A catalog record for this book is available from the Library of Congress.

ISBN:	HB:	978-1-3502-8801-0
	PB:	978-1-3502-8805-8
	ePDF:	978-1-3502-8802-7
	eBook:	978-1-3502-8803-4

Series: Bloomsbury Advances in Digital Language Learning and Teaching

Typeset by Integra Software Services Pvt. Ltd.

To find out more about our authors and books visit www.bloomsbury.com
and sign up for our newsletters.

Contents

List of Figures	xi
List of Tables	xii
Acknowledgements	xiii

Introduction	1
1. Why TBLT and technology?	1
2. The role of the teacher	2
3. Language awareness	3
4. Research gaps in TBLT and technology	4
5. TBLT and the four skills	5
6. Mobile-Assisted Language Learning (MALL) and TBLT	6
7. Organization and summary of the chapters	7

Part 1 From Standard to Digital Task-Based Language Teaching

1	From Task to Process: Key Concepts in TBLT	13
	1. Introduction	13
	2. Historical background	14
	3. Task-based approaches	15
	4. The key concepts of TBLT	16
	5. Designing a task-based curriculum: main steps	20
	6. Planning a task-based lesson	21
	7. Issues in TBLT	22
	8. Tasks for assessment	25
2	Theoretical Approaches in Task-Based Language Teaching	27
	1. Introduction	27
	2. Cognitive-interaction theories	28
	3. Sociocultural theories	34
	4. Conclusion: are cognitive and sociocultural perspectives incompatible?	38

3	Moving Forward: A Framework for Technology and TBLT	41
	1. Technology, CALL and TBLT: the apparent revolution	41
	2. Adapting TBLT to digital contexts	42
	3. Tasks in technology-mediated TBLT	43
	4. Pedagogic language tasks and pedagogic technology tasks	44
	5. Technology-mediated TBLT: a new framework	46
	6. Integrating TBLT and technology: key challenges	48
	7. Technology-mediated TBLT in the literature	49
	8. A new framework for new learners?	53
	9. The role of the teacher	54
	10. The technology-mediated TBLT framework in this volume	54
	11. Conclusions	55
	Appendix 1	56
	Appendix 2	59
	Appendix 3	59
	Appendix 4	60
	Appendix 5	60

Part 2 Technology-Mediated TBLT in Practice

4	Task-Based English Language Teaching in Secondary Education	63
	1. TBLT in secondary education	63
	2. Challenges in implementing TBLT in secondary education	64
	3. Technology and TBLT: a step ahead	67
	4. TBLT across different secondary school educational contexts	68
	5. The context of this volume	71
	6. The Italian secondary school system	72
5	TBLT, Technology and English Writing Skills	75
	1. Introduction	75
	2. Literature review	76
	3. Methodology	81
	4. Findings	86
	5. Discussion	89
	6. Pedagogical implications	90
	7. Conclusion	90
	Appendix 1	91
	Appendix 2	92

6	**TBLT, Technology and English Reading Skills**	93
	1. Introduction	93
	2. Literature review	94
	3. Research questions	97
	4. Methodology	98
	5. Analysis	103
	6. Results	103
	7. Discussion	107
	8. Conclusions	109
	Appendix 1	110
7	**TBLT, Technology and English Listening Skills**	113
	1. Introduction	113
	2. Review of the research	114
	3. Methodology	117
	4. Analysis	121
	5. Qualitative results	122
	6. Discussion	126
	7. Conclusion	128
8	**TBLT, Technology and English Speaking Skills**	131
	1. Introduction	131
	2. Research questions	132
	3. Theoretical underpinnings	132
	4. Technology mediation in TBLT and CALL research	133
	5. Literature review	133
	6. Methodology	136
	7. Procedures	138
	8. Data collection	140
	9. Analysis	140
	10. Results	141
	11. Discussion	144
	12. Implication for teachers	147
	13. Conclusions	147
	Appendix 1	149
	Appendix 2	150
	Appendix 3	150

9	Conclusions: The Future of TBLT and Technology in Secondary Education	153
	1. Introduction	153
	2. Summary of key findings	156
	3. Implications for practice: EFL teachers	161
	4. Implications for policy makers and institutions	163
	5. Contributions	164
	6. Limitations of the study	165
	7. Future directions for technology-mediated TBLT in secondary education	166

References	168
Index	188

Figures

1.1	Task classroom implementation cycle	21
3.1	Example of technology-mediated TBLT task planning	45

Tables

5.1	Research design	83
5.2	Results and descriptive statistics of the grammar pre-test	87
5.3	Results and descriptive statistics of the grammar post-test	87
5.4	Comparisons between focus on content and focus on form group for accuracy and complexity ($N = 20$)	88
6.1	A sample technology-mediated TBLT lesson focused on reading	101
6.2	A sample EFL lesson activity for the control group	102
6.3	Descriptive statistics of the vocabulary pre- and post-test	104
6.4	Descriptive statistics for Summative Assessment Test – Grammar	106
6.5	Descriptive statistics for Summative Assessment Test – Vocabulary	106
6.6	Descriptive statistics for Summative Assessment Test – Reading Comprehension	107
7.1	Main Project outline	119
7.2	Post-test t-test results for the Focus on Vocabulary and Focus on Language groups	126
8.1	Research design	137
8.2	t-test results for Overall Global Achievement score for B1 Preliminary Speaking paper at pre-, post- and delayed post-test	142
8.3	Descriptive statistics Speaking Subskills – Pronunciation (Post-test)	142
8.4	Descriptive statistics Speaking Subskills – Discourse Management	143

Acknowledgements

I would like to thank all the Italian secondary school students for their time, dedication and enthusiastic participation in the case studies. I am particularly grateful to the EFL teachers for their trust in my vision of this research study and for the time they spent studying, discussing and planning together.

My gratitude also goes to the series editors and reviewers for their in-depth comments on the manuscript. I am particularly grateful to Michael Thomas for his immense support and encouragement.

Introduction

1. Why TBLT and technology?

My practical experience of task-based language teaching (TBLT) and technology in secondary schools started about ten years ago when Apple iPads were widely distributed to lower and upper secondary schools in the north of Italy through a 'technology for schools' project funded by 'Regione Lombardia'. Tablets were organized in classroom sets and teachers were strongly encouraged to make use of them in their lessons. The project was meant to generate innovation in secondary school education practices. However, the delivery of technological hardware was not accompanied by any teacher development courses and innovation did not happen. As a language teacher in a school, I was expected to be the first to implement new practices in my classroom. I suppose the link that my colleagues made was mostly related to English being the language of the internet. The assumption was: easy access to EFL content online, easy English language teaching practices. At the time, I wished they were right. They were not.

Since then, I have constantly investigated and implemented TBLT practices inside the classroom (as a teacher) and beyond it (as a researcher). TBLT is a language-teaching approach focused on what learners need to 'do' with the language rather than on what they need to 'know' about it (Norris, 2009). In TBLT the focus is mainly on communication and meaning, although attention to form is not neglected (Ellis et al., 2019). The increasing use of computers and the internet for language learning and teaching has occurred in lockstep with the emergence of TBLT in language education (Park, 2012) and the potential synergies between computer-assisted language learning (CALL), second language acquisition (SLA) and TBLT immediately seemed very pertinent (Chapelle, 1998; Chapelle, 2001, 2009). The question of whether the TBLT methodology is appropriate for secondary school settings has been widely discussed (see for example, Lai, 2015) and is still an open debate. With the growing research interest in the use of computers and mobile technologies in formal language learning, a lively debate continues on whether the integration of technology and tasks is beneficial for intermediate and lower intermediate school learners. At the same time, technology-mediated TBLT practices are becoming increasingly popular.

Van den Branden et al. (2009) recognized how changes in language education are often responses to new technologies, so just as language laboratories changed the way EFL was approached, the same is probably now happening with mobile devices in language education. This book has been designed to help both teachers and researchers implement technology-mediated TBLT practices in secondary education. As research often fails to provide meaningful examples of classroom practice with regard to specific contexts, this volume focuses on the specific context of secondary state school EFL classrooms. Through a series of narratives of four case studies the book addresses some of the issues raised in TBLT such as the role of focus on form. The aim is to provide teachers and researchers with opportunities to reflect on their practice and observe how TBLT can be implemented in digital and blended settings to foster language acquisition among young adolescent learners.

The main idea behind the volume is that TBLT is not a monolithic approach to language (Ellis et al., 2019) and it can be applied in different educational contexts with different designs. As such, with this book I would like to shed light on TBLT practices in technology-mediated secondary EFL classrooms by presenting practical case studies supported by research and literature.

What makes TBLT and therefore, technology-mediated TBLT so appealing is the fact that the approach has many variations and possible applications. It is tremendously flexible and can fit a variety of different formal and informal contexts. It is also particularly relevant nowadays when the boundaries between formal and informal learning are blurring and even the classroom is no longer meant to be a fixed and static place, but a mobile educational environment where the student and the device are flexible in terms of tools, concepts and cultural understanding.

2. The role of the teacher

Increasingly, teachers are invited to innovate their teaching methods using mobile devices without having any proper training in this, with the result that they tend to just 'add' technological activities instead of 'integrating' them into their standard teaching. In addition, they lack systematic professional development and this leads to a very basic use of computers and mobile devices for language learning. As East (2021) has recently pointed out, if what researchers discover does not really happen in class and teachers do not feel comfortable in integrating technology and tasks, then there is a need to further explain how to do this. As often happens with major changes, there are steps which can be taken to move towards innovative practices. Regardless of the cultural context in which they operate, secondary school teachers often share the same concerns about a TBLT approach (Lai, 2015). One of these relates to explicit grammar teaching and language learning as they see the TBLT approach as strongly focused on communication and students therefore potentially having difficulties with language forms. As a result, teachers continue to work with the standard presentation-practice-production (PPP) methodology as they feel secure in this.

Although TBLT is a student-centred approach, the role of the teacher is crucial. After all it is the teacher that 'brings TBLT to life' (Van den Branden, 2006) by designing and implementing effective tasks for students. To overcome some teachers' misconceptions, teachers need to be aware of the key principles of TBLT and also to be fully involved in the design and implementation of technology-mediated practices. Some questions remain: are teachers really secure with the PPP approach? Can technology-mediated TBLT help them move from a standard PPP approach to a dynamic and reliable TBLT approach? The case studies in this volume attempt to answer these questions by providing real-life classroom examples of the integration of tasks and technology. The studies presented here are also useful for reflecting on the different dynamics and issues faced by teachers in implementing TBLT in digital contexts.

3. Language awareness

This volume has been designed for researchers and language teachers and is intended as a step towards meeting learners' and teachers' needs in the context of secondary education. One of the most significant needs of teachers and language learners, particularly in the Italian school system, is to be aware of the language features they can use to communicate effectively, so they are often drawn to focus on form activities. Whilst I recognize that the pure TBLT approach does not allow for language-awareness activities, I believe that tasks, and specifically digital tasks, can be designed to foster communication and language awareness (although not necessarily grammatical awareness). In this respect, the studies illustrated in this volume are more oriented towards a task-based curriculum that includes both focused and unfocused tasks (Ellis, 2003; Ellis et al., 2019).

This is not intended as a return to a structural approach but aims to redirect students' attention to linguistic forms that are either essential or very useful in performing a particular task.

4. Research gaps in TBLT and technology

The planning and design of the studies presented in this volume have been informed by the TBLT research agenda recently suggested by Smith and González-Lloret (2020). The agenda identified a series of research areas and tasks in the field of technology-mediated TBLT that need to be addressed to move the field forward. Some of these research tasks are discussed in this volume. These are:

1) What is the effective role of technology in facilitating the completion of a task? That is, why are certain technologies supportive of specific tasks and others not?
    The technologies used in the studies in this volume have a specific role in the completion of the tasks.
2) Selecting the technology for the task-based technology-mediated research in accordance with the specific teaching and learning context in which it will be implemented (Smith & González-Lloret, 2020). The technology used in the secondary school where the case studies took place was mainly related to mobile devices and Google applications. This strongly influenced the design and implementation of the TBLT tasks. In order to maximize the benefits for learners, technologies need to be appropriate for the language activities proposed by the teacher.
3) Learners are not always aware of all the possibilities technologies offer and sometimes do not make use of them (Smith & González-Lloret, 2020).
    The applications and devices used for the case studies presented here have been scrupulously explored by the teachers so as to inform learners about them. Students' use of these technologies has been constantly observed by the teacher. In the case study on listening, students were also interviewed about their practices in order to observe any link between behaviours and outcomes.

Smith and González-Lloret (2020) conclude with an important consideration about the digital divide and our role, as researchers and teachers, in equipping learners with a broader understanding of issues of social justice and intercultural communication. I believe that young adolescents need to be informed about the opportunities technology-mediated learning provides to connect language learners and make cross-cultural learning available to more students around the globe.

5. TBLT and the four skills

As digital and mobile learning environments are becoming more common in secondary school language educational settings, I chose to implement a technology-mediated task-based (TBLT) approach for the design and implementation of tasks focused on the four skills: reading, writing, listening and speaking. TBLT has been implemented in different settings and with different methodologies around the world (see for example, van den Branden & van Gorp, 2021). As stated above, the main idea behind this approach is the focus on what people, and learners in particular, need to be able to *do* with the language, and therefore what kind of tasks should be introduced in an EFL curriculum. The TBLT approach has been chosen particularly because of two key assumptions: (1) exposure to large amounts of high-quality input is necessary for language learning and (2) learning a language is enhanced by a meaningful, and purposeful use of the language (Solares, 2014). In his book on task-based language teaching, Nunan (2004) identified seven key principles behind the TBLT classroom design. These are:

1. Scaffolding: students need to have a supporting framework in order to activate learning.
2. Task dependency: each new task should be built upon the previous, so that students can learn step by step.
3. Recycling: to master a specific language function students need to use and re-use it in various situations.
4. Active learning: students should use the language actively to maximize their learning.
5. Integration: tasks should be able to teach the link between communicative, grammatical and semantic meaning.
6. Reproduction to creation: students should be taught to move from rehearsal to creative production of a specific function.
7. Reflection: students should be aware of their learning process.

The reading, writing, listening and speaking tasks designed for this study were inspired by these principles. Moreover, the participants in the study were also preparing for the Cambridge B1 Preliminary certificate examination, and therefore some of the tasks analysed were adapted from the Cambridge ESOL general guidelines. The Cambridge Preliminary is an external language examination at B1 level of the Common European Framework of Reference for Languages (CEFR). It is a test of the different areas of language ability and includes four papers around the four language skills of reading, writing, listening and speaking. Tasks are often organized reflecting Nunan's key principles. For example, writing tasks are built upon each other creating a sequence of activities that guides students' learning; vocabulary is often recycled in the different papers (reading, listening etc.) and students are asked to use the language functionally. The exam can be either computer- or paper-based. Depending on how a secondary school manages the process, learners can either follow a specific preparation course as an extra-curricular activity or it is included in the school's annual English programme, as was the case in the school involved in this study. For the speaking paper, learners perform a face-to-face interaction with another learner while two examiners act as facilitators. The writing paper requires learners to be able to write two pieces of writing of different text types, such as reports, articles, reviews and essays. For this reason, teachers model the writing tasks to provide learners with practice of the text types required for the examination.

6. Mobile-Assisted Language Learning (MALL) and TBLT

The technological devices used in the case studies presented in this volume are mainly mobile devices (e.g. smartphones, tablets and new generation laptops). Students were often provided with a classroom set of Google new generation laptops (Chromebooks). These portable devices allowed students to connect to the Google for Education suite and access all the applications needed to perform the tasks. The use of mobile devices to assist foreign language learning has been a reality for almost twenty years now (Kukulska-Hulme, 2006). In particular, the studies in this volume look at how mobile devices may have an impact on learners' development of the four English language skills in a secondary school environment in Italy. Productive skills are particularly challenging for students since these skills require them to internalize their learning and manipulate it. The main question that guided the studies in this volume is whether mobile technologies, such as Chromebooks, allow educators and students to do things in second language education settings that they could not otherwise do, from a task-based language teaching and learning perspective. Mobile language learning has its own peculiarities. According to Naismith et al. (2004), mobile language learning brings the online dimension of learning to the face-to-face setting. Thanks to easy access to Wi-Fi networks inside and outside school, learners and teachers can have access to the internet whenever and wherever they need. They can search for content, access teachers' and students' online notes, read books, share links and contribute to an ongoing lesson (Kukulska-Hulme, 2012). They can also access content offline through the increasing number of mobile apps that provide this type of service. The use of mobile devices and laptops in the language classroom provides learners with technological support in addition to the standard teacher-learner support. As explained in Godwin-Jones (2017) thanks to online and offline learning tools, students can correct, modify and refine their work. The use of the spelling and grammar checker, for example, provides them with immediate feedback. It is suggested that checking their language assignments helps keep learners engaged with their task (Gabarre et al., 2014).

I believe the two fields of Mobile-Assisted Language Learning (MALL) and TBLT are strongly interrelated and this interconnection should be further investigated for various reasons. Firstly, the research literature on MALL indicates that many studies have focused on a descriptive analysis of specific language-teaching applications, and in particular on those focusing on listening and reading skills (Chen & Chung, 2008; Chih-Kai & Hsu, 2011; Huang et al., 2012; Sandberg et al., 2011). However, Chang and Hsu (2011) observed that in addition to improving reading comprehension, future studies should also consider investigating speaking, listening and writing proficiency functions. Some of the studies presented in this volume attempt to address this gap by analysing the use of mobile devices and apps for listening, speaking and writing tasks. The four case studies focus on the development of reading, writing, listening and speaking skills supported by the use of Chromebooks or other mobile devices, and they are intended to inform both MALL and technology-mediated TBLT practices in the secondary EFL classroom, considering also the limited research in this field in Italy.

7. Organization and summary of the chapters

This book illustrates the development of task-based language teaching approaches in relation to the evolution of digital technologies. It highlights how technology-mediated TBLT principles can support English as a foreign language

(EFL) learning and contribute to an understanding of the new classroom dynamics. Drawing on the key theoretical concepts of TBLT, the book discusses the integration of tasks and technologies from a secondary education perspective that is often under-represented in the TBLT literature. It looks at how the EFL secondary classroom has been recently re-conceptualized as a social place whose boundaries extend far beyond the traditional school setting. The volume has also been designed to address some specific challenges related to the Italian EFL context as for example the concerns about teaching grammar explicitly or the need to prepare students to meet the requirements for state exams and language official examinations.

This book provides theoretical approaches and examples of classroom implementation by presenting four case studies on the different L2 skills (reading, writing, listening and speaking). The idea of technology integration permeates all the studies. Digital technologies are fully integrated and a clear digital literacy outcome is embedded in the tasks (e.g. use glossed e-books, produce and publish a podcast). The terms 'digital tasks' and 'technology-mediated tasks' are used interchangeably throughout the volume.

The volume is organized into two main sections. The first section focuses on the theoretical approaches to TBLT and highlights the key concepts behind this methodology. This section also looks at the recent development of a technology-mediated TBLT framework and its implementations in various EFL educational contexts. The second section presents four case studies of secondary school EFL learners in Italy. Each case study focuses on a different language skill, providing examples of classroom practices in blended and online learning settings. The studies use both quantitative and qualitative data collection methods. Pedagogical recommendations are provided for teachers at the end of each case study. The book adopts a multimodal approach and aims to provide scholars of Applied Linguistics and TBLT practitioners with theories and implementation practices to understand the ways in which technologies are shaping tasks and mediating students' learning processes.

The first section of the volume includes three chapters that are intended to provide the reader with the essential concepts behind TBLT, SLA principles and technology integration. The volume is framed by a chapter on the key concepts of TBLT that will be taken up in the subsequent chapters. The chapter looks at the different definitions of 'task' in foreign language and technology-mediated contexts. The essential principles behind the TBLT approach are then outlined, including task design and implementation. This chapter also introduces the debate around focus on form activities in TBLT and its relevance for the case studies presented later in the volume, and it concludes with a description of performance-based assessment in TBLT. Chapter 2 presents the main SLA theories behind research into CALL and TBLT: cognitive-interaction and sociocultural theories. The chapter aims to illustrate how different task types are related to different theoretical approaches. It also discusses issues related to the implementation of TBLT. Chapter 3 is an introduction to the technology-mediated TBLT framework. By highlighting its main principles and characteristics, the chapter provides an overview of the opportunities offered by technology-mediated TBLT practices, but it also presents a series of challenges that researchers and teachers face in secondary school settings.

The second section of the book consists of five chapters. Chapter 4 is a review chapter on the implementation of (technology-mediated) TBLT in secondary education in different cultural and geographical contexts around the world and serves as a background to the chapters that follow. It references literature on the implementation of TBLT in Asia, Europe, New Zealand and South America and also looks at the concerns related to the implementation of TBLT in secondary education, proposing some possible indications for overcoming key issues. This chapter is followed by four case studies implemented in a lower-secondary school in Italy. Each case study focuses on a different skill. Chapter 5 presents a study on the impact of technology-mediated pre-task activities on learners' written accuracy. Chapter 6 focuses on the design and implementation of extensive reading tasks for vocabulary learning using e-books on mobile devices and Chromebooks. Following a mixed-method approach the study aimed to measure vocabulary learning through extensive reading. The third case study (Chapter 7) is an investigation into the use of multimodal captioned videos to develop learners' listening skills. This study took place entirely online due to the Covid-19 emergency. Following an experimental design, students were divided into two groups (an experimental group and a control group) to see whether a different task focus in the pre-task had an impact on students' learning. Finally, Chapter 8 investigates the use of podcasts in the planning and rehearsing of learners' speaking performances. The study looked at the role technological tools played throughout the task cycle in mediating and scaffolding learning. Analysis showed encouraging results in terms of improved pronunciation and fluency. The volume concludes with a short chapter on pedagogical implications and offers insights for future research directions.

In sum, as a teacher and researcher I am fully aware of the challenges of implementing technology-mediated TBLT practices with secondary school learners, but I am profoundly enthusiastic about the positive learning outcomes this approach can offer to young adolescent learners. From a pedagogical perspective, technology is mobile and, as such, so are learners. Technology is a distracting tool, but it is also a powerful learning and inclusive tool that can be integrated into EFL practices. I offer this volume to present studies in which technologies and TBLT principles have been methodologically integrated into a lower-secondary school curriculum, thereby sharing these practices with researchers and practitioners to support them in their implementation of a technology-mediated TBLT framework.

Part One

From Standard to Digital Task-Based Language Teaching

1

From Task to Process: Key Concepts in TBLT

1. Introduction

TBLT is an approach whose primary focus is on meaning. It has been very popular since the 1980s because of its clear role in developing students' communicative competence. As Ellis noted (Ellis et al., 2019), it is neither a monolithic method that must be strictly followed, nor a fixed approach to language teaching. Its flexibility has been one of the major characteristics that make TBLT an approach that is applicable to a variety of different educational contexts from primary education to higher and informal settings. It continues to be a topic of interest and debate (East, 2021) and some aspects of it remain controversial. It is, in a sense, still innovative as issues relating to TBLT are the subject of lively discussion in journals and recent book publications. The TBLT approach has its roots in Communicative Language teaching concepts. In assessing second language technology-mediated tasks in this volume, I will consider the recent changes in language teaching methodologies and their impact on classroom teaching and learning contexts, including in the role of teachers and learners. For the last three decades, researchers of second language acquisition have recognized that the modality of learners' engagement in communicative classroom activities plays an important role in their development (Kahn, 2012).

Language learning and teaching has experienced a series of significant changes over the last forty years, mostly due to the need to find effective methods (Power & Shrestha, 2009) of fostering second and foreign language learning. What is striking is that there has been a clear move away from a traditional teacher-centred method, such as grammar-translation, to more student-centred methods such as Communicative Language Teaching (CLT) and Task-Based Language Teaching (TBLT). This volume has been designed to investigate the use of technology-mediated TBLT approaches in the EFL classroom. In the first part of this chapter, I will provide an overview of the two approaches and review the relevant studies on CLT and TBLT's integration with technology.

2. Historical background

2.1 Communicative language teaching

A communicative approach to language teaching uses realistic life situations based on the lives of students to foster language learning and develop their functional competence (Canale & Swain, 1981). A communicative (or functional/notional) approach is organized according to functions (e.g. describing, inviting, apologizing) that learners need to know in order to address real-life situations. Communicative activities are interactive and clearly relate to students' experiences, thus motivating learners to communicate in meaningful ways about subjects of interest (Richards & Rodgers, 2001). The main objective of communicative language teaching is to develop learners' communicative competence in a target language (Littlewood, 2007). It represents the response to the need for *'genuine communication in L2 classrooms'* (East, 2021: 34). As stated by East (East, 2008: 14) 'language exists for purposes of *real* communication with *real* individuals in *real* contexts'.

In his analysis of CLT over forty years, Littlewood (Littlewood, 2014) identifies two different versions of CLT: a communicative perspective on language and a communicative perspective on learning (Littlewood, 2014: 351). A communicative perspective on language is about what we learn, not specifically in terms of language structures, but in terms of communicative functions. Examples of classroom activities related to this approach are activities in which learners are asked to 'do things with the language' (Wilkins, 1976) such as role-plays, pair work discussion, use of authentic materials etc. On the other hand, a communicative perspective on learning focuses on how we learn a language in terms of natural acquisition, with no or limited help from a teacher (Terrell & Krashen, 1983). For these reasons, the communicative perspective on learning is identified as the strong version of CLT, while the communicative perspective on language is the weaker version. Although innovative in many ways, both versions (weak and strong) were viewed as incomplete (East, 2012) or too extreme (Long, 2015). This led to the emergence of the TBLT approach.

2.2 Input from SLA research

Second language acquisition researchers also investigated the need for communicative activities in language learning. In 1967, Corder (Corder, 1967) was already arguing that learners acquire the grammar of a language following a 'natural route' as they have their own 'built-in' syllabus. That is, students do not learn grammatical structures one by one, but acquire them in no specific order, and often concurrently. Based on these premises, Krashen and Terrell (1983) developed *The Natural Approach*, a classroom perspective that was student-oriented, with a primary focus on meaning and incidental acquisition. In this model, students master a language by 'acquiring' it unconsciously, rather than by 'learning' it consciously through a set of rules (Krashen, 1985). This is the principle that underpins the TBLT approach.

3. Task-based approaches

Stemming from some CLT concepts and techniques, the task-based language teaching approach (TBLT) is based on the idea of identifying and delivering what learners need to be able to *do* in the new language. However, it is not purely focused on communication as in the strong CLT, or on grammar as in the weak CLT. TBLT aims to merge the need for both fluency and accuracy by providing students with real-world tasks. TBLT is an approach whose primary focus is on meaning, but it also 'draws students' attention to linguistic elements *in context*, as they arise *incidentally* in lessons' (Long, 2000: 185).

In this volume, as in, for example, Littlewood (2014), Nunan (2004) and Richards (2006), TBLT is seen as a logical development of CLT (East, 2012) in which communicative tasks play special roles. Tasks are the real-world activities that people do in their daily life (e.g. answering the phone, making breakfast, playing sports). Some of them are simple, some are complex; some are related to language, some are not (Long, 2015).

In order to further clarify the use of the terms CLT and TBLT, it is important to say that the two terms are often considered under the same umbrella, TBLT in particular being viewed as a specific realization of the CLT framework (Hu, 2005; Littlewood, 2004; Nunan, 2004). However, this volume considers TBLT as an approach with its own identity (Ellis, 2003; Estaire & Zanon, 1994; Nunan, 2004; Willis, 1996). Consequently, in the following chapters only the term TBLT will be used.

4. The key concepts of TBLT

To understand TBLT and its relationship to this study, it is important to clarify what a task is and the key concepts behind TBLT.

4.1 What is a 'task'?

There is no single definition of a task. Back in 1985, Long (1985) defined a task as one of the numerous things that a person performs in any context of everyday life, such as work, school, or free time. Following this definition, Nunan (Nunan, 1988) added that a task should be a meaning-focused activity and 'a communicative act in its own right' (p. 10). In the last twenty years, many definitions of tasks have been proposed and the term 'task' has often been adapted to fit language-learning contexts, ranging from Van den Branden (2006) who defined it as 'an activity in which a person engages in order to attain an objective, and which necessitates the use of language' (2006: 4) to Samuda and Bygate's (2008) 'holistic activity which engages language use in order to achieve some non-linguistic outcome while meeting a linguistic challenge, with the overall aim of promoting language learning, through process or product or both' (p. 69). As already mentioned, Long (2015) has proposed a broader definition in which tasks are real-world activities that people perform in their daily life (e.g. answering the phone, making breakfast, playing sports). Some of them are simple, some are complex; some are related to language, some are not.

All these definitions emphasize the idea that tasks should provide meaningful and motivating communication activities that learners can perceive as relevant, including beyond the language classroom. However, the large number of task definitions has not been helpful for the design and implementation of the TBLT approach in formal and informal contexts and has led to a variety of designs and some confusion about the criteria behind the implementation of TBLT.

More recently, Ellis et al. (2019) have claimed that the proliferation of definitions has its origins in the confusion over distinguishing between task-as-workplan (i.e. the material that constitutes a task) and task-as-process (i.e. the language produced during a task). They argued that the starting point can only be the task-as-workplan, as the task-as-process, or the language performed by students, is very often unpredictable. On the other hand, the materials used to foster communication (task-as-workplan) can be designed based on specific TBLT criteria. From this perspective tasks are intended as activities with a primary focus on meaning and language use, as opposed to exercises that are activities where the only focus is on form (Ellis, 2003). Ellis and Shintani (2014) proposed a selection of four main criteria to define a task-as-workplan.

The task designer/researcher makes a prediction based on task design criteria. The role of the TBLT researcher is to see if the predictions were accurate or not. That is why it is crucial to work on a task-as-workplan and not as a process (Ellis, 2003). The studies presented in the second section of this volume aim to investigate the task-as-process to confirm that the task-as-workplan resulted in the intended communicative activity in English as a foreign language (Ellis et al., 2019).

4.2 Task types

Input-based vs output-based tasks

Tasks can be generally divided into two macro areas: input-based and output-based tasks. In input-based tasks learners usually read and listen to texts, and are not required to produce language (whether written or spoken), unless they wish to. On the other hand, output-based tasks are product-oriented as they require learners to produce either written or spoken language (Ellis, 2003). Output-based tasks can result in a product or 'outcome' that can be used for evaluation. In reaching the outcome of the task, learners are engaged in a 'task process' that is 'any language process(es) used in working towards an outcome' (Samuda & Bygate, 2008), including the use of language to collaborate with peers, share information etc.

Both 'task as a product' and 'task as a process' are important, as learners need to engage in a process to reach the target task and conversely, there is no process without the need to achieve a product (Samuda & Bygate, 2008). Due to this study's focus on the development of specific productive and receptive sub-skills, the tasks considered for investigation and analysis are comprised only of output-based tasks with a strong focus on the task product.

Focused tasks vs unfocused tasks

Another important distinction in TBLT is that between focused and unfocused tasks. The aim of unfocused tasks is to 'elicit general samples of language' (Ellis et al., 2019) whereas focused tasks are designed to draw learners' attention to a specific language feature by creating 'a communicative context for its use' (Ellis et al., 2019). Due to the context considered in this volume (secondary school settings), the type of tasks generally implemented in the case studies presented here are mainly focused tasks. The reasons for this are presented in the following paragraphs.

Real-world vs pedagogic tasks

Real-world tasks are examples of authentic real-life situations in which learners often perform the target task by taking on the roles involved in the situation. For example, if the target task is 'buying a new backpack for a trip', one student will be the shop assistant and the other will be the customer looking for a specific backpack. Pedagogic tasks are different as they may not recreate the real-world situation, but they still foster the development of the same language functions. For example, learners are required to describe a picture representing the 'buying a new backpack' situation. Pedagogic language tasks are often preferred in secondary school settings where teachers have to deal with large classes of young learners. A question posed here is whether a TBLT course designed for secondary EFL students should contain only pedagogic tasks or also include real-world tasks, and how technology could help in mediating and realizing real-world tasks in this context.

4.3 Tasks in second language learning

At the basis of TBLT is the idea that students are given functional tasks that ask them to focus on meaning exchange and to use language to address real-world situations, with no specific linguistic purposes. However, the key concepts of TBLT have also been largely used in second language acquisition research (SLA); for example, tasks have been used to elicit language, to work on negotiation of meaning and an increasing number of studies show how TBLT can effectively promote language learning (Ellis, 2003; Lee, 2020; Nunan, 2004; Swain et al., 2001). As Long (1985) suggested, to be effective tasks should be based on learners' needs. This proved to be valid in the context of English for specific purposes (Sarani & Sahebi, 2012; Tsai, 2015), where a group of adult learners need to develop a specific skill (e.g. reading specialized texts, interacting in the foreign language). In such a context, for example, learners are required to write in English, but will never have to speak it (Long, 2015). On the other hand, in EFL secondary school settings learners need to be able to practice all four skills (reading, writing, listening and speaking) as it is not a specialized context. As noted in Van den Braden (2006) research on TBLT in the general English language classroom is less common, especially in secondary school settings. This is probably due to the fact that it is not easy to identify target task needs in foreign language settings (Cameron, 2001) and therefore to design tasks for secondary EFL learners. In a study conducted with middle school students, for example, Park (2015) noted how the needs identified and planned for by the teachers were different from the ones identified by students.

Based on these premises, 'how can teachers design and organize activities to stimulate and support learners reaching these language learning goals?' (Van den Braden, 2006: 2). The studies presented in this volume aim to identify language learning goals for secondary EFL learners focusing on communicative functions. Each case study will also look at how technology-mediated tasks can enhance TBLT.

4.4 Tasks in technology-mediated language teaching and learning

TBLT and CALL (Computer-Assisted Language Learning) both developed in the 1980s and since then their popularity has grown consistently, initially in parallel and then as a mutual support as they in fact complement each other. CALL offers TBLT the possibility of developing multimodal and flexible tasks. Learners can quickly access a variety of inputs from different sources both synchronously and asynchronously and can easily produce complex outputs. Moreover, while working on language tasks they also develop other skills such as, for example, digital literacy.

Tasks in technology-mediated contexts cannot merely translate face-to-face exercises into a digital context. Therefore, as Gonzalez-Lloret (2017) recommends, a clear definition of a digital task is needed. Based on the definitions above, a technology-mediated task should (1) have a primary focus on meaning, (2) be based on learners' needs, including their preferences for digital tools and their digital literacy, (3) be authentic, (4) offer opportunities for self-reflective learning and also (5) provide additional gains beyond language learning (e.g. intercultural exchanges, discourse analysis skills) (Chapelle, 2014; González-Lloret, 2017). The development of technology-mediated TBLT will be explored in Chapter 2.

5. Designing a task-based curriculum: main steps

Although many task-based designs have been developed (e.g. Wilkins, 1996; Ellis, 2003), most include the following elements (Norris, 2009):

a) Needs analysis – this is the 'first stage in the design of a TBLT program' (Long, 2017); in order to identify the tasks to be included in the curriculum, a needs analysis should gather information about language necessities, learning needs, context etc.
b) Task selection and sequencing – based on the needs analysis, tasks are then organized into group types and articulated into a frame.
c) Materials and instructions development – when organized tasks are delivered to learners, materials should provide learners with (1) relevant input supported by authentic materials (2) activities that have been manipulated in order to ensure sufficient focus on form (3) scaffolded, meaning-oriented, interactive activities and (4) *target-task performances* (Norris, 2009: 4).
d) Teaching – in a TBLT environment the teacher plays a key role in organizing and providing learners with communicative tasks, but also in monitoring and enhancing understanding of language use.
e) Assessment – through several modalities of assessment, students' task-based learning is regularly evaluated (Norris, 2009).
f) Programme evaluation – in task-based programmes the evaluation of the experience is crucial in understanding and improving those aspects of the TBLT design that enable teachers to better implement classroom tasks.

As will be explained in the following chapters, the studies presented in this volume focus on elements b, c and d, with some needs analysis aspects provided by the first phase of each study. Moreover, given the different approaches to TBLT and the local context of this study, the TBLT approach used follows the indications in Ellis (2003) and Ellis et al. (2019), particularly regarding the focus on form in all phases of the TBLT and the integration with traditional approaches. There was an important shift from the TBLT principles of Skehan (1998) and Long (1985, 1991) who rejected traditional approaches, to the most recent by Ellis (2003, 2019). It is important to note that Ellis (2003) introduces the possibility of integrating traditional approaches into TBLT, which could make TBLT easier for teachers to implement in their own curriculum.

6. Planning a task-based lesson

Although implementing TBLT in an EFL classroom requires flexibility and attention to the context, and there is therefore no fixed structure for classroom work, it is possible to identify three main phases in the task classroom implementation cycle (Ellis, 2003) as shown in Figure 1.1.

1) A *pre-task phase* in which the target task is introduced, and learners are exposed to language in use, to motivate and prepare them for the main task and to facilitate learning. This phase usually includes activities such as reading/listening to a text, watching a video etc. in which the language is not manipulated. This helps learners to see language in context and activates their previous knowledge and motivation. During this phase, the teacher usually provides a language input without working on or modifying it. There are various methodological options for this stage, including pre-task planning (students have time to plan the main task performance), modelling (the input serves as model performance) and focus on form (learners are explicitly exposed to a grammar rule before the main task).

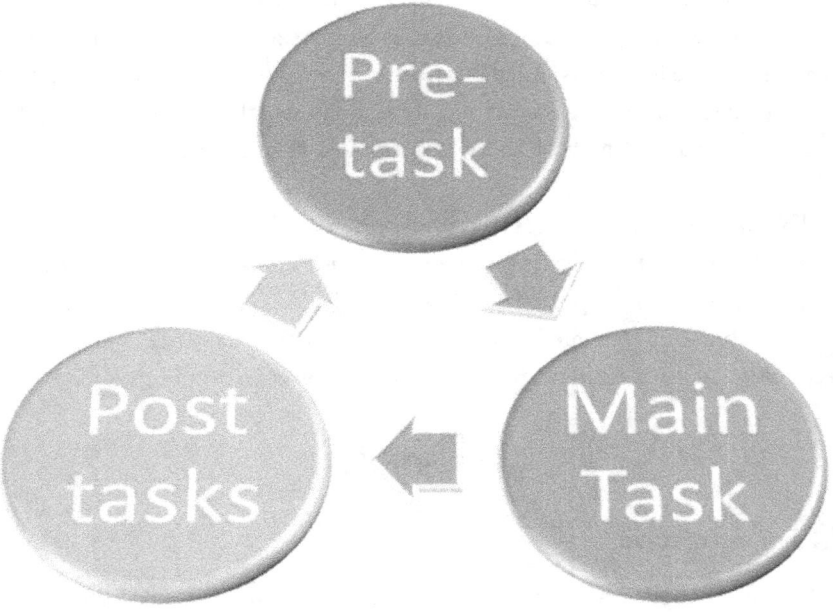

Figure 1.1 Task classroom implementation cycle

2) *Main task phase* in which learners can start noticing and manipulating the target language forms and functions. According to Ellis (2003), by manipulating a task it is possible to make learners focus on different aspects of the language. The role of the teacher here is therefore to raise students' awareness of new forms and facilitate a first-production stage by using interactive activities in which learners can collaborate, negotiate, solve problems and start using the language iteratively. At the end of this phase the teacher can provide learners with specific feedback or with general explanations on forms, functions etc. Following several uses of the language form and functions similar to the ones met at the pre-task phase, during the main task stage learners produce what they have learned in the previous stages. Depending on the curriculum, this can be in the form of a short presentation on a specific topic, a long written text (e.g. an article, a review – see Chapter 5), an interview etc. In this phase, teachers should replicate real task context and situations as much as they can: providing an audience for the presentation, creating a newsletter for articles or reviews etc.
3) The last stage is usually a *post-task* phase. Teachers and learners can decide to reflect on the performed tasks by looking at different aspects including form, planning, accuracy, fluency etc. The post-task stage can serve as language learning enhancement, but, as Norris (2009) points out, it can only work if there is a 'focus'. A list of errors cannot be the right way to reflect on language forms, whereas a list of common patterns that emerged during the performance can improve learners' awareness of language.

The task design and lesson cycle presented here (Figure 1.1) can be complemented by the specific use of technological tools such as mobile devices. This integration is supported by recent studies on TBLT and CALL/MALL, and a technology-mediated TBLT framework that fosters full integration of technology in the second language curriculum has been proposed.

7. Issues in TBLT

7.1 Focus on form

Focus-on-form plays a crucial role in TBLT. Long first introduced the concept to refer to situations in which learners notice a linguistic form during the performance of a communicative task (Long, 1991). It is an implicit process and contrasts with standard structure-based approaches where specific linguistic aspects are explicitly taught to learners. More recently, Long (2015) refers to focus-on-form as involving:

> '(…) a reactive use of a wide variety of pedagogic procedures to draw learners' attention to linguistic problems in context, as they arise during communication in TBLT, typically as students work on problem-solving tasks (…)
>
> (Long, 2015: 317)

What is important here is the focus on a 'reactive use' to address a communication problem and the idea that focus-on-form is not a single approach, but a 'variety of pedagogic procedures'. While Long (2015) saw focus-on-form only as a reactive process, Ellis (2016), on the other hand, recognized that focus-on-form can happen pre-emptively, that is for example, when a teacher or a student expects the use of a specific linguistic form to perform a task. It can also take the form of a recast, or an explicit error correction performed by the teacher.

Although controversial, the introduction of focus-on-form is one of the main developments of TBLT. It draws attention to the fact that an exclusive focus on meaning does not necessarily lead to a better performance or faster learning. A study conducted by Ellis (2015) demonstrated how focus-on-form can foster second language acquisition. Moreover, studies have increasingly recognized the importance of focus-on-form at different stages of the TBLT cycle. Although TBLT research generally adheres to the principle that no explicit linguistic instructions should be provided at the pre-task stage (Willis, 1996; Willis & Willis, 2013), a growing number of studies recently have investigated providing learners with strategies to focus-on-form such as planning and modelling (Ellis et al., 2018; Sharafi-Nejad et al., 2016; van de Guchte et al., 2019). The effects of pre-task planning and modelling on learners' linguistic competence will also be discussed in Chapter 5.

According to Willis and Willis (2013), the post-task stage is the most favourable stage for focus-on-form activities. At this stage the communicative activity is completed, and the teacher can invite learners to reflect on the linguistic structures. Specific language activities can be based on what learners found challenging or on the task-as-workplan. The effect of metalinguistic explanations, task repetition and post-task transcription activities have been the subject of recent studies (Foster & Skehan, 2013; Hassanzadeh-Taleshi et al., 2021; Hsu, 2017a; Shintani et al., 2016).

There is growing recognition that focus-on-form activities in TBLT are needed to foster linguistic awareness and language acquisition.

Nevertheless, the main focus should always remain on meaning and communication. It is the combination of both meaning-focused and language-noticing activities that can strongly contribute to language learning, particularly in secondary school settings where teachers are often concerned with the volume of grammar teaching required (see for example van de Guchte et al., 2019).

7.2 Task-supported or task-based?

In the language classroom, tasks are selected to be part of a *task syllabus*, which consists of a series of *pedagogic tasks*. *Pedagogic tasks* are the activities that students and teachers work on in the language classroom (Long, 2015). It is important to underline that the EFL context of language education in secondary schools in Italy can be described as 'task-supported' rather than 'task-based'. As Samuda and Bygate (2008) argue, in a task-supported environment tasks are 'used to enrich the syllabus or to provide additional learning opportunities. However, tasks are not used for assessment purposes and the syllabus may be defined by categories other than tasks' (2008: 59). Most Italian teachers are familiar with the TBLT approach through short teacher development courses and handbooks in which often standard communicative activities (e.g. interviewing someone) and exercises are relabelled as *tasks* without any connection with students' real lives.

In this context, the communicative approach and the task-based (or task-supported) learning approach seem to be the most widely used approaches by English language teachers in Italy. These approaches appeal to many learning styles (linguistic, visual, kinaesthetic etc.) and make substantial use of collaborative learning activities.

As Sung (2010) points out, a review of the current literature on TBLT and CLT shows that the teaching context is a crucial factor in determining whether TBLT can be successfully implemented in the classroom (Sung, 2010). Some researchers (Bax, 2003; Holliday, 1997) take the position that CLT is not equally suited to all contexts while others (Hiep, 2007; Liao, 2004; Shrestha, 2013) claim that issues associated with particular contexts do not necessarily negate the usefulness of CLT. Considering the potential of CLT and TBLT to suit various classroom situations (including the iPad language classroom), and the fact that it is common practice in Italy to use these approaches, this study will only investigate TBLT classroom situations.

8. Tasks for assessment

The final stages of a TBLT curriculum are students' assessment and programme evaluation. Assessment in TBLT is often performance-based. According to Brown and Hudson (1998) and Gonzales-Lloret (2017), performance-based assessment should evaluate how students use the target language and their ability to manage and solve authentic tasks.

In TBLT, assessment is conceived mainly as formative feedback so that learners can be motivated to improve their performance until they are able to perform the task correctly. In formative assessment teachers get information on how learners perform a target task, their engagement, and the problem-solving strategies they employ to accomplish the task. Formative assessment also provides teachers with information on how successful tasks can be designed and implemented. In the context of secondary school education, as for example in the case studies presented in this volume, assessment of students' learning is crucial. Teachers need to use both formative and summative assessments. Summative assessment involves the evaluation of learners' achievements. The role of the teacher is to test and assess if learners have reached specific language and communication outcomes. In TBLT, outcomes are strictly related to the target tasks planned at the beginning of the programme, usually based on specific students' needs and more generally on the needs of the age group/level.

The use of tasks for assessment purposes has contributed to a general move in the field of language testing away from an evaluation of students' knowledge of the language (i.e. their linguistic proficiency) to a more integrated approach that tests the ability of students to accomplish specific target tasks (e.g. writing an email, interviewing someone). Students' personal preferences and characteristics are part of the performance-based assessment, together with the context in which it takes place. However, as Bachman (2002) first and Ellis et al. (2019) later pointed out, a 'needs based approach is not appropriate for all learners' (Ellis et al., 2019: 20). In the case of secondary school EFL learners, the context of this volume, the purpose of the assessment is to evaluate learners' communicative skills within a general English target domain, so it is not the *situational authenticity* of the task that drives learning, but the *interactional authenticity* (e.g. tasks that draw on familiar contexts and situations).

One of the main issues related to performance-based assessment of secondary school EFL learners is establishing clear criteria and rating scales that allow teachers to easily evaluate if students can perform a task and how well they do so in terms of linguistic knowledge, pragmatic abilities and intercultural skills. In the latest update of the Common European Framework of Reference for Languages (CEFR, 2020), the Council of Europe aimed to provide educators with a series of descriptors of language teaching, learning and assessment that also includes mediation, online interaction and intercultural competence. Similar to the main concepts of TBLT, the CEFR descriptors relate learning aims to real-world language use with a view to a more integrated action-oriented learning. The framework also attempts to set up a profile of needs for learners at different levels to help users identify which language tasks are relevant for a particular group of learners.

Although assessment is a crucial component of the TBLT curriculum, there is still little literature on this subject. A few studies have focused on the definition and design of TBLT assessment (Byrnes et al., 2006; Norris, 2009), but studies on assessment implementation remain scarce. More recently, Norris (2016) attempted to provide a review of different types of TBLT assessment, including examples. He identified Language Education Assessment as one of the four areas where evaluation tasks can make a significant contribution (see for example, van Gorp & Deygers, 2013). He also underlined the importance of supplementing the TBLT curriculum, instruction and assessment in second and foreign language learning to provide students with a coherent learning track and aligned outcomes.

A final case that has recently been proposed is that of students' self-assessment. If properly guided, learners are able to assess their own task performance. Butler (2019) has recently investigated how young learners respond to self-assessment items and demonstrated the crucial role of the context of implementation. Students' ability to properly assess their own work, for example, depends on whether they are asked to assess a specific task or a generic condition, or whether questions are asked immediately post-task in a specific context or in a decontextualized situation. The attention given to young language learners' self-assessment is growing rapidly and educators and researchers are interested in its relevance to students' learning and formative assessment in general.

Ultimately, in contexts where assessment is intended to evaluate learners' ability to accomplish a task, use language meaningfully or solve a problem in a specific context, TBLT principles can provide a powerful contribution to the design of task-based assessment items in both formal and informal contexts.

2

Theoretical Approaches in Task-Based Language Teaching

1. Introduction

SLA theories have provided a theoretical basis for TBLT (technology-mediated language learning) and CALL (computer-assisted language learning) realities for the past twenty years. In this chapter, I examine the primary hypotheses that have guided TBLT research and technology-mediated TBLT studies in particular, providing a companion to the preceding chapter. In particular, I look at the two most prominent theoretical frameworks: the cognitive-interaction and the sociocultural (SCT) models. Drawing on current studies in the field (Oskoz & Elola, 2016; Ziegler, 2016), this chapter analyses the connections between the different theoretical views and the various types of tasks. Since both theories place an emphasis on interactions, it is crucial to compare and contrast research conducted from both theoretical perspectives to see what similarities and distinctions exist. The chapter also discusses the importance of teachers' professional development and TBLT knowledge and offers the results of various evaluation studies (such as action research). Finally, it proposes an integrated perspective on SCT and TBLT, addressing the key concerns addressed in relation to the use of SCT in TBLT. Examples of experimental (e.g. González-Lloret & Nielson, 2015) and descriptive studies (Shintani, 2016a) in TBLT are presented together with some evaluation studies (e.g. action research). This also led to some important reflections on the role of teachers' professional development and understanding of TBLT. Finally, I discuss the main concerns that have been raised in connection with the use of SCT in TBLT, proposing an integrative view of the two theories.

2. Cognitive-interaction theories

Cognitive-interactionist theories have informed many of the studies in the field of SLA and TBLT (Long, 1983; Long & Porter, 1985). The interactionist approach suggests that interaction fosters L2 development as it activates the mental mechanism responsible for acquisition. The work of Long (1983, 1985) contributed to the development of the cognitive interaction theory in relation to the foundational principles of TBLT. Long agreed with Krashen's input hypothesis, underlining how a *comprehensible input* fosters language learning, but he was concerned about how to make the input *comprehensible* to students (East, 2021). One of the most effective strategies to make input more comprehensible is the *negotiation of meaning*. In face-to-face interaction, language learners often experience some sort of communication breakdown, that is when one of the speakers needs to adjust their language to make the message clearer, to make sure that the other speaker understands. Hence, during interaction learners negotiate the meaning by processing the input and, consequently, modifying their output. Tasks are particularly useful in this sense as they provide learners with modified input, feedback and opportunities to evaluate their interlanguage and produce output (Ellis & Ellis, 2000; Long, 2015).

2.1 What is interaction?

One of the key models in SLA and TBLT theories is that 'learners are exposed to input through interaction' (Ellis et al., 2019). But how do we define interaction? Traditionally, interaction has been defined as the exchange of face-to-face communication between two or more people. However, in the last twenty years, innovations in computer-mediated communication and in language teaching have contributed to a broadening of the traditional definition. Nowadays, interaction also occurs in technology-mediated contexts and tasks, as demonstrated by the growing interest in this research field (Gonzales-Lloret & Ortega, 2014). Interaction in technology-mediated tasks has its own characteristics which will be analysed further in the following paragraphs. Regardless of the context in which interaction takes place, it can involve two learners (two-way communication), for example when two participants both talk and contribute to an interaction, or only one participant (one-way communication) as, for example, in the teacher-class mode. In the former, both participants produce input and generate output; in the latter, it is instead only the speaker who produces the input and learners simply receive it. This distinction is crucial as it leads to two different types of tasks (see Chapter 1): output-based tasks and input-based tasks.

A popular misunderstanding is that input-based interactive tasks are not modifiable and are therefore less comprehensible as the listener normally does not speak. Nevertheless, research has demonstrated that the input provided in input-based tasks is, in fact, flexible as the speaker often modifies it according to the listener's ability to understand. In secondary school settings, for example, teachers often adjust their language in order to make the input *comprehensible* to learners. In a study conducted by Shintani (2012), young Japanese learners were exposed to the same listening tasks and teacher input for five weeks. The analysis showed how the input provided by the teacher changed over time to facilitate students' comprehension.

In the secondary education EFL context, it is often the student who is asked to produce the input (one-way task), for example when a learner is providing his/her classmates with information about an event that is happening soon (e.g. a concert date, how to buy tickets, how to get there). In this case the learner must make the input *comprehensible*, ensuring understanding by repeating key information, adjusting vocabulary etc. That is, by using a series of *discourse management* strategies that help to get the message across. In the school context, where classes are quite large and tasks are limited by time constraints, teachers and students can also make use of strategies that foster comprehension. For example, the teacher can draw students' attention to a particular language form (e.g. remember to use the imperative to give instructions) in the pre-task stage to prevent issues in the task performance; also, students can ask pre-emptive questions (e.g. is it ok to use the continuous form?). In this respect, TBLT research is split into two strands. Long (2015) supports the idea that learners need to use discourse management strategies and repairs only when a problem occurs during task performance. Learners should be able to react to problems raised during interaction. On the other hand, Ellis (2016, 2017) recognizes the specificity of some contexts, such as the language classroom, and proposes also using interaction to prevent problems by deploying pre-emptive strategies or eliciting key language features, as this favours acquisition.

As stated above, technology-mediated interaction has attracted the attention of researchers and practitioners from different fields (e.g. informal learning, education, second language learning) and continues to do so. Technology-mediated interaction here is intended as the communication that occurs mainly or entirely through digital technologies (Bower, 2019). For example, in the case of a lesson delivered online, the videoconferencing tool mediates the interaction between peers. Technology-mediated interaction can be synchronous, real-time interaction, either written (e.g. text messages, chat) or spoken (e.g. videochat, video conferences), where learners communicate instantaneously and in the same time session; or asynchronous, delayed interaction, where participants do not communicate at the same time, but write/record messages using digital tools and send them to the receiver who will read or listen to them in a different session. Technology-mediated interaction differs in some aspects from face-to-face conversation, and is characterized by its own features. In particular, it appears to be beneficial to acquisition as it provides learners with rich input, provides dynamic peer-to-peer feedback and offers opportunities to focus on form. A group of studies focusing on synchronous technology-mediated environments, for example, showed how task-based interaction through written text-chat could boost vocabulary learning (Smith, 2004), improve accuracy through corrective feedback (Sauro, 2009) and generally enhance L2 language development as it provides learners with a visual representation of their own writing (Pellettieri, 2010).

The growing interest in technology-mediated tasks can be in part explained by the possibilities that digital tools offer for interaction. The situations in which language learners can interact are no longer limited to the formal and physical language classroom but can go well beyond it. Learners can choose from a wide range of synchronous and asynchronous communication modes, and this consequently opens for them a variety of authentic inputs.

2.2 Implicit and explicit learning

A series of cognitive processes are involved in SLA, including implicit learning, noticing and attention to form. A strong form of TBLT sees implicit learning, as opposed to explicit learning, as the central cognitive process behind SLA (Long, 2015). Whereas the latter refers to the use of intentional and conscious learning operations, the former involves learning naturally, without consciousness of doing so (Ellis & Ellis, 2000). People, particularly children, acquire language spontaneously with no explicit focus on form (explicit learning). That is, when exposed to an input they learn without paying conscious attention to linguistic features. On the other hand, adults, as they age, appear to lose the key mechanisms that allow them to acquire language naturally, so adult learners tend to rely on explicit language teaching and intentional learning. In order to learn, their attention needs to be consciously guided towards specific language features. However, Long claimed that 'implicit learning is still possible in adults' (Ellis et al., 2019), but is limited to certain areas such as word order or basic associations between form and meaning. He does not dismiss focus on form and explicit learning but limits them to spontaneous interventions which are often aimed at solving problems that have arisen during the task performance. For example, when a student notices a linguistic structure during spontaneous peer-to-peer interaction and asks the teacher for clarification, he is eliciting some sort of focus on form to overcome communication problems and accomplish the task goal. In this case, focus on form favours implicit learning as it fosters automatization. Although Long (2015) recognized the importance of focus on form and explicit learning in facilitating language acquisition in adults, he considered it complementary to implicit learning as the main focus of TBLT must remain on meaning (Long, 2000; Long, 2015).

Ellis et al. (2019) presented a more recent development of cognitive-interactionist theories in TBLT that allows for attention to form during the performance of a task in addition to the strong focus on meaning recognized by Long (2015). Adults have a limited capacity for implicit learning, so drawing learners' attention to linguistic forms activates the conscious awareness of language features (noticing) and fosters implicit knowledge (Ellis et al., 2019).

2.3 Noticing

Several studies have demonstrated that noticing is a necessary condition for learning a second language (Izumi, 2002; MacKey, 2006; Mackey et al., 2000). Some studies on the use of digital tools in TBLT (e.g. Pellettieri, 2010; Smith, 2004) have also claimed that technology-mediated tasks may promote the noticing of specific language features and aspects of learners' interlanguage. For instance, Pellettieri (2000) demonstrated how learners made excellent use of the additional time typically involved in text-chat interactions. The extra time allowed them to detect and notice specific language features. Compared to face-to-face interaction, technology-mediated interaction offers more opportunities to pause and reflect on language, while also easing communication as the learner feels less constrained by turn-taking and timing (Ziegler, 2016). These benefits are particularly relevant in synchronous written interactions as learners are able to see their interaction, reflect and then act on it (Pellettieri, 2000; Smith, 2004). It is clear that in both face-to-face and technology-mediated interaction, the interactionally modified input tends to encourage noticing more than the pre-modified input does, probably because learners have more time to process the input (Ellis et al., 2019).

2.4 Task-based interaction studies in the language classroom

Cognitive-interaction theories have been used as a theoretical framework in a large number of studies in TBLT. Early research in this area focused on task-based learner interaction and performance, in which the core of analysis is task-based language production during a task performance (Plonsky & Kim, 2016). On the other hand, a more recent area of prolific research addresses the processes involved in TBLT (e.g. noticing) and what impact they have on L2 acquisition (see, for example, Shintani, 2015). These are usually defined as 'task-based learning outcome studies' as the focus is on L2 development. Similar to the studies presented in the second part of this volume, these studies usually follow a pre-test – post-test – delayed post-test design. In this short review, I will first look at task-based language performance studies and then move on to task-based learning outcome studies.

Analysing learner language and performance is a crucial concept in SLA that has been used over the years to measure the efficacy of certain language teaching methodologies, but also more broadly to test SLA theories (Plonsky & Kim, 2016). Most of these studies in TBLT focused on how different task designs, complexity and implementation impact the types of interaction that foster language acquisition. Given the enormous increase in online teaching and learning in the last few years, the need to better understand how technology-mediated tasks impact interaction is fundamental. The study of Gurzynski-Weiss and Baralt (2015) investigated the interaction of twenty-four Spanish-as-a-foreign-language learners in face-to-face and synchronous computer-mediated chat (SCMC) environments to see whether learner-modified output after feedback showed examples of noticing. Students participated in recall sessions immediately after the interaction to measure what they noticed. A stimulated recall session is a meeting in which learners are stimulated through video or audio prompts to recall the learning processes employed during the task performance. Results showed that in both modes, learners' partially modified output predicted their noticing of language features. Also, it was only in the face-to-face mode that noticing led to fully modified output, showing that feedback efficacy is stronger in face-to-face interactions. In their previous study Gurzynski-Weiss and Baralt (2014) also found no differences in the perception of corrective feedback in technology-mediated and face-to-face interaction. Similarly, Jepson (2005) found that repairs were more frequent in face-to-face conversation than in web chats. On the other hand, these results are in contrast with those of Lai and Zhao's study (2006) which demonstrated how text-based online chat fosters noticing of learners' language features and mistakes. The study analysed data from conversation recordings and stimulated recall sessions to measure instances of noticing interactional feedback and one's own errors. Smith (2003) came to the same conclusions. Although technology-mediated interaction has its benefits, it appears that features inherent in this type of interaction can moderate some of the advantages. Sauro (2009) for example, noticed that the slight delay of the recast in SCMC mitigates the efficacy of feedback. As Ellis et al. (2019) warned, TBLT performance studies can offer a general overview of the implementation of a task impact interaction, but, on the other hand, they cannot be considered fully reliable as different variables (which possibly interact with each other) are involved.

The second strand of research focuses on TBLT and learning outcomes by looking at the impact of different task features and conditions on L2 acquisition. By investigating different treatment groups researchers are able to assess the effect of task types and interactions on various language aspects including lexis, grammar and pragmatic features (Kim, 2012; Kim & Taguchi, 2015). The implementation of these studies with young learners in primary and secondary education has also begun to receive attention. Kim and Taguchi (2015), for example, investigated the effect of task complexity in the learning of request-making through collaborative writing with Korean high school learners. Although the results showed no significant differences in learning outcomes, participants who completed more complex tasks showed more frequent language-related episodes (LREs). Shintani (2015, 2016a) also looked at the use of input-based tasks to achieve communicative competence with young Japanese learners. Learners were exposed to the same task over a period of five weeks. The data showed promising results, demonstrating how modified input can help to direct learners' attention to certain target language features. Although in input-based tasks learners are not required to provide an immediate response to the input, they can do so, using either L1 or L2. Shintani's study is an example of how interaction fosters language learning even with beginner level learners.

Cognitive-interaction theories have also served as a framework for several technology-mediated TBLT studies. For instance, González-Lloret (2003) reported the results of a study based on the design of a series of interaction-focused digital tasks to foster L2. The technology-mediated task required learners to negotiate meaning and interact orally. Data were analysed following SLA principles and demonstrated that well-designed digital tasks foster the use of key language acquisition strategies (e.g. meaning-making, interaction moves).

2.5 Cognitive-interaction theories in TBLT: main concerns

One of the main principles of cognitive-interaction theories in TBLT is that interaction and negotiation of meaning trigger implicit language learning and lead to L2 acquisition. However, interaction works when it favours noticing, and focus on form is needed to make sure that input has been fully internalized. TBLT activities need to be informed by these principles, but since interaction is a multidimensional concept and is also quite versatile (see chat interactions), cognitive-interactionist researchers need to investigate it in its various dimensions. The studies presented in this brief literature have shown that interactionally modified input promotes noticing, especially in digital interaction, probably because learners have more time to react. Also, authentic interaction can work successfully with young beginner learners as well as in secondary education, particularly with input-based tasks, although literature in the field is still limited. In addition, interaction has an impact on long-term language acquisition, so studies that focus on long-term effects are needed.

3. Sociocultural theories

So far, I have examined how TBLT studies have drawn on cognitive interactionist principles. On the other hand, around 1990 a new application of sociocultural theory (SCT) (Lantolf et al., 2014) emerged in TBLT studies. Learning a second language now is more a socially constructed activity than a pure acquisition of knowledge (Lantolf & Appel, 1994). SCT sees the classroom as a social context that fosters language development, while also allowing explicit attention to form during the performance of a task. The interaction between students, teachers, tasks and technology mediates, scaffolds and activates the conscious awareness of language features (noticing). Although the theoretical relevance of SCT is not always recognized in TBLT (e.g. Long, 2015), tasks are clearly influenced by social dynamics and research studies in this area continue to grow. Cognitive and sociocultural researchers are still, in a sense, in opposition to each other, as a few aspects of SCT in TBLT may sound inappropriate to one school of TBLT researchers. For instance, the idea of using explicit teaching of language to foster declarative knowledge (see Lantolf et al., 2014) may be understood as being totally in contrast to Long's principle of implicit learning (Long, 2015). The following paragraphs aim to illustrate how both theories can contribute to the development of TBLT. Some of the studies presented in this volume (see Chapters 6 and 8) have fruitfully applied SCT as a theoretical guide, considering its suitability for promoting collaboration as well as experiential and social learning. In this second part of the chapter, I will first define the principles behind sociocultural theory, and then review some key studies related to TBLT.

3.1 Key concepts in sociocultural theory

Mediation

One of the key concepts of sociocultural theory is that the human mind is *mediated* (Lantolf & Thorne, 2006). Mediation is the process that links the individual to the social. Human behaviours are structured and controlled by symbolic and material artefacts (Swain, Kinnear, et al., 2011). All higher mental processes, such as attending, predicting, monitoring, planning and inferencing are mediated by tools that are symbolic (such as language) and material (such as computers, smartphones or tablets) (Lantolf & Appel, 1994; Lantolf & Thorne, 2006). Vygotsky (1978) distinguished between signs which mediate our actions through symbolic representations, and tools which mediate our actions through objects (such as technologies) (Swain, Kinnear et al., 2011). The use of a tool necessarily implies cultural mediation, and the way people use it daily shows its constitution both temporally and historically (Thorne, 2003). Thus, tool use shifts according to content. For instance, a computer or digital tool may function primarily as a family information medium, or it can be used as a collaborative writing tool in the language classroom. Therefore, in a teaching and learning context, mediation indicates the interaction between a tutor (and/or a book, a mobile device) and their learner in relation to the issues encountered by the learner and the progressive support given by the tutor. This interaction must be relevant to the learner. Since tools and signs are not neutral, we can expect that the use of different tools, such as mobile technologies and laptop computers (in the instance of this volume), can offer different possibilities for developing language skills including speaking and writing (Hampel & Hauck, 2006).

Zone of proximal development (ZPD)

The interaction that occurs during mediation between the learner and the teacher, or with other peers, or indeed with digital tools, facilitates a type of acquisition that the learner could have not achieved working on their own. This area of supported and co-constructed learning is called the zone of proximal development (ZPD). The ZPD is particularly relevant to TBLT as it is social interaction that triggers its creation. How exactly this learning mechanism works is a question that has already attracted cognitive interactionist researchers: what type of interaction enables L2 acquisition processes? For SCT it is the co-constructed interaction (teacher-student, student-student, student-students, students-digital tools etc.) that allows the creation of a ZPD and therefore supports language learning. There are various ways to assist and support learners during interaction. One of the most important is scaffolding.

Scaffolding

The ZPD represents the area in which students need a little extra support to comprehend material. However, they cannot do this on their own and need to be scaffolded. Learning can be scaffolded by the various media involved in the classroom interaction (people and tools). For instance, in terms of reading, mobile devices such as tablets can serve as excellent tools that scaffold students' reading abilities (Morgana, 2018). Learning can also be measured in terms of the quantity of scaffolding learners need to complete a task correctly (Aljaafreh & Lantolf, 1994). In this respect, SCT sees learning as the change in the amount of scaffolding learners need to perform a task, rather than the quantity of information learned. Scaffolding is a crucial construct for TBLT. In his book on task-based language teaching, Nunan (2004) identified scaffolding as the first of the seven key principles behind the TBLT classroom design, stating that students need to have a supporting framework for learning to be activated.

Personalization

Personalization is another key concept supported by sociocultural theory (Vygotsky, 1978). Personalization focuses on learners' choice, autonomy and agency. In particular, in a technology-mediated learning environment, learners can enjoy a higher degree of agency. Activities are designed for different learners to meet their individual learning styles and learning methods and these can be modified at the level of both tools and activities (see for example Ziegler, 2016). The case studies presented in this volume have been designed to investigate how a technology-mediated TBLT approach can be implemented with secondary school learners with different learning styles, and the impact of this on the development of reading, writing, listening and speaking skills.

3.2 Sociocultural studies in the TBLT classroom

Many of the TBLT research studies based on cognitive-interaction theories do not mention the role of mediation in the language classroom, with only a few mentioning scaffolding. In SCT task-based studies that involve the use of digital tools, mediation refers to the interaction between a learner and a teacher and the technological tool (e.g. a computer, mobile device, an application) in relation to the problems and any positive language learning outcomes experienced by both the learners and the teachers, considering that individuals change artefacts (tools), and that these, in turn, change individuals (Vygotsky, 1978). Mobile technology use, for example, plays a leading role in the process of meaning-making related to the mediated nature of the human mind (Viberg & Grönlund, 2012). SCT is particularly relevant to technology-mediated TBLT in secondary education because the focus of the research is on the EFL classroom, which is viewed as a site of sociocultural practices.

There are a number of classroom studies based on Vygotskian sociocultural theories; these studies have 'focused on the tools learners use to control their own second language development' (Kahn, 2012: 91). The types of tasks informed by theoretical frameworks associated with Vygotsky's sociocultural theories can offer opportunities for students to help shape their own language-learning setting and trajectories, and their own learning results (Pellerin, 2014). Task-based language teaching tasks performed with digital tools are very much related to this idea of individual mastery, where learners become familiar with tasks and topics and internalize the use of such mediators (e.g. laptop computers) (Kozulin et al., 2003).

The Neumanns (2014) have investigated the use of touchscreen tablets by young children in supporting early literacy development within a SCT framework. The results showed that tablets could potentially contribute to the development of children's literacy skills (e.g. alphabet knowledge, emergent writing). However, they suggest that the ideal use of tablets for early literacy learning should consider the type of scaffolding (Wood et al., 1976) used by teachers at school or parents and the availability and quality of tablet applications. More practical studies investigating different learners and contexts (e.g. age, gender, nationalities) are needed to identify positive aspects and any issues with digital interactions through scaffolding by teachers, parents or peers.

Pellerin (2014), similarly to the studies presented in this book, examined how the use of mobile devices in language classrooms could support the redesign of task-based approaches for young language learners. The research, informed by the sociocultural principles of ZPD, mediation and scaffolding, provides evidence of how mobile technologies allow young language learners to create their own learning setting and meaningful language tasks with the help of cognitive tools. She followed a qualitative interpretative research design (Hinkel, 2011; Richards, 2003), and used collaborative action research (Burns, 2009). The study involved sixteen primary teachers from Grade 1 to Grade 4. The findings provide evidence that the use of tablets contributes to the creation of authentic and meaningful language tasks; because of the multimodal nature of the touchscreen devices, learners were engaged, and they developed greater autonomy (Pellerin, 2014). By mediating their learning, the devices helped learners to create their own learning situation using different modes (e.g. touching, using video and audio tools).

As stated above, since 'artifacts and tools are not neutral' (Oskoz & Elola, 2014: 118), there are numerous ways students can use them and, therefore, multiple different possibilities for language development. Tasks themselves mediate learning, and task mode (e.g. mobile-based tasks) strongly influences how foreign language learners approach the L2 (Oskoz & Elola, 2014). In their study on collaborative writing using digital tools and tasks, Oskoz and Elola employed the key SCT constructs of mediation and scaffolding to design learning tasks that promoted social learning and collaboration. The study involved university students of an advanced Spanish writing course. Students were required to complete collaborative writing tasks (argumentative and expository essays) using web chats and wikis. Results showed that these two social tools mediated learning in different ways. Chats were used for fast, synchronous communication that was more focused on the macro aspects of the writing. On the other hand, the more asynchronous nature of the wiki spaces encouraged learners to focus more on grammar development and editing. Overall, the study supported the SCT views of mediation and scaffolding; during interactions via social tools learners helped each other and created the ZPDs that foster language acquisition.

To sum up, the research on SCT and TBLT has a lot to offer in terms of how tasks can be implemented in the language classroom. Research on collaborative work and technology-mediated tasks has demonstrated how learners' interactions constitute opportunities for scaffolding and mediation. Students themselves realize the importance of social participation in language learning.

4. Conclusion: are cognitive and sociocultural perspectives incompatible?

Although SCT entered the realm of SLA relatively late compared to cognitive-interaction theories, it has since become quite popular among researchers and practitioners. The main difference between the two approaches is that SCT sees learning as socially constructed whereas cognitive interactionists see it as a purely mental activity. Cognitive SLA researchers in TBLT have dismissed SCT as it does not provide a solid theoretical framework for TBLT and the design of a TBLT curriculum. In fact, in a sense the key concepts of mediation, scaffolding and ZPD may sound somewhat inconsistent and appear not to interlock in a series of methodological steps that support the design of a curriculum (Swain, Kinnear et al., 2011). This could be an issue, especially for secondary school teachers, who need to have a syllabus to support their teaching throughout the school year. On the other hand, SCT supports teachers in their choice of how a task should be implemented to foster language learning (Ellis et al., 2019; Oskoz & Elola, 2014). It goes well beyond the task design to explain why certain choices facilitate learning and others do not. It has also demonstrated that social participation is an integral part of the learning process.

Are the SCT and cognitive interaction perspectives incompatible? The question still remains open. However, more than twenty years ago, Ellis (2000) already argued that both positions have a contribution to make to the development of TBLT. The structured approach of cognitive interaction perspectives offers a solid framework for ground task-based curriculum design and general directions, while SCT principles support teachers in the implementation of task, helping them to choose the right tools and strategies as they go along (Ellis et al., 2019). I argue that the mutual benefits of the two perspectives appear to be particularly relevant in the specific context of technology-mediated TBLT in secondary schools. EFL teachers need to be supported both from a theoretical and an experimental point of view and provided with the tools to answer key learning questions. Does interaction need to be complemented by explicit instruction? Are input-based tasks more appropriate for elementary language learners? In what ways can technology-mediated tasks help foster language acquisition processes? The following chapters will try to answer these questions by looking at the latest developments in TBLT and technology and their impact on secondary school instruction. Both the Vygotskian sociocultural theory (SCT) of education and the cognitive interaction hypothesis served as theoretical foundations for the studies in this volume. Case studies on reading and speaking (chapters 6 and 8) were informed by SCT and the concepts of mediation and scaffolding, whereas those on writing and listening were based more on cognitive-interaction principles.

Moving Forward: A Framework for Technology and TBLT

1. Technology, CALL and TBLT: the apparent revolution

Language teaching and technology have been affecting each other both within and beyond the formal boundaries of the language classroom for more than thirty years now. A series of adjectives have been applied to this mutual relationship: 'innovative', 'emerging', 'ground-breaking' or simply 'new' as if the relationship between these two elements were non-standard and therefore, in a sense, revolutionary. Are we still talking about innovation? Or are we talking about the reality of language teaching? A reality that is made up of language-learning practices which are supported by technology, and which are simultaneously formal and informal, synchronous and asynchronous, incidental or explicit, very often crossing the boundaries of the language classroom. In reality, integrating language teaching and technology is at this point 'an imperative' (González-Lloret & Ortega, 2014). However, the use of technology to foster second language learning is a complex challenge for all players involved, including teachers, researchers and administrators.

One of the main concerns associated with technology has been that from a pedagogical perspective, technologies (e.g. smartphones, tablets, new generation laptops) can only serve as entertainment and lack a solid educational purpose in the background that supports them. To address this issue, the authentic nature of TBLT appeared to make it the most appropriate methodology to support computer-assisted language learning (CALL) research. Back in 2001, Chapelle (2001), in his investigation into the possibilities offered by CALL, SLA and task-based models, warned that anyone researching the field should be aware that technology-mediated tasks have their own distinctive features and

'To meet the challenge, the study of the features of computer-based tasks that promote learning should be a concern for teachers as well as for SLA researchers who wish to contribute to knowledge about instructed SLA.'

(p. 2)

Since then, there has been a significant amount of research, which has focused on CALL and teaching with a specific emphasis on task-related opportunities and issues (Thomas & Reinders, 2010). In their book on TBLT and technology, Thomas and Reinders (2010) provided a series of international studies that focused on the link between second language TBLT and CALL in different contexts. Stemming from Chapelle's work (2001, 2003), their research investigated how the traditional theory of TBLT tasks can foster an understanding of technology-mediated tasks, but also how technology in TBLT can contribute to reshaping theory and research on tasks. CALL research, specifically, has often responded to the changes in the use of technologies inside and outside the classroom, moving from a behaviourist to a more integrative approach (Thomas & Reinders, 2010; Warschauer, 1997). One of the key elements that emerged from their analysis is the 'less restrictive and diversified approach' to tasks very often present in CALL research, in contrast to the traditional classroom-based TBLT research.

In the technology-mediated TBLT research agenda proposed by Smith and González-Lloret (2020), the authors argued that research on technology and TBLT should carefully consider the affordances of technology, the various learning contexts, the notion of task, particularly task complexity and sequencing, and the match between technology and task. This chapter is divided into three parts. The first focuses on the adaptation of TBLT to digital contexts and the technology-mediated TBLT framework proposed by Gonzáles-Lloret and Ortega (2014). The second part provides a brief overview of research on TBLT in mobile-assisted language learning (MALL) and CALL contexts. In the final part, the roles of the learner and the teacher are discussed, focusing in particular on how technology-mediated tasks influence EFL learners' and teachers' behaviours and identity.

2. Adapting TBLT to digital contexts

The synergy between technology and TBLT offers great opportunities for language learning. On the one hand, tasks can be enhanced by the use of digital tools and mobile technologies; on the other, TBLT offers a grounded methodological framework for the integration of technology in language learning (Lai & Li, 2011). However, adapting the standard TBLT model to digital contexts is not straightforward and there are various aspects that implementers need to keep in mind. The affordances of the technology, for example, are a crucial aspect. Each digital tool and technology has its own special features and functions that allow language learners to do particular things with the language. Matching the task learning outcome with the right technology is, in fact, one of the major challenges of adapting TBLT to digital contexts.

Doughty and Long (2003) and González-Lloret (2015) provided a number of recommendations for adapting task-based learning concepts to the digital learning environment. González-Lloret (2015) describes in detail how to plan and deliver technology-mediated TBLT lessons. Naturally, the affordances offered by any technology interact with the digital expertise of the participants and the nature of the activity itself. Students must be taught how and when to use technology, even if the general objective is comprehensible. In some instances, it may not be possible to directly transfer every task that works well in the traditional face-to-face format to the technology-mediated learning environment (Blake, 2016) and vice versa. For instance, as the case studies presented in this volume show, technology-mediated tasks often allow students extra time for pre-planning, and this can improve speaking accuracy, enable greater complexity and possibly help learners feel less frustrated. Meanwhile, the use of podcasts, for example, encourages learners to produce more complex speaking outputs, enhancing fluency and pronunciation (see Chapter 8).

3. Tasks in technology-mediated TBLT

As Smith and Gonzáles-Lloret (2020) point out, there is an important difference between technology-mediated and technology-enhanced tasks. In schools, for example, teachers tend to include some use of technologies in their lessons for motivational purposes and without a solid rationale behind it. However, when we talk about technology-mediated TBLT we are referring to the full integration of technology and tasks in the L2 curriculum (González-Lloret & Ortega, 2014). Moreover, the selection of a task in technology-mediated TBLT should follow five key principles: (1) the task should primarily focus on meaning; (2) it must be goal-oriented, requiring learners to produce a communicative outcome; (3) each task should respond to learners' needs by engaging them in the use of linguistic, but also non-linguistic resources; (4)

the task has to be as authentic as possible and reflect situations that learners could encounter in their real life outside formal contexts; and finally (5) a task should stimulate self-reflection to help learners develop metacognitive strategies (González-Lloret & Ortega, 2014).

In other words, over the past few decades, there has been a remarkable increase in the number of learning environments and resources available. As Ziegler (2016) observed, to reach the full potential of technology-mediated TBLT, tasks must be structured in a way that not only stimulates learners' need to communicate information, hence offering various opportunities for interaction and L2 growth, but also incorporates learners' digital and technological literacy and competence (González-Lloret & Ortega, 2014), recognizing these areas as resources and skills that must also be cultivated for successful TBLT implementation. Based on these indications, a technology-mediated TBLT curriculum would include both pedagogic language tasks and pedagogic technology tasks to allow students to work holistically and develop learning strategies they can apply in different contexts. The case studies presented later in this volume aimed to integrate both tasks to foster learners' language skills and digital literacy.

4. Pedagogic language tasks and pedagogic technology tasks

Before proceeding further, it is essential to clarify the differences between pedagogic language tasks (PLT) and pedagogic technology tasks (PTT). In a technology-mediated TBLT classroom, language and technology constantly interact with each other (González-Lloret, 2014), therefore a curriculum based on these principles has to include both task types, organizing and sequencing them in terms of their complexity. For example, in a lesson plan where the main task is to create a video presentation for tourists, PLTs would include listening comprehension activities based on multimodal videos for tourists, such as identifying key information, and lexical activities related to the contexts of art and theatre, city attractions etc. At the same time, PTTs would be to use the browser to gain more information about the topic, explore the location through a 3D map, create a voice-over interactive presentation for tourists etc. As already stated, it is crucial to provide learners with technological tasks that will enhance their knowledge, allowing them to 'do things' that would not be possible or would be substantially different with pen and paper. Clearly, it is the pedagogic language task that usually drives the pedagogic technology tasks. For example, secondary school EFL students would need to learn how to write an informal email so one of the PLTs could be to 'write an email to your friend about your weekend'. In the task design phase, it is crucial to consider the task (writing the email), but also the language involved (e.g. texts about past events, vocabulary for free-time activities), the technological tool needed to write the text (email), and learners' digital literacy (how good they are at and feel about using email software). Teachers must be aware that it is necessary to have different PLTs and PTTs to meet learners' needs. Figure 3.1 shows an example of technology-mediated TBLT planning. Students had to undertake a standard PLT first (to read and learn the opening and closing expressions of a standard informal email), followed by a PTT in which they were required to write, use software (Mail), read and cross-check their writing. The built-in checking function of the software also supported them in the self-evaluation of their written performances.

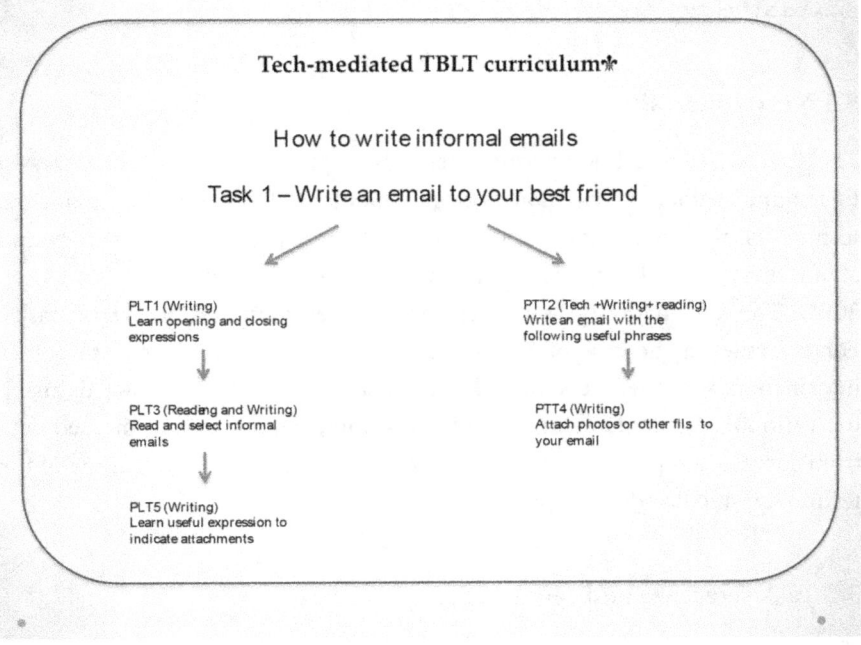

Figure 3.1 Example of technology-mediated TBLT task planning

5. Technology-mediated TBLT: a new framework

It is widely accepted that language teaching and technology influence each other both inside and outside the language classroom, that technology is often a crucial aspect of language practice (Motteram, 2013) and that, in line with these premises, technology and tasks should be carefully evaluated, including according to their social and pedagogical impact. As stated earlier in the chapter, in this context, a TBLT approach to second language acquisition seems particularly relevant, considering the range of new, real-world tasks that different technologies could offer. Following this notion, González-Lloret and Ortega (2014) introduced a new framework for the reciprocal integration of technology and tasks, which they defined as 'technology-mediated TBLT'. It is a methodological framework for technology-mediated task design and implementation. The framework opens up a new practice based on the concept that 'the choice of technology used for language learning is not neutral'. The key idea behind the framework is that 'pedagogic tasks should take full advantage of a chosen technology' (p. 8) and that the relationship between tasks and technology should be reciprocal. The technology-mediated TBLT programme cycle includes various steps, as presented below.

5.1 Needs analysis

The first step of technology-mediated TBLT planning is a needs analysis; this should gather information not only about the tasks, but also about the technological tools involved in the lesson, about learners' digital literacy and about the availability of the technological tools required (González-Lloret, 2014). The information gathered will serve to select and classify target tasks. For example, in the case of the studies illustrated in this volume, to gather information about learners' digital literacy and their attitudes towards using the various tools available in the EFL classroom, the research team used data from surveys and pilot studies that were conducted before the beginning of the technology-mediated TBLT project.

5.2 Task selection and sequencing

The second step of the planning relates to task selection and sequencing. Tasks need to be relevant to learners, should provide rich and authentic input and opportunities for corrective feedback (from peers or teachers), and promote collaborative work (Chapelle, 1998; Long & Doughty, 2009). For example, some of the tasks used in the Italian secondary school investigated in this volume (e.g. speaking – Chapter 8) have been adapted from the Cambridge Preliminary certificate standard tasks, making them particularly relevant to students. Exam preparation courses in this school were not primarily task-based or technology-mediated, so this research, in a sense, provided an opportunity for learners to prepare for the Cambridge exam using a different approach and for teachers to innovate their teaching. Additionally, well-designed tasks in a technology-mediated context are particularly beneficial for L2 communication as they create a virtual space where participants (learners and teachers) can interact synchronously and asynchronously. For instance, in a MALL context, learners can write an essay in class and the teacher can give feedback on it in real time (synchronous interaction), or they can perform a collaborative writing task, such as story writing, completing it from different places at different times (asynchronous interaction). Multimodality is also crucial for secondary school EFL learners. The research team involved in the case studies presented here (Chapters 5–8) always tried to select, design and modify tasks, making sure that learners could use three different modes: text, audio and video. Very often learners undertook interactive problem-solving tasks involving pair work and group work discussion. In some speaking tasks, for example, they were asked to role-play characters in a specific situation and they had a few minutes to discuss the topic and agree or disagree on something (e.g. the best tourist options in a big city). They were asked to record the conversation, or to look for specific information on their Chromebooks. The teachers and the researcher had weekly meetings to discuss and evaluate how the planned tasks unfolded for learners as they progressed.

5.3 Technology-mediated TBLT assessment

The last step of the technology-mediated TBLT planning is assessment. In technology-mediated TBLT, assessment is usually performance-based and is designed to give students information on how they can improve their L2 performance (González-Lloret, 2015). Usually learners perform a task, similar to a real-life task, and receive a score for their performance. They are evaluated on the basis of a series of criteria that assess their ability to use the language, accomplish a communicative task, solve problems or negotiate interactions. The goal is to test learners' ability to use the language rather than their knowledge about the language, thus reflecting the approach taken by the Council of Europe in the Common European Framework for Languages (CEFR) (Council of Europe, 2001). Although assessment was not the main goal of all the case studies presented here, I believed there was scope for investigation in this area and we consequently designed a few tasks to help learners self-monitor their oral development and teachers evaluate speaking performances using a performance-based assessment scale (see for example Chapter 8). Each student completed different speaking tasks using a voice recorder or other similar apps (e.g. podcasting apps). They were allowed to record the tasks and listen to them as many times as they wanted before sending them to the teacher and receiving feedback. In the post-task phase, they were often asked to self-evaluate their speaking tasks according to criteria provided by the teachers, such as pronunciation, intonation, range of vocabulary etc. Unfortunately, the study did not include any statistical comparison between their own evaluation of their performance, and those of the teachers, but the study includes comments made by the teachers on students' speaking performances.

6. Integrating TBLT and technology: key challenges

The key challenges in implementing a technology-mediated framework are strictly linked to the three main requirements for a full integration of technology and TBTL: (1) teachers must be aware of the definition of task; (2) technology is not neutral, as different technologies offer different affordances; and (3) a full integration of technology-mediated tasks works only when embedded in a full TBLT curriculum (González-Lloret & Ortega, 2014). First, being aware of the task type and the linguistic and non-linguistic objectives a teacher would like to reach is not easy. Teachers must be well-informed about TBLT design principles as well as about learners' needs and desires. A complete needs analysis can be helpful in planning the right target tasks.

Secondly, as González-Lloret points out, it is important to understand the distinction between the 'mere extensions of tasks to online environments' and a 'technology-mediated TBLT' (2014: 5) where technology and tasks are truly integrated. This means that the planning, delivery and performance of pedagogic tasks should all be fully supported by the technological tool chosen, and this should enhance the standard pen and paper activity, instead of simply translating it to a new medium. Teachers may not have sufficient training to recognize the possibilities offered by the digital tool chosen for investigation and therefore may find it particularly difficult to match learning objectives with the correct technology. Chapters 5–8 will provide examples of technology integration for reading, writing, listening and speaking tasks. Finally, as recommended by González-Lloret (2014), technology needs to play a key role in all the different stages of the TBLT curriculum, including needs analysis, assessment and evaluation. An ELT secondary teacher who would like to implement technology-mediated practices in their classroom also needs to be supported by colleagues and administrators as full integration requires a thorough analysis of a school's needs, affordances and learning objectives, which apply across the school curriculum, not only in the foreign language.

To sum up, there are three key requirements to consider when planning to implement this framework. First, teachers, researchers and educators should work with a definition of task that is based on TBLT principles. Then, they should be aware of the impact that technology integration is having on language learning and knowledge in general, inside and outside the classroom. Finally, they need to work towards a complete integration of technology and tasks in the school curriculum. It can be challenging, but teachers and administrators can overcome difficulties by investigating learners' needs, planning and sharing best practice.

About twenty years ago, Warschauer (2004) stated that learning English was becoming a tool for accessing the internet, using technology and communicating with others online and offline. It was no longer the opposite, with technology being used as a tool to learn English. I believe this is a crucial idea that learners should be aware of. In a technology-mediated model, language learning is not only an objective, but is also a medium to help learners succeed in L2 technology tasks. It follows that research and theory on TBLT should consider various mediating aspects of technologies in communication inside and outside the language classroom (Motteram & Thomas, 2010). Chapters 5–8 will present a comparison between the traditional TBLT curriculum and the technology-mediated TBLT curriculum.

7. Technology-mediated TBLT in the literature

7.1 Task-based approaches within CALL and MALL

As the case studies presented in the second section of this volume remind us, there are various technologies that can support EFL learners in accomplishing language tasks, and mobile technologies (including Chromebooks) provide an example of this.

Over the last thirty years, researchers in the field of language learning and technology have provided evidence of the impact of different types of technological tools on language acquisition (Chapelle, 2009; Levy & Stockwell, 2006; Warschauer & Healey, 1998). Many of them have explored new strategies for CALL and task-based language learning (e.g. Chapelle, 2014). Among different types of technologies, in the last decade the use of mobile devices (e.g. smartphones, tablets, new generation laptops) has had a huge impact on the second language classroom, often going beyond the borders of those classrooms. In particular, some studies have explored the use of mobile technologies to reconceptualize task-based language teaching and learning approaches (e.g. Canto et al., 2014; Lys, 2013; Pellerin, 2014; Solares, 2014).

These studies proved particularly relevant for the research projects presented in this volume. Pellerin (2014), for example, conducted a study on a second language young learner classroom of French students using mobile devices (iPods and tablets). The study, informed by Vygotskian's key sociocultural concepts of scaffolding and the zone of proximal development (ZPD), aimed to demonstrate how the use of such tools can support the design of language tasks. The choice of SCT supports the dynamic view of tasks as potentially modifiable by learners (Ellis, 2003). Pellerin states that one of the most positive aspects of using a mobile device is that 'learners can directly interact with the interface' (Pellerin 2014: 11), and this provides opportunities to 'create and design their own learning tasks', supporting the idea that this factor makes learning a productive, engaging and focused activity. Another crucial aspect that informs this study is that 'the physical and functional affordances provided by the iPods and iPads contribute to greater learner engagement, which in turn increases learners' motivation to learn because they develop a sense of control and ownership over their learning' (Pellerin 2004: 11). Moreover, iPods seem to manage to bridge different learning styles and therefore they can be very useful in the young learners' foreign language classroom. Although the study investigates crucial aspects of the integration of mobile devices into the language classroom, very often the analysis of the data is incomplete. As is clearly expressed in this study, the increase in motivation and engagement is a common and crucial aspect in MALL. However, it would be beneficial to have detailed examples of the changes in learners' engagement and motivation. These two concepts of engagement and motivation will be further investigated in the results of the present study (see Chapters 6, 7 and 8).

In their attempt to design a technology-mediated TBLT framework, González-Lloret and Ortega (2014) presented a series of studies in the field with a specific focus on key concepts of TBLT, from needs analysis to evaluation. Sharing a common focus with this volume, their research includes five empirical studies that explore task design, selection and sequencing, that is, the steps highlighted in this volume. These investigations include learners from different countries and cultural backgrounds studying English or Spanish as a foreign language in higher education. Moreover, the studies present a wide range of communicative tasks and goals for learners to achieve. The studies in this section consist of a short introduction followed by sections on methodology, data collection and analysis, discussion and limitations. Some of them address the use of a technology-mediated TBLT approach to develop second language writing skills. For instance, Adams et al. (2014) examine the role of prior knowledge in EFL writing in text chat where learners undertook an interactive problem-solving task. They found that accuracy and the complexity of language production were only affected by prior knowledge to a limited extent. Moreover, an action research study conducted in Mexico with EFL learners proved to be important for some of the case studies in this volume. Solares (2014) investigated a multi-stage online writing task with three different groups who were engaged in three instructional designs with and without technology-mediated tasks. The three groups were interviewed about their perceptions of the usefulness of tasks and technology; a small group of students who had benefited from using technology was also interviewed a few months later. Interestingly, the study provides information about implementing successful tasks in a textbook-bound context, providing encouragement for teachers who want to redesign existing tasks. In particular, learners seemed to have reached the same linguistic competence, but there was a quite significant difference in their perception of task design and its link with technology. However, the study has some limitations, especially in its design: for instance, the lack of a survey on digital literacy at the beginning of the study, and the choice of the students in each group being arbitrary, as it would have made a stronger case if it had had clear criteria behind it.

Similar to Solares (2014), Oskoz and Elola (2014) presented a classroom study on the design and integration of sub-tasks to develop genre knowledge using Web 2.0 tools (social media and wikis). A sociocultural theoretical background informed the study. Remarkably, the authors attempted to overcome the standard task and technology design by also targeting two writing genres (argumentative and expository essays). Oskoz and Elola found that writing collaboratively made students feel more engaged in the writing process, and they started to develop critical thinking skills. Despite the encouraging results of both studies, they do have some methodological limitations, such as the insufficient information about learners' digital literacy and the lack of a pen-and-paper group. Nevertheless, these studies will potentially inspire follow-up studies, which may provide further data and evidence. Although several studies showed various ways to enhance the quality of a TBLT curriculum through the full integration of technology (Canto et al., 2014; González-Lloret, 2014; Oskoz & Elola, 2014; Sauro, 2014; Solares, 2014), the question of how to integrate language tasks and new technologies into a complete L2 secondary school curriculum remains largely under-researched.

7.2 Task-based approaches and sociocultural theory

The communicative and task-based approaches have been strongly influenced by sociocultural principles. In a sociocultural classroom where Vygotskian ideas are applied, the teacher encourages learners to engage in dialogue with both the teacher and each other, and to think by asking questions of each other (Brooks & Brooks, 1999). Moreover, collaboration is seen as the most effective means by which sociocultural learning can be established (Lantolf & Appel, 1994; Woollard, 2010). In a student-centred language classroom context, mobile technologies can play a key strategic role, moving from being simply the presentational devices used in a teacher-centred context to having a more collaborative function, where learners are asked to use and identify cognitive strategies that facilitate their learning (e.g. cooperative, non-linguistic, problem-solving strategies). Furthermore, tasks themselves mediate action and interaction, and the way they are designed and presented could also influence how learners orient themselves (Lantolf & Appel, 1994). In a study conducted with first-year university students in Taiwan, Sung (2010) examined the effects of three communicative language teaching-based projects that included the use of technology (e.g. blogs, videos). The results showed that students had a positive reaction to communicative tasks, the projects reinforced authentic communication and they fostered student autonomy, stimulated creativity, and promoted independent language learning. Moreover, the use of technology helped them to work on all four language skills. Although the results were positive, the study did not include a needs analysis, so some students were not skilled in the use of technology (e.g. in the blog project). As Nunan (1991) suggests, it would be beneficial for instructors to collect information about learner needs, as well as institutional and social needs, before designing the curriculum since TBLT activities aim to cover what learners need and consider important. In this respect, the following paragraph looks at the profile of twenty-first-century language learners and the skills they need to maximize the benefits of a technology-mediated TBLT approach.

8. A new framework for new learners?

The complex landscape of the digital generation has been an area of debate for years (Buckingham, 2006; Hernández-Martín et al., 2021; Olofsson et al., 2015; Seiz Ortiz, 2017), and the definition of the digital generation itself is still problematic (Prensky, 2001). Generally, digital natives are people who feel comfortable using digital tools and devices as they were born in the digital era (Dingli & Seychell, 2015). A common misunderstanding in applying this definition to the school and education context is that all digital learners are highly competent in the use of such tools, especially for learning (Erstad, 2010). Twenty-first-century adolescents and young adults are keen users of digital media and technology, but this does not necessarily mean that they are aware of the possibilities these media offer for language learning. As such, the technology-mediated TBLT framework lays the foundations for a digital approach to the L2 classroom, while at the same time presenting a series of stimulating challenges for all the actors involved. First, the technology-mediated TBLT approach requires learners to be more independent in their learning (Thomas, 2012), meaning that they develop new learning strategies and become aware of the mediation role of digital tools. Secondly, digital learners in TBLT are required to be more confident in the target language as the focus of communicative tasks is mainly on meaning and they are required to produce real outputs (e.g. a podcast, publishing a blog post). Previous studies on the integration of TBLT and technology have also identified a number of challenges related to the lack of technology skills or intercultural understanding and communication (Hampel & Hauck, 2006). Lai and Li (2011) also noted that students may not be ready to collaborate with other peers using digital technologies and this may inhibit task performance. Thomas (2012) reported a similar issue with Japanese learners in an online language learning context. Although motivated and engaged, students found it challenging to collaborate digitally using the target language, so they mainly relied on their L1 (Japanese). To sum up, digital technologies are engaging for secondary school language learners, and their use contributes to increased learner motivation. However, digital learners are not always competent and skilled enough to easily undertake technology-mediated tasks, particularly collaborative tasks.

9. The role of the teacher

Many studies on the integration of technology devices into the language classroom have pointed out a series of issues related to the role of the teacher. Twenty years ago, in the Futurelab literature review of languages, technology and learning, Milton (2002) already warned that 'it is a very common feature of technology-based language teaching materials, that they are technology-led rather than pedagogy-led'. Teachers may in fact risk focusing and planning their TBLT around a technological tool instead of integrating it into the task lesson cycle. In order to overcome this issue, teachers need to have a clear idea of what a task is and what type of task they would like to implement. As Ellit et al. (2019) noted, in TBLT language teachers often have different ideas about what a task is, so teacher training courses on TBLT and technology are crucial to improving teachers' ability to implement this framework. Colpaert (2004) suggests that, as a first step, the teacher should put more emphasis on the importance of developing the language-learning setting rather than focusing on the role of technologies. The focus should therefore be on the learner first, ahead of the technology.

Nevertheless, the successful use of any tool in language learning needs reflective thinking (Chinnery, 2006). Ultimately, teachers may be concerned about the workload entailed in planning and implementing technology-mediated language tasks (East, 2014) and this is a valid concern as there are only a few publications with practical instructions on how to implement a technology-mediated TBLT framework. The aim of the case studies presented in this volume is to contribute to addressing these issues by providing teachers and researchers with real-life examples of secondary classroom implementations.

10. The technology-mediated TBLT framework in this volume

As detailed above, all the changes and innovations in technology and language teaching led González-Lloret and Ortega (2014) to introduce a new framework with the aim of combining technology and tasks, in what they define as 'technology-mediated TBLT'. The team involved in this research (myself as a researcher and two EFL teachers) decided to implement this framework to develop the reading, writing, listening and speaking skills of EFL secondary school learners. As suggested by González-Lloret and Ortega (2014), I considered technology, and mobile technologies in particular, as part of the full planning cycle of a TBLT curriculum, from needs analysis to assessment and evaluation. For example, the needs analysis conducted for the tasks in the present research that involve the use of different mobile technologies (e.g. Chromebooks, smartphones) considered not only the language skills needed to perform the tasks in question, but also the learners' digital literacies, access to Wi-Fi connections, need for technological support etc. I also considered the teachers' attitudes towards the digital tools and mobile devices, and their motivation for introducing new technology-based tasks into their teaching, being aware that this aspect will potentially have strong bearing on the view of technology-mediated TBLT as an innovative practice (Hubbard, 2008).

11. Conclusions

The main aim of this chapter was to introduce and review the use of technology and TBLT approaches in language education. The first part looked at the key concepts behind the technology-mediated TBLT framework as conceptualized by González-Lloret and Ortega (2014) and the challenges related to its implementation. The chapter also included a discussion of the problems identified and offered suggestions as to how these might be addressed. In the second part of the chapter, the task-based language-teaching concepts in relation to CALL or MALL were presented and analysed. Many studies suggest that the integration of technology and tasks helps to reconceptualize TBLT and learning. The studies reviewed in this chapter explored students' and teachers' use of technology in relation to specific second language tasks. It should be noted that the results of the studies reviewed are encouraging in all the areas analysed. However, research in this field is still limited, and often related to specific tasks rather than the design of a technology-mediated TBLT curriculum. The chapter also described the most common elements to consider when implementing a technology-mediated TBLT, such as the students' profile, the role of the teacher, the social nature of new technologies, task complexity and sequencing, and multimodality. Finally, the chapter outlined the technology-mediated TBLT framework's design principles as implemented in the case studies presented in the following chapters. In particular, the four case studies presented in this book are empirical investigations into the integration of pedagogic language tasks and technology language tasks. Chapter 5 explores the impact of digital writing pre-tasks on learners' accuracy; Chapter 6 is an action research study in which technology language tasks were implemented in an e-book extensive reading programme; Chapter 7 reports on an online classroom study of a multimodal video-based task; while Chapter 8 illustrates how speaking tasks can be designed to be integrated and performed with mobile devices and a podcasting application.

Appendix 1

Pilot study

A. F2F Interview for students and teachers

Notes:

- This interview takes place at the beginning of the project; students will start using the iPad in the EFL classroom just a few days after this interview. Teachers have received the iPads only fifteen days before this interview. They are familiar with the device, but they've never used it in class.
- Students and teachers will answer the same questions.
- Students have already completed a quick online survey with ten multiple choice questions on the same topic.
- All the questions will be audio recorded and transcribed.
- Each interview lasts about 10 minutes.
- The F2F interviews serve two aims:
    1. to have a general idea of the students' and teachers' perception of the use of the iPad for language learning to design future tasks.
    2. to get their level of 'technology acceptance'.

Questions

1. How do you use your smartphone/tablet in your free time?
2. Do you think the iPad is a useful tool to learn English? Why?
3. Do you know any apps for learning English? Have you ever used any of them?
4. Can you mention five things you can do with your iPad to learn English?
5. What would you like to do with your iPad during English lessons?
6. Is there anything you don't like about the use of the iPad?

B. Questionnaire for students (completed using Google Forms)

1) Have you ever used mobile devices before having it at school?

2) If yes, what did you know?
    games
    agenda
    watching movies
    etc.

3) How long do you use your tablet/smartphone at home?

4) How did your parents react to the fact that you were going to use mobile devices at school

   very enthusiastic
   not so much
   no particular reaction
   they gave you a not-to-do list right away

5) Do you think technologies will change the way you learn English at school?

   Yes
   No

6) Do you think mobile devices and digital tasks will be useful to learn English?

   Not at all
   A lot
   Average
   Just a bit

7) Do you think the Chromebook will be useful to take notes?

   Not at all
   A lot
   Average
   Just a bit

8) Do you think the Chromebook will be useful to do writing tasks?

   Not at all
   A lot
   Average
   Just a bit

9) Do you think the Chromebook will be useful to do listening tasks in class?

   Not at all
   A lot
   Average
   Just a bit

10) Do you think the Chromebook will be useful to do reading tasks in class?

   Not at all
   A lot
   Average
   Just a bit

11) Do you think the Chromebook will be useful to do speaking tasks in class?

   Not at all
   A lot
   Average
   Just a bit

12) Do you think your classroom is well equipped for the use of mobile devices?

   Yes
   No

13) Do you think your English teachers are well prepared to teach with mobile devices and digital technologies?

   Yes, very well
   Not at all
   Just average

14) Are you expecting to create materials or presentation with your Chromebook?

   Yes
   No

15) Would you prefer studying on e-books?

   Yes
   No

16) What are you expecting from the use of mobile technologies and digital tools in the English classroom?

   I'll improve my listening skills.
   I'll improve my reading skills.
   I'll improve my speaking skills.
   I'll improve my writing skills.

Appendix 2

Examples of technology-mediated tasks

A. You and your partner have a budget of 20 euros for today's lunch and a 45-minute break. Look at the menu of your favourite restaurants on the Deliveroo app, find special deals, check for delivery timing. Discuss your choices with your partner and agree on what to order.

B. Your friend has just arrived at the train station but you are late to pick him up. Leave him/her a voice message on WhatsApp, and ask him to walk towards your place. Check the easiest directions on the interactive map and give him/her directions.

Appendix 3

Correspondences between the features of the CALL tasks developed by Chapelle (2001) and those of the technology-mediated TBLT framework presented in Gonzales-Lloret (2014) with examples from the studies presented in the volume.

CHAPELLE (2001)	GONZALES-LLORET & ORTEGA (2014)	EXAMPLE OF TASKS FROM THIS VOLUME	
		Writing and reading	Speaking and listening
Authenticity	Holism	Reading a crime story from the BBC website	Listening to a podcast on Anchor or Spotify
Meaning focus	Primary focus on meaning	Focus on key structures in context to convey meaning (use of narrative tenses)	Focus on key expressions for public presentation
Learner fit	Learner centredness		B1 Preliminary modelled speaking task
			Focus on intonation, pronunciation and fluency
Language learning potential	Reflective learning	Use of collaborative writing activities.	Interactive tasks: e.g. discuss with your partner key features to include in the presentation.
Positive impact	Reflective learning		
Practicality	X		
X	Goal-orientation	Write a crime story	Production of a podcast

Appendix 4

Common task type implemented in the case studies

GOAL	Development of EFL Reading, Listening, Speaking and Writing skills
Task types	• Mixed – simple skills (e.g. listening for gist) as well as multiple skills (e.g. reading, inferring meaning from context) • Individual tasks (e.g. information gathering via web searches) • Interactive tasks (e.g. sharing of information via classroom, discussions, interviews) • Interactive tasks (e.g. sharing comments with peers and teachers, recording a discussion, negotiating meaning)

Appendix 5

Examples of Pedagogic Language Tasks (PLT) and Pedagogic Technology Tasks (PTT)

TBLT CLASSROOM CYCLE	TYPE OF TASK (Tech-mediated – Pedagogic)	TECHNOLOGY USED
Substantial input	Tech task – video watching	YouTube
	Pedagogic task – Find key information on after school activities (timing, types etc.)	Google docs (shared)
Pedagogic task	Tech task – find information on official school websites	Google Web browser
	Pedagogic task – Answer comprehension questions, focus on key vocabulary	Google docs (shared)
Target task performance	Tech task – create a webpage, add key information, videos, visuals and internal/external link	Google sites voice recorder search engines
	Pedagogic task – You need to promote the after-school activities of your school: produce a short video.	Google docs (shared) Camera – video editing tool.

Part Two

Technology-Mediated TBLT in Practice

4

Task-Based English Language Teaching in Secondary Education

1. TBLT in secondary education

Secondary education is a quite complex landscape. Depending on the national school systems, students attending secondary schools are normally aged between eleven and eighteen years old. As Steinberg (2014) identifies, this is the age of opportunity. Brains are more malleable and minds are wide open to learning opportunities. As researchers and educators, we should take advantage of this attitude, be attentive to needs and feel a sense of responsibility to offer young adolescent learners the best possible chance to learn a second language. On the other hand, conducting second language investigations in secondary schools has always been problematic. Classes are large, teachers do not always collaborate with each other, and learners are minors, which implies a series of important ethical considerations that could prevent researchers from carrying out investigations. Despite the fact that it can be a challenging context, research in secondary school settings is extremely necessary, particularly in the context of second- and foreign language education.

In my experience with secondary school students, I have noticed that they often complain about the lack of opportunities to interact in the second language in their weekly EFL lessons. At the same time, their teachers are always looking for language activities that are relevant to the students' lives, to motivate them. In these circumstances, implementing the essential TBLT principles appears to be the appropriate response to learners' and teachers' concerns. Instead, the reality is quite different and the implementation of TBLT practices in secondary education is scarce and often quite challenging. Despite the large volume of research into TBLT and technology in the last twenty years (see, for example, González-Lloret & Nielson, 2015; Tavakoli et al., 2017; van de Guchte et al.,

2015; Ziegler, 2016), only a relatively small number of studies have focused on secondary school settings (for example, Park, 2012; Solares, 2014; Zheng & Borg, 2014). There are obviously various reasons why research has focused on higher education or primary school settings; difficulty in data collection and teachers' attitudes are probably the most common. On the other hand, the literature in the field of TBLT and secondary schools has demonstrated that TBLT is a flexible methodology and, when properly adapted, it leads to encouraging results in terms of language learning and proficiency. There is a need for an adjustment of TBLT towards a more 'situated version of task-based teaching' (Carless, 2007).

This chapter is divided into two parts. The first part illustrates the opportunities and challenges offered by TBLT and technology-mediated TBLT in various geographical contexts. The second part presents a detailed description of the Italian secondary school system and its implications for the research studies presented in the second section of the volume. I argue that TBLT is suitable for state schools, and a technology-mediated TBLT approach should be strongly recommended to address and overcome some of the issues raised by students and teachers in this context.

2. Challenges in implementing TBLT in secondary education

Research studies in the field of secondary education and TBLT have identified a series of challenges that have sometimes prevented TBLT from being implemented in the language classroom (Carless, 2007; Carless, 2015; Lai, 2015). Carless (2007, 2015), for example, found that TBLT could only work with secondary school teachers and learners if adapted to a weak version that emphasized focus on form techniques and activities, adjusted tasks to official language examination requirements and focused more on reading and writing task-based activities rather than listening and speaking ones. So far, challenges in implementing TBLT in secondary education settings can be categorized into four areas: learners' proficiency, grammar instruction, stakeholder examinations and teachers' knowledge. Local and cultural peculiarities can vary from one educational context to the next, but generally, the literature has demonstrated that most challenges are the same across different secondary school settings, both nationally and internationally.

2.1 Low-proficiency learners

There is a shared consensus among most secondary school teachers that TBLT can only be effective if implemented with advanced foreign language learners. Secondary school young adolescents are, in fact, usually elementary or lower-intermediate learners, and this inevitably would exclude them from learning with a TBLT approach. This non-issue, as Long defined it (Long, 2016), has been supported by various studies in the field. Bruton (2005), for example, evaluated the use of TBTL practices in state secondary schools, concluding that task-based language teaching is very limited for secondary school foreign language classrooms as it fails to maintain accuracy. Similarly, Swan (2005) suggests that task-based teaching is most suitable for advanced learners as lower-level learners need to receive the necessary input, and this is not possible with large classes in secondary schools. Large classes are, in fact, the reality in secondary schools, but this is not linked with input quantity and quality or with any TBLT principles (Long, 2016). Teachers can provide the necessary authentic input to pre-intermediate learners even if classes are large, and especially with the support of technology-mediated tasks.

2.2 Grammar instruction

A second common issue identified with tasks in secondary school classrooms is that TBLT approaches do not offer a sufficient focus on grammar and this could be detrimental for pre-intermediate learners who need to learn grammar structures. This represents a huge challenge for traditional language teachers who are used to the standard presentation of a language form, followed by controlled practice activities. The concerns come from a quite common misunderstanding about focus on form in TBLT (Long, 2016). The fact that the TBLT lesson cycle does not include the explicit teaching or pre-teaching of grammar rules does not imply that TBLT neglects focus on form (Ellis, 2003; Ellis et al., 2019; Long, 2015). In its pure form, TBLT allows for spontaneous focus on form only after the task work (if necessary). To address secondary teachers' concerns about introducing grammar forms before the task work, a growing body of research (Ellis, 2009, 2016, 2021; van de Guchte et al., 2019) has focused on the opportunities to guide learners' attention to form without directly teaching it at the pre-task stage, for example, by modelling and planning (see also Chapters 5 and 8).

2.3 Examination focus

Most secondary schools' curricula are strongly influenced by the internal and external language examinations that learners have to take either at the end of their schooling or during their second or third year. In Italy, for example, students need to take an official state examination at the end of the third year of lower-secondary school, which includes an EFL written and oral examination. Most students also take the external Cambridge ESOL examination to certify their English level (e.g. Preliminary B1 or Key A2). As noted in Carless (2007), examination requirements often guide the type of tasks and methodology used in classrooms. Teachers would not be willing to try new approaches if they did not find them relevant in terms of preparing learners for the official examinations. I argue that the flexibility of technology-mediated TBLT allows teachers to adapt test preparation tasks following TBLT principles. For example, the case studies presented in Chapters 7 and 8 have attempted to adapt Preliminary B1 tasks to fit into a technology-mediated TBLT lesson cycle.

2.4 Teachers' attitudes and knowledge

Apparently, secondary school-language teachers around the world share a hesitancy about (technology-mediated) TBLT (van Den Branden, 2006; Lai, 2015). Teachers from eastern and western countries face the same challenges as they share the same beliefs about language teaching. The standard PPP methodology continues to rule the language classroom despite changes in school policies and educational management. In Italy, for example, the TBLT approach is strongly advocated in the latest Ministry of Education guidelines, but these recommendations do not seem to be officially implemented in schools. Similar situations have been reported in studies on European and non-European countries. Carless (2015) reported that despite the TBLT official syllabus, Hong Kong teachers did not implement it widely and continued to work with a weak version of TBLT. According to van den Branden (2006), some Belgian teachers felt uncomfortable managing noisy group work as they did not want to give up control of the classroom. Similarly, van de Guchte et al. (2019) found that Dutch teachers prioritized accuracy and complexity, preferred to follow textbooks and complained about the time constraints of the curriculum to teach other skills. A study by Ogilvie and Dunn (2010) found that Canadian pre-service teachers failed to utilize TBLT during their teaching training in schools, despite receiving significant training in TBLT methodology. This was due partly to their perception that children could not acquire a language by undertaking tasks that did not include any pre-taught linguistic information, and partly due to the cultural norms in the schools, which placed emphasis on teacher authority and the comprehensive covering of learning content. Thus, these findings confirmed the widespread idea that western culture still relies largely on teacher-centred approaches.

Another crucial challenge that inhibits technology-mediated TBLT is the lack of teaching expertise in task-based approaches and technology. Teachers often feel that they have limited knowledge of methodology and this inevitably affects their attitudes towards new practices as well as the outcomes of TBLT implementations. Ellis et al. (2019) reported that when learning outcomes are not reached, it is mostly because teachers do not have a clear idea of what a task is and how they are going to implement it in their teaching. Sometimes students report that, despite technology being integrated in TBLT, they perceived teachers to be insufficiently skilled, both in methodology and in the management of technology, to support their learning (Morgana & Shrestha, 2018).

3. Technology and TBLT: a step ahead

The challenges presented above confirm how implementing TBLT practices in secondary school is commonly perceived as particularly demanding and sometimes disadvantageous for lower-level learners. Some misconceptions are quite hard to change, but data-driven research can contribute to the gradual transformation of secondary language teaching practices.

These observations also generated a series of reflections on how much TBLT should be adapted to make it suitable for schools, and how appropriate such modifications would be in terms of changing TBLT principles excessively. In this context, a technology-mediated framework, as advocated by González-Lloret and Ortega (2014), would be particularly useful. The framework could support teachers to overcome the challenges that prevent them from using TBLT practices. For instance, technology allows teachers to enhance input and modify activities to suit large classes. It is also useful in providing personalized and synchronous/asynchronous feedback and focus on form activities (when needed).

4. TBLT across different secondary school educational contexts

The literature suggests a series of possible adaptations to the standard TBLT model to suit different contexts, as each context has its own implications. The following paragraphs present studies on the implementation of TBLT practices in secondary education settings in various geographical areas.

4.1 Asia

A large body of research has been conducted in secondary settings in Asia (see, for example Littlewood, 2007; Thomas & Reinders, 2015). The studies mainly focus on teachers' perceptions and only a few of them looked at classroom implementation practices.

Park (2012) conducted a study with thirty Korean middle-school students to investigate the design and implementation of TBLT lessons to develop learners' writing skills. Participants were divided into experimental and control groups. The experimental group followed a TBLT approach, while learners in the control group followed the standard teacher-centred methodology. Results from pre- and post-test scores for writing showed that the experimental group outperformed the control group, thus demonstrating how TBLT practices foster L2 communicative competence without interfering with the development of linguistic knowledge. However, Carless (2007, 2015) did not have the same positive experience in Hong Kong. In his study of teachers' beliefs and attitudes towards TBLT practices, he found that task implementation was only possible if adapted to the school contexts and if explicit grammar tasks were implemented and examination requirements were satisfied. Zheng and Borg (2014) reported similar findings with regard to the challenges Chinese secondary school teachers faced in implementing TBLT in large classes and the need to provide a strong focus on grammar. The review paper by Lai (2015) identified all the issues in TBLT secondary education in the Asian context, underlining two important ideas. First, the generalization that the learning styles of Asian students are incompatible with TBLT due to cultural reasons, which is unjustified. Secondly, most if not all of Asian teachers' concerns about TBLT in secondary classrooms are not specific to the eastern culture but are widely shared with their western colleagues.

4.2 Australia

Studies in the New Zealand context have investigated the secondary language classroom from the teachers' perspective (East, 2012; Erlam & Tolosa, 2022). Recently, Erlam and Tolosa (2022), in their book on a TBLT teacher training programme and its classroom implementations, reported encouraging results on the importance of teachers' professional development in TBLT. Teachers in the study learned about TBLT and how to implement tasks in schools over a period of four years. The study investigated implementation in multiple foreign language contexts with beginner-level learners. At the end of the experiment, teachers felt comfortable using the TBLT approach and in the second part of the study successfully implemented it as an innovative approach.

4.3 Europe

The European experience of TBLT in secondary schools does not differ substantially from those in Asia and New Zealand in terms of the challenges faced in implementing TBLT in secondary schools. However, studies from Belgium documented and measured the impact of language policy innovations taken by the government (van den Branden, 2006; van den Branden et al., 2009; van den Branden & van Gorp, 2021). The Dutch Flemish project was implemented with the idea of changing the education system using the innovative approach of TBLT. Drawing on Duran's (1994) research into task-based syllabuses in Flemish secondary education, van den Branden (2006) discussed to what extent the main principles of TBLT can be implemented in general L2 classes and also transferred to content language integrated secondary classrooms (CLIL classrooms). Van Gorp and Bogaert (2006) presented a practical study on the design and manipulation of language tasks to support learning Dutch for academic purposes. Examples taken from the study showed how the manipulation of task features enhances L2 learning. More recently, van de Guchte et al. (2019) have investigated the impact of a different focus at the pre-task stage on secondary learners' proficiency in the Dutch context. Teachers interviewed before the project expressed concerns about grammar teaching and TBLT. By comparing two different groups performing two planning and modelling tasks with a different focus (on language and content), the study aimed to demonstrate that a focus on content does not necessarily interfere with language proficiency in terms of knowledge of grammar structures. Apart from Belgium, there are no government language policies in Europe that explicitly foster the implementation of (technology-mediated) TBLT in secondary school education. However, in 2013 the European Commission funded the PETALL project (Pan-European Task-based Activities for Language Learning). The main aim of this project was to develop and encourage the use of technology-mediated TBLT practices across ten European countries (Germany, Greece, Hungary, Italy, the Netherlands, Portugal, Serbia, Spain, Turkey and the UK). Over three years (2013–16), universities and schools involved in the project worked in tandem to develop tasks to be implemented in secondary schools (Lopes, 2016). Tasks were trialled and revised according to a series of criteria based on the CEFR. Unfortunately, to the best of my knowledge, the research results on the classroom implementation of tasks are yet to be published.

4.4 South America

Perspectives on secondary education in South America are not frequent in the literature. The study by Solares (2014) is particularly relevant for this volume as it implemented technology-mediated TBLT practices. Solares (2014) investigated a multi-stage online writing task with three different groups using three instructional designs, with and without technology-mediated tasks. The three groups were interviewed about their perceptions of the usefulness of tasks and technology; the small group of students who benefited from the use of technology was also interviewed a few months later. Interestingly, the study provides information about implementing successful tasks in a textbook-bound context, and it provides encouragement to teachers who want to redesign existing tasks. In particular, learners seemed to reach the same linguistic competence, but there was a quite substantial difference in their perception of task design and its link with technology. Although the study has some limitations, it is one of the few examples of research studies in TBLT and technology. The South American context is also quite challenging in terms of traditional approaches to language learning. However, Solares's study (2014) demonstrated how the teacher was able to overcome difficulties (e.g. traditional textbooks) to implement innovative practices without this having a negative impact on students' language learning and linguistic competence.

Literature from different cultural secondary education contexts has shown how teachers' concerns about the implementation of TBLT (and its integration with technology) are commonly shared. Although teachers in eastern and western contexts tended to have similar beliefs on second language practices and were generally unwilling to implement TBLT practices, there are opportunities to overcome the issues and these lie in technology-mediated TBLT practices, as the case studies presented in the following chapters attempt to demonstrate. It is also important to remember that students also need to be trained in technology-mediated practices as they are often not aware of the affordances of the technology and tasks, and of the opportunities offered by their mutual combination. A study by Kim (2013) found that including video modelling to help students focus on useful language while completing a task improved their performance in the activity. In a semester-long TBLT training programme, Lai and Lin (2015) showed that students developed more positive attitudes and performed better in tasks as a result of learning the concepts and processes of TBLT and developing essential affective and cognitive strategies.

5. The context of this volume

Mobile devices and new generation laptops such as Chromebooks are becoming popular and many schools in Italy and all over the world (Lin, 2014; Pegrum et al., 2013) are integrating them into everyday classroom settings. As observed by Sekiguchi (2011), many educators have high expectations for the use of these devices in the classroom as it may allow EFL learners and teachers to discover new methods of learning and teaching.

The administration and the English language teachers in the lower secondary schools involved in the studies presented in this volume became interested in the phenomenon and made the decision to trial the integration of Chromebooks, online applications and TBLT practices with their students as part of a research project which was also designed to increase teachers' knowledge as part of their professional development. All four case studies took place in a state lower-secondary school in Milan, Italy, in which the school administration had recently decided to implement a classroom-based MALL project in some of its classes. In the case studies presented here, the participants were Italian eleven- to fourteen-year-old secondary school students who were taking part in general English language classes in accordance with the Italian Ministry of Education requirements. In 2020, immediately after the first and main lockdown triggered by the Covid pandemic, the classes had been provided with a classroom set of Chromebook devices for their in-class work. Students in state schools all follow the same curriculum and receive the same amount of EFL lessons. However, since lower secondary state schools in Italy are mainly local, students tend to go to school close to where they live. Specifically, the school where these projects took place has been classified as a high-achieving school with most of the students coming from high socioeconomic backgrounds.

6. The Italian secondary school system

In Italy, education is organized into four stages:

1. preschool from three to five/six years (scuola dell'infanzia)
2. primary school (scuola primaria), which typically spans the ages of six to eleven
3. lower secondary school (or middle school), from ages eleven to fourteen (scuola secondaria di primo grado)
4. high school, from ages fourteen to nineteen (scuola secondaria di secondo grado).

There are both public and private schools in Italy. Many of the latter are referred to as 'paritarie' since they must adhere to the Italian national regulations and procedures. Essentially, they are similar to public schools but are privately operated and so charge fees. The public education system in Italy is free for all children resident in Italy, regardless of nationality. Education is compulsory for every child between the ages of six and sixteen. State nursery schools are also free and have motivated teachers and reasonable class sizes. In the past, the educational system enjoyed a favourable reputation, but it is today considered to be too traditional, especially in foreign language education. It tends to emphasize rote memorization and obedience over creative thought. On the other hand, the quantity of knowledge students acquire in subjects such as history, literature, philosophy and art history in the Italian system is astounding compared to other countries. Infrastructure is not always good, although plans have recently been made to develop new infrastructure.

Primary school (scuola primaria) begins at age six and lasts for five years. Free schooling and textbooks are provided. The curriculum comprises Italian, English, geography, history, mathematics, science, technology, music, art, physical education and religion. Formerly known as scuola media, the next level is now known as scuola secondaria di primo grado, or lower secondary school, where students study until they reach the age of fourteen. Historically, compulsory education ended at fourteen. The minimum school leaving age has now been increased to sixteen. While secondary level education is free, books must be purchased. Students must pass a formal examination ('esame di terza media') before progressing to high school. In Italian schools, if a student fails too many subjects, he or she is required to repeat the entire year (rather than a single subject or group of subjects).

Methodologically, the EFL context of language education in secondary schools in Italy can be described as task-supported rather than task-based. As Samuda & Bygate (2008) argue, in a task-supported environment, tasks are 'used to enrich the syllabus or to provide additional learning opportunities. However, tasks are not used for assessment purposes and the syllabus may be defined by categories other than tasks' (2008: 59). Most Italian teachers are familiar with the TBLT approach through short teacher development courses and handbooks where often standard communicative activities (e.g. interviewing someone) and exercises are relabelled as *tasks* without having any connection to students' real lives.

TBLT, Technology and English Writing Skills

Case study 1 – The Role of the Pre-task in Learners' Written Accuracy

1. Introduction

While secondary school teachers are fully aware that digital tools already play a key role in second language education, both within and beyond the classroom, the sudden switch to online education during 2020 accelerated the need for more research on how digital tasks can support English language teaching in secondary schools (Bailey & Lee, 2020). The period of sustained lockdown impacted all levels of education in Italy. Secondary school students were particularly significantly affected as the way they were learning English changed radically. Even after the lengthy lockdown, learners continued to alternate between periods of face-to-face and online learning, requiring teachers to redesign tasks for a blended approach. Various studies on the impact of the pandemic on English language education have claimed that there are characteristics of online and blended learning that are worth investigating (see, for example Moorhouse & Kohnke, 2021). For instance, English language teachers had to design and adapt language tasks for synchronous and asynchronous online teaching. Despite this being a challenge, it also provided an opportunity for further reflection, particularly in the context of research into technology-mediated TBLT. Due to the peculiarities of online and blended teaching, the integration of tasks and technology is no longer simply encouraged but is required. Based on these premises, there are, without doubt, questions that secondary school EFL teachers need to reflect on and this case study has been designed to answer some of these questions. First, how can we design effective technology-mediated pre-tasks to develop learners' writing skills? Secondly, given the concerns of Italian EFL teachers about learning grammar, how does a different focus in the pre-task impact the main task performance?

As stated in the first part of the volume, task-based language teaching (TBLT) has been of interest to a significant amount of research in the field of computer-assisted language learning (CALL) and second language acquisition (SLA) (Ellis et al., 2019; Hubbard & Levy, 2016; Thomas & Reinders, 2010; Ziegler & González-Lloret, 2022) as both fields benefit from mutual opportunities. However, some researchers and practitioners remain concerned about the value of this approach in foreign language learning. EFL teachers in Italy, for example, tend to discard the use of purely meaning-focused activities, as they think it is inappropriate for elementary EFL learners. In fact, one of the main concerns about TBLT is the widespread opinion that the lack of explicit focus on form (grammar rules) could negatively impact students' language learning (Sato, 2010). Nevertheless, TBLT encourages and enables attention to form through implicit meaning-related activities (Ellis, 2009; Long, 2015), even if explicit focus on form is not advocated.

With these points in mind, this chapter reports on a case study of the effects of pre-task modelling and planning on students' learning of narrative tenses (the past simple and past continuous) through technology-mediated tasks. This study is part of a broader study on technology-mediated TBLT and focus on form in secondary school education. Preliminary results from a pilot study have been illustrated in Morgana and Thomas (2023). Students in the study were assigned to two different guided planning approaches (focus on form and focus on content). A final written task was used to measure the effects of the pre-task approach on students' performance in terms of attempted use of the target structure (accuracy) and number of words, subordination and coordination (complexity). The study also addressed teachers' concerns about explicitly teaching grammar in TBLT. In fact, Italian EFL teachers choose to teach grammar rules in the pre-task phase, even if coursebooks follow a communicative approach design. The study's main aim was to investigate whether paying explicit attention to form at the pre-task stage through technology-mediated tasks would lead to more accurate use of the selected narrative tenses (past simple and past continuous).

2. Literature review

2.1 Explicit focus on form in the pre-task

In the standard TBLT classroom cycle (Willis, 1996), learners follow three steps: a pre-task stage, followed by the main task; and a final post-task stage in which they perform some (optional) post-task activities. The pre-task stage has been identified as the stage of the TBLT cycle in which noticing and focus on form techniques appear to be most beneficial for learners (Ellis et al., 2019).

There are several strategies for drawing attention to form at the pre-task stage. Among these, modelling (van de Guchte et al., 2019), planning (Ziegler, 2018) and visual input modification (Lee & Huang, 2008) are becoming popular and have been investigated most extensively. However, research in this area has often led to inconsistent results as, for example, reported in Park (2010). In fact, pre-task planning and modelling have been shown to be relevant strategies for improving fluency and complexity, but they have mixed effects on accuracy (Foster & Skehan, 1996; Ortega, 1999; Park, 2010).

The conditions in which a task is performed, in addition to the choice of the sort of task to be undertaken, are not neutral. As the tasks will affect students' language ability in terms of accuracy, fluency and/or complexity (Skehan, 2003), the teacher must select them with care. In this regard, pre-task activities play a crucial role in highlighting target language elements and engaging students with the task's content (Van de Guchte et al., 2016). In prior research investigations, the subject of whether explicit grammar instruction in the pre-task is beneficial has proved highly controversial. Some scholars believe that an explicit emphasis on language can increase accuracy, particularly in EFL circumstances (Littlewood, 2007). Others (Foster & Skehan, 1996; Skehan, 2022) believe that focusing attention on an area of language may prevent learners from focusing their attention on other aspects. This last attitude has its roots in the cognitivist principle that people's capacity to process information is limited. Other researchers, such as Ellis (2016), have demonstrated how a focus on grammar at the pre-task stage risks directing the student's attention to form, negatively affecting the communicative purpose of the task; that is, students become more concerned with producing accurate language than with fluency and meaning-making. However, a pre-task emphasis on form may result in more frequent use of the desired feature throughout the task performance and even in the post-task period (Ellis et al., 2019). In accordance with this perspective, this chapter examines a study that includes explicit grammar instructions in the pre-task and analyses the effects on EFL learners' accurate language use.

2.2 Planning

Planning is an essential component of the pre-task stage, and its potential has been extensively studied by scholars (Ellis & Yuan, 2004; Ellis, 2005; Foster & Skehan, 1996, 1999; Ortega, 1999; Ryu & Lee, 2018; Ziegler, 2018).

Both guided and unguided tasks have enhanced the performance of spoken activities, resulting in greater fluency. Research also reveals positive benefits in terms of complexity. However, the impacts of pre-task planning on accuracy are inconsistently demonstrated. According to a number of research studies, specific planning conditions have little effect on accuracy. Foster and Skehan (1996, 1999), for example, studied the effect of guided and unguided pre-task planning on the subsequent performance of an oral activity. Students in the guided group (the detailed group, as described by the authors) produced more complex utterances, but the difference in correctness was not statistically significant. A further study undertaken by Foster and Skehan (1999) with L2 learners yielded comparable results: students were exposed to various planning sources (teacher-led, individual and group planning), with each planning group focusing on specific aspects (language vs content). As anticipated, different effects were observed depending on the source of planning, but these were not attributable to the differential between focus on language and focus on content.

In contrast, more recent research has indicated that pre-task planning positively affects accuracy (Ellis, 2009, 2016; Mochizuki & Ortega, 2008). In his evaluation of the influence of pre-task preparation on fluency, complexity and accuracy, Ellis (2009) found that thirteen of the nineteen research studies included reported a positive impact on accuracy. Mochizuki and Ortega (2008), for instance, worked with a cohort of fifty-six Japanese secondary school EFL students to investigate the impact of pre-task guided planning conditions with a focus on grammar (relative clauses) on learners' fluency, complexity and accuracy in the performance of an oral narrative task. The students worked under various conditions (guided planning, unguided planning and no planning). Compared to the other two groups, pre-task guided planning fostered a more precise use of relativization. Thus, the study indicated that beginner L2 students may require more grammatical resources during planning time to attain their linguistic goals.

Van de Guchte et al. (2016) investigated the impact of pre-task modelling on learners' task performance. As in Mochizuki and Ortega (2008), the pre-task planning included a specific focus on form (locative prepositions), with the purpose of comparing the impacts of two different pre-task foci (focus on language versus focus on content) on accuracy and complexity. Forty-eight German as a foreign language secondary school students participated in the study. They were randomly assigned to two different planning conditions (one with a focus on language and the other on content). Having watched a modelling film which demonstrated how to do the primary activity, all students completed a modelling task during the guided planning period. The results showed that students' speech performance was affected by the pre-task planning. Specifically, in the immediate post-test activity, students in the focus-on-language group outperformed students in the focus-on-content group, using the target structure more frequently and more accurately. At the delayed post-test, however, no significant difference was observed. This could be because the focus-on-language group did not receive specific focus-on-form instructions and grammatical explanations, which likely hindered their long-term acquisition processes.

Ellis, Li and Zhou's (2019) experimental study involving seventy-two eighth-grade EFL students assessed the effect of pre-task explicit teaching on an orally-focused activity. Two oral dictogloss tasks that enabled learners to construct past passives were performed by two groups: the explicit instruction task group, which received a brief grammar lesson followed by practice exercises, and the task-only group, which undertook the identical task without pre-teaching. The explicit instruction group produced more frequent but less precise and sophisticated target language, calling into doubt the effectiveness of directing attention to linguistic form prior to task performance.

The experimental study conducted by Kim (2013) investigated pre-task modelling as a type of planning approach in connection with Korean junior high school students' understanding of question structures. Over a period of five weeks, two groups, a pre-task modelling group and a no-modelling group, completed a pre-test consisting of three dyadic tasks and two post-tests. The modelling group engaged in guided planning by watching pre-task movies, whilst the other group did not. Data were obtained from students using think-aloud procedures and examined according to language-related events. The findings demonstrated positive implications for focus on form and learners' question development among students in the pre-task modelling group.

2.3 Planning in technology-mediated EFL writing

Learning to write is an essential objective of every EFL course and pre-task planning has proved to be largely accepted by EFL teachers around the globe as it supports process writing (planning, editing, revising), an approach commonly used in the classroom (Ellis, 2021). However, although a relatively large number of studies have examined how pre-task planning affects L2 written performance, only some have reported positive results (e.g. Ellis & Yuan, 2004) while others have found no or very limited impact of pre-task planning on learners' writing performance (e.g. Johnson et al., 2012). Very little research to date has looked at pre-task planning and writing performance in technology-mediated contexts

(Adams et al., 2014; Hsu, 2012, 2017; Ziegler, 2018). The research conducted by Ellis and Yuan (2004) studied the effects of various planning types on fluency, complexity and precision. In particular, they evaluated whether pre-task planning or online planning activities improved the accuracy and complexity of texts produced by forty-two EFL undergraduates. Similar to the present study, students were required to compose a narrative based on a collection of connected images. The three planning conditions included no planning, preparing prior to the assignment and online planning. The participants in the online planning group did not have any pre-task preparation time, but had unlimited online planning time. The pre-task planning group had 10 minutes to plan prior to the task and limited online planning time (75 minutes). In the pre-task and online planning stages, form was not explicitly emphasized. Students in the online planning group, who were not hindered by time constraints, wrote more correct texts than those in the pre-task planning group. However, the pre-task planning group scored better than the other groups in terms of syntactic diversity and fluency.

Hsu (2012) examined the impact of pre-task planning time on the complexity, accuracy and fluency of written text-chat learners. Thirty intermediate English learners were randomly allocated to the conditions of having either 10 minutes' pre-task planning or no planning. All students were given unlimited planning time within the task and worked individually with the researcher to perform a narrative story-telling task based on a sequence of images. Findings demonstrated that there were no significant differences between the two groups on measures of complexity, accuracy and fluency, indicating that strategic pre-task planning had no substantial effect on learners' performance. Hsu (2017) compared the effects of rehearsal in conjunction with within-task planning to those of within-task planning alone. As in Hsu (2012), students in the rehearsal group were given 10 minutes of planning time during which they were encouraged to take notes that were afterwards discarded, and unlimited time to perform the task. Both conditions resulted in higher levels of complexity, while learners in the rehearsal group also used grammatical verb forms with greater accuracy. Similar to Hsu (2012, 2017), Ziegler (2018) examined the effects of pre-task planning time in synchronous text-chat by analysing composition processes and written products. Forty-four intermediate EFL learners completed three collaborative picture narrative tasks with varying amounts of pre-task planning time. Chat scripts were analysed for complexity, accuracy and fluency. Results showed no significant differences across the different planning times for any of the three areas (fluency, accuracy and complexity), although students who had the longest planning time slot (3 minutes) used a wider range of lexis than the other groups.

Adams et al. (2014) explored planning in task-based computer-mediated writing with forty-five university-level EFL learners in Malaysia. The participants were assigned to one of three experimental conditions (planning, online planning or no planning) and given the task of writing a wiki page on an engineering project in English for specific purposes (ESP). Students in the unlimited online planning group created more precise language than students in the other groups, confirming the findings of Ellis and Yuan (2004).

Based on this analysis, technology provides potential to create and implement several forms of synchronous or asynchronous writing tasks which could facilitate second language acquisition processes. However, there are still some areas that require further investigation. These studies took place in higher education settings, often under laboratory conditions. In addition, all experimental planning sessions in the studies were unguided with no particular focus on language or content. Technology-mediated written tasks were also focused on one-to-one text chat interactions. Further research is required to determine which types of language-learning tasks can facilitate the development of writing skills in both formal and informal situations.

3. Methodology

3.1 Context of the study

The case study presented here aims to address the gaps in the literature by examining the effects of guided planning on students' written task performance under two conditions (an explicit focus on form or focus on content) at the pre-task stage in a blended learning context. Twenty-four EFL secondary school students were asked to perform a main writing task similar to the one presented in the pre-task (a crime story). The independent variable considered was planning under two different conditions: 10 minutes of guided planning with a focus on content and 10 minutes' guided planning with an explicit focus on grammar. The correct use of the target structures – the past simple and past continuous – constituted accuracy in this context. In addition to integrating both complexity and accuracy as in previous research, and similar to Van de Guchte et al. (2016), this study also featured the concept of modelling. As part of their planning time learners read and listened to a crime story similar to the one they were asked to produce in the main task. The guided planning group ($N = 12$) focused on the use of narrative tenses in the story, while the others ($N = 12$) focused on content (crime, sequence of events). The study investigated the following research question:

1) How do modelling and planning under different conditions (explicit focus on form vs focus on content) in the pre-task impact learners' written accuracy and complexity?

Based on the positive results of previous studies, it was hypothesized that the guided planning group (with a focus on form) would outperform the content-focused planning group in terms of accuracy, as they had been guided towards the noticing and use of target language features in the pre-task activity. Additionally, I hypothesized that learners in the focus on content group would produce more complex texts as focusing on content while listening to/reading a story may foster creativity. Finally, I expected that when more complex language was used, this would have a negative impact on accuracy, as explained by Skehan's (1998) trade-off hypothesis.

3.2 Participants

Twenty-four thirteen- and fourteen-year-old EFL learners (at the A2 level of the Common European Framework of Reference for Languages; CEFR, Council of Europe, 2001) from a lower secondary public school in Italy participated in this study. There were thirteen girls and eleven boys. The majority of students were native Italian speakers, but two had Chinese heritage and two were multilingual (Italian/Spanish). The teacher divided them into two groups: a guided planning group with a focus on content ($N = 12$) and a guided planning group with a focus on form ($N = 12$). To guarantee balance and homogeneity between the two groups, students were assigned to their respective group based on their Oxford placement test scores from the beginning of the school year. The groups contained the same number of students at CEFR levels A1, A2 and A2+. The Italian national secondary curriculum requires that students receive three hours of English instruction per week. Due to the Covid-19 health emergency, all lessons took place under blended learning conditions, partly remotely using the Google for Education workspace, and partly face-to-face. The platform included a bundle of applications that students could use synchronously during the lessons, such as a word processor (Google Docs), a videoconferencing tool

(Google Meet) and a presentation tool (Google Presentation). During classroom lessons each student was also provided with a new generation laptop device which they used to perform the tasks (Chromebook).

3.3 Research design and procedure

This study followed a pre- and post-test research design carried out over a period of four weeks (see Table 5.1). Learners took a pre-test on the use of the target structure (the past simple and past continuous) at the beginning of the study, with the identical test being administered a week after the end of the investigation as a post-test. Students' written productions in the main task were collected and analysed for accuracy and complexity using T-unit measures. The two-phase pre-task on the crime story (Phases 2 and 3 – modelling and planning) was carried out under two conditions: focus on content and focus on form.

3.3.1 *The crime story*

The main task (Phase 4) involved a picture-based crime story writing task. This type of task was chosen to make the study comparable to previous studies in the field and because students were already familiar with this type of story from their Italian literature classes.

Table 5.1 Research design

Timing	Focus on content	Focus on form
Phase 1 **Pre-test**	Cloze grammar test on a crime story	
Phase 2 **Pre-task (Modelling)**	Model observation (Crime story) Instructions focused on content (30 minutes)	Model observation (Crime story) Instructions focused on language (30 minutes)
Phase 3 **Pre-task (Planning)**	Guided planning time (15 minutes) Story outline	Guided planning time (15 minutes) Story outline
Phase 4 **Main task (Story writing)**	Writing task performance	
Phase 5 **Post-test**	Cloze grammar test on a crime story	

3.3.2 Pre-task modelling

As a pre-task, all participants read and listened to a picture-based crime story taken from their digital course book (Bowen & Delaney, 2019). The story was 1,943 words long and comprised multimodal input such as images, sounds and a voice actor as the narrator. The story's language was at the A2 level of the CEFR and included coordinate and subordinate clauses, time expressions linked to the past simple and past continuous tenses (e.g. when, while), and crime- and mystery-related vocabulary (Morgana & Thomas, 2023). Both groups received guided planning instructions on a digital handout which was distributed to the set groups by the teacher via Google classroom. Learners in the focus on content group were asked to observe features of a crime story (type of events, characters etc.), while the focus on form group was instructed to focus on the use of verbs in the past simple and past continuous forms. On the observation sheet, a brief discussion of the grammar rules was also supplied. Students in the focus on form group were required to produce ten written examples of the use of the past simple and past continuous from the story (see Appendix 1). This first phase took place online using the video conferencing tool Meet. Students from both groups were informed that they could make notes on the handout while reading and listening to the story. Students were given 5 minutes after the conclusion of the story to answer general comprehension questions before submitting their notes to the teacher (Morgana & Thomas, 2023). All participants in the study were fully aware that the subsequent main task consisted of re-writing the crime story.

3.3.3 Pre-task planning

Phase 2 of the study (pre-task planning) took place at school in the standard classroom using a classroom set of Chromebooks. Students were already familiar with this type of mobile device as they had been trained on them since the beginning of the school year. Also, Chromebooks were frequently used by other teachers (e.g. Maths, Geography). For the main task, learners were separated into two different classrooms where they received instructions for the main writing task. Three research assistants helped the teacher monitor this phase to guarantee that the tasks were performed by both groups following the same procedure. All learners had 15 minutes of planning time to write their outline of the crime story before performing the main task. The focus on content group did not receive any specific instructions on the target language to be used in performing the task, but they had information on the main features and strategies used to write an effective crime story (see Appendix 2). Learners in the focus on form group were provided with a grammar bank handout in English, featuring explanations on how to use the past simple and past continuous to narrate a story, as well as examples of time expressions. Participants were strongly encouraged to make use of the extra information during story planning as they would not be able to use the digital handouts during the main task performance (Motchizuki & Ortega, 2008). Students were expected to plan the task in English (L2). During the planning and writing time, neither group could access any other resources such as the internet or online dictionaries, thanks to the use of the lockdown browser. The instructor/researcher was able to monitor the preparation time using Google Docs, and all students made use of the entire 15-minute session. At the end of the preparation period, students uploaded their outlines to Google Classroom. At that stage, outlines were collected for research purposes so no personalized feedback was provided.

3.3.4 The main task

Students performed the main task immediately after the pre-task planning. Both groups received a series of pictures from the story. Learners were required to rewrite the crime story they had heard and read in the model, providing all the details and features they could recall. The task lasted 60 minutes. Students did not request any extra time. A week later, all students performed the post-test on the use of narrative tenses.

3.4 Data collection

Two types of data were collected for this study. As in Morgana and Thomas (2023), a pre- and post-test was administered, consisting of forty cloze items on the use of narrative tenses (past simple and past continuous). The test was created by the teacher/researcher and validated by two native English teachers who took the test. When multiple answers were possible, the test was adjusted to include fewer possibilities. Twenty learner written tasks were also collected and analysed for accuracy and complexity using T-unit measures.

T-unit analysis has been widely used to measure the syntactic complexity of written and spoken texts (Gaies, 1980). The T-unit usually consists of a main clause and all the subordinate clauses with the structures that are attached to or embedded in it (Hunt, 1965). Larsen-Freeman (1978) has widely used T-unit analysis as a valid measure to evaluate the quality of EFL student written texts. Additionally, more recent studies have used it to measure fluency in EFL writing (Ishikawa, 1995; Jiang et al., 2019; Sasaki & Hirose, 1996) or in relation to syntactic complexity and accuracy in TBLT (Housen & Kuiken, 2009). T-unit measures used in this study include the analysis of the number of words per text, number of sentences per text, T-units per text and error-free T-units per text.

Anonymity and confidentiality were protected in accordance with the British Educational Research Association (BERA) ethical framework. Informed consent was obtained from the students' parents and they and their children consented to participate in the study.

4. Findings

4.1 Pre- and post-test

The same procedure used in the pilot study (see Morgana & Thomas, 2023) was adopted for the pre- and post-tests. The tests were administered immediately before and immediately after the pre-task/main task work. The test was designed to measure students' proficiency in the target language features (narrative tenses) before and after the intervention. It was conducted using Google Forms and automatically graded by the system according to criteria defined by the teacher. To verify the validity of the results, each test was double-checked by the instructor/researcher.

Table 5.2 shows the results of the pre-test, revealing no statistically significant differences between the two groups. As confirmed by the results, both groups performed better in the post-test (see Table 5.3), indicating that the written work had an effect on their knowledge gain of narrative tenses.

In conclusion, it appeared that both groups began the project with comparable proficiency in the use of narrative tenses in stories. In addition, as indicated by the pre- and post-tests, all students' proficiency in the targeted language elements had increased following the intervention. Although students in the focus on content group did not receive any explanations on the target structure, they were able to perform at the same level as the focus on form group, thus contradicting the first hypothesis that a focus on form would increase the accurate use of the language structure compared to the focus on content group. These findings support Foster and Skehan (1999) and Ellis, Li and Zhou (2019), but in a sense conflict with Mochizuki and Ortega (2008), Van de Guchte et al. (2016) and Adams (2014), who did find differences between the experimental

Table 5.2 Results and descriptive statistics of the grammar pre-test

	PRE-TEST – Focus on content	PRE-TEST – Focus on form
Number of tests	12	12
Mean	26.000	25.667
SD	4.729	4.539
Shapiro-Wilk	0.919	0.918
P-value of Shapiro-Wilk	0.274	0.268
Minimum score	18.000	19.000
Maximum score	32.000	33.000

Note: Maximum possible score 40/40.

Table 5.3 Results and descriptive statistics of the grammar post-test

Descriptive statistics		
	POST-TEST – Focus on content	POST-TEST – Focus on form
Number of tests	12	12
Mean	32.000	31.500
SD	4.178	4.815
Shapiro-Wilk	0.934	0.963
P-value of Shapiro-Wilk	0.423	0.828
Minimum score	27.000	25.000
Maximum score	40.000	40.000

Note: Maximum possible score 40/40.

and non-experimental groups. However, although the pre- and post-test were designed to measure learners' knowledge of the target structure, they are more focused on receptive knowledge and do not provide specific information on the accurate use of the target structure. To complement these results, I conducted a T-unit analysis of students' written productions in the main task.

4.2 T-unit analysis of the written crime story task

The twenty written tasks (rewriting a crime story) produced by both the focus on content group ($N = 10$) and the focus on form group ($N = 10$) were coded for accuracy and complexity (see Table 5.4). Fluency is normally assessed

Table 5.4 Comparisons between focus on content and focus on form group for accuracy and complexity ($N = 20$)

Measure	Focus on content group	Focus on form group	Difference
Accuracy: Target structure error-free T-unit	73.8% (110/149)	87.7% (115/131)	+13.9% (Focus on form)
Complexity: Words per T-unit	10.5	7.5	+ 3 words per T-unit (Focus on content)
Complexity: Subordination per T-unit	1.5	1.2	+ 0.3 (Focus on content)

through word/time ratio. In this study, fluency was not assessed as the teacher provided students with the number of words they should achieve (120 words), so all written texts were of a similar length. No significant difference was found between the two groups in terms of the number of T-units (Focus on content= n149 T-units overall; Focus on form= n131 T-units overall). Students in both groups produced an average of 14 T-units per text.

Accuracy

T-unit analysis revealed that the focus on form group outperformed the focus on content group in the correct use of the target structure (115 error-free T-units out of 131).

Complexity

As expected, the focus on content group produced longer T-units, although compared to the focus on form group these were not particularly complex in terms of subordination. There are various possible reasons for this. For instance, since teenage EFL learners tend to connect short main clauses with 'and, but, or and because' they tend to use relatively few words for each individual T-unit, that is, each main clause usually only has one short subordinate clause attached to it. However, as their L2 competence grows, they begin to use a range of language structures such as prepositional phrases and subordinate clauses that increase the number of words/T-unit. This confirms what Hunt (1977) argued in his studies that there is a progressive order in which students acquire the ability to perform different types of embedding.

5. Discussion

The purpose of this case study was to investigate the effects of technology-mediated pre-task planning on EFL learners' written performance. To do so, learners were divided into two planning groups with two different conditions: focus on content and focus on form. All tasks were performed in a digital environment, namely Google classroom, using blended learning methods. Similarly to Van de Guchte et al. (2019) and Morgana and Thomas (2023), this study used the guided listening and reading of multimodal input as a model for planning.

Overall, the findings indicate that there were no significant differences across the different pre-task planning conditions (focus on content vs focus on form) in terms of receptive knowledge of the target structure. My initial hypothesis that learners in the focus on form group would outperform learners in the focus on content group in the grammar post-test was not confirmed by the test results. This outcome may have a number of explanations. Learners from both groups were exposed to the multimodal input (the listening and reading of the crime story). Although the focus on content group did not focus on language explicitly, it may have noticed meaning and form at the same time without any excessive cognitive burden. Additionally, EFL secondary school learners in Italy are used to focusing on grammar in the pre-task and may have focused on form spontaneously, even if they belonged to the focus on content group.

On the other hand, findings from the written text analysis showed that the focus on form group outperformed the focus on content group in the correct use of the narrative tenses. Although they produced shorter texts, they were able to rewrite the story using appropriate and correct verb tenses. Thus, pre-task planning with a focus on form has an impact on learners' written accuracy, even with pre-intermediate EFL learners. This confirms the results of both Van de Guchte et al. (2019), where students in the focus on language group used the target features significantly more often and more accurately than the focus on content group, and those of Mochizuki and Ortega (2008).

Considering the results of the post-test, the fact that the focus on content group produced more complex but less accurate texts may be explained by Skehan's trade-off hypothesis (2007). The limited capacity for attention may have influenced learners' performance in the main task (i.e. rewriting the crime story) as students were more focused on conveying the meaning and organizing their own ideas.

6. Pedagogical implications

Pre-task planning is one of the areas that could potentially benefit from technology-mediated TBLT being used as a more multimodal and engaged task approach (Ellis, Li & Zhu, 2019; Mochizuki & Ortega, 2008). The blended learning mode that the health emergency situation dictated proved to be an opportunity to develop and adapt innovative teaching practices. This study may have important implications for teachers and educators as it was carried out in real classroom conditions with an entire class of secondary school learners. First, the capabilities of the technology promoted language awareness because the digital writing tool enabled students to easily revise and restructure text (and, subsequently, their ideas). According to previous research (Morgana & Thomas, 2023), students feel comfortable using the Google for education digital platform as they are able to receive immediate feedback, access the digital story and listen to it at their own pace, and make use of all the process writing strategies (editing, revising etc.). Secondly, teachers may want to design pre-tasks following the multimodal input modelling strategy, using stories and videos that students can easily access and manipulate to guide their learning. The multimodal input can be directed at form, content, lexis or specific language functions. Finally, this study focused on technology-mediated pre-tasks in a blended learning context, thus demonstrating how a well-designed task as a workplan can be easily adapted and frequently enhanced by technology. For example, learners from this study could eventually write and publish their own illustrated crime story.

7. Conclusion

This study was designed to address Italian teachers' concerns about the teaching of grammar at the pre-task stage. Some research in EFL argues in favour of the importance of grammar teaching (e.g. Littlewood, 2007), but most TBLT researchers (e.g. Ellis et al., 2019; Long, 2015) dismiss the explicit teaching of grammar rules in the pre-task, as learners will have the chance to notice and practice this in the communicative tasks that follow. Based on these premises, this study sought to examine the impact of pre-task planning with a different focus (on form vs content) on learners' knowledge of a goal structure (narrative past simple and past continuous tenses) in a technology-mediated context. The case study presented in this chapter is part of a larger study on the impact of technology-mediated TBLT in the EFL secondary classroom. A pilot study on pre-task guided and unguided planning has been conducted previously (Morgana & Thomas, 2023). The students' questionnaires conducted during the pilot study also served as a needs analysis for this research.

Overall results indicated that technology-mediated tasks appeared to have an effect on students' learning, but learning was mainly guided by the type of task rather than by the technology itself. This is a common aspect of technology-mediated TBLT studies (see, for example, Solares, 2014) indicating that it is the task design and its successful integration with technology that fosters language learning. A variety of innovative learning possibilities for the pre-task stage have been identified. Students can be guided towards content, form or meaning-making through multimodal input and careful planning. This case study has also demonstrated that carefully designed digital pre-tasks could be successfully implemented in most educational contexts including online, distance and blended education. Moreover, a careful selection of the appropriate digital tools (e.g. the use of breakout rooms) could enhance students' and teachers' experience. However, one of the main challenges for educators is to acquire the right expertise to effectively design technology-mediated tasks. Future studies should look at how to provide specific training for instructors to help them overcome these obstacles and exploit the opportunities presented by the integration of a technology-mediated TBLT curriculum in secondary education.

Appendix 1

Focus on content and focus on language instructions

Model observation (Crime story)

Instructions focused on content

1) Read and listen to the Crime story. You are allowed to scroll through the text and review parts of the text.
2) What are the steps of the crime story? How are events sequenced?
3) Besides how the story is structured, what makes it interesting?
4) What do the main characters do to solve the story?

Model observation (Crime story)

Instructions focused on language

1) Read and listen to the Crime story. You are allowed to scroll through the text and review parts of the text.
2) Write down five sentences using narrative tenses?
3) Write down three time expressions used with narrative tenses.

Appendix 2

Student's sample written task (Focus on language group)

Task: Re-write the crime story

> It was a dark winter night, two women were walking around the city to look for a car to rent. It was snowing and it was very cold. No one could see anything from outside. A man offered his car to the women, but they didn't accept. After that, they went in the library. There was a man sitting on a small table. He was drawing a map. Then, he saw two men coming inside the library and he left. He left the drawing on the table and one of the two women went there and took it. It was a map. The two women were curious and decided to follow the map. They took the car of the strange man* (stranger) and went outside the city. Suddenly, they arrived in a forest. It was snowing and they couldn't see anything outside. They heard a sound, a shot from a gun. They were scared, but went to see what happened. Two men were running with a little boy on their shoulders. He was kidnapped. The women called the police. Then they followed the men and tried to save the boy, but they took them. At the end the police arrived and saved the little kid and the two women. The policeman was the man they met at the library and drew the map.

TBLT, Technology and English Reading Skills

Case study 2 – E-reading Tasks for Vocabulary Learning: The Chromebook Classroom

1. Introduction

Among the four language skills (reading, writing, listening and speaking), reading and writing are the most complex. While children listen and learn to speak spontaneously, reading and writing need to be taught. Moreover, reading involves the cognitive challenges of understanding the message and being aware of the communicative purpose of the text. It follows that comprehending a foreign language written text is one of the most sophisticated real-life tasks that L2 learners face. In this respect, EFL instructors and educators are well aware of the importance of vocabulary learning and the consequent regular, meaningful interactions with target vocabulary. They also know that EFL classroom time for formal reading instruction is restricted, and that opportunities to engage students in developing English reading skills outside of the classroom are also quite limited. Extensive Reading (ER) is one of these possibilities.

English as a Second Language (ESL) and English as a Foreign Language (EFL) researchers have been studying ER for over twenty years. The primary benefits of ER are improved vocabulary and reading comprehension. Extensive studies have been conducted in the field of ER vocabulary acquisition ((Brown et al., 2008; Pigada & Schmitt, 2006; Webb & Chang, 2014). In terms of reading abilities, reading competence and speed have been measured using various tests and programmes (Beglar & Hunt, 2014; Milliner, 2017). Prior to 2010 and the widespread adoption of tablet devices in everyday life, ER depended greatly on the availability of a large collection of graded reading books because it was primarily based on printed materials. As a result, its implementation was extremely expensive for both institutions and students (Davis, 1995). With the ever-increasing availability of electronic devices in classrooms and in students' homes, graded readers and other reading resources for ER can be accessed with the click of a mouse or the tap of a finger. This remarkable transformation in the availability of materials has spawned a new field of ER study: ER on electronic devices. As such, the number of studies investigating the use of e-books in ER beyond the language classroom has been rapidly expanding.

On the other hand, teachers have been looking for opportunities to integrate ER projects, which are mainly performed outside the language classroom, with in-classroom work to maximize students' learning outcomes. In this scenario, the rapid development of technology-mediated TBLT and the growing interest in its implementation in secondary school contexts appears to offer the methodological answer to teachers' needs.

This study examines vocabulary acquisition through an e-reading and technology-mediated TBLT project on mobile devices inside and outside the language classroom. As meta-analysis shows (Jeon & Richard Day, 2016), there is little published material on the use of e-books in ER projects involving eleven- to thirteen-year-old EFL learners in lower secondary schools; thus, this project aimed to fill this research gap. The study participants were fifty second-year Italian secondary school students from two separate classrooms. Half of them engaged in an ER and technology-mediated TBLT project during a four-month period using the Oxford Learners Bookshelf platform.

2. Literature review

2.1 Extensive reading on e-books

As observed in Morgana and Pavesi (2021), there are three main advantages to using smart and mobile devices rather than printed materials for Extensive Reading. First, EFL learners can access online libraries of graded readers, such as the one used for this study (Oxford Learners' Bookshelf), which provide vast quantities of reading material at the appropriate level (Cote & Milliner, 2015b). Second, electronic devices provide access to multimedia features such as audio narration, and to glossaries or dictionaries (Huang, 2013; Lai & Chang, 2011; Larson, 2009). A number of studies have reported that the capabilities of multimedia devices have a positive effect on reading motivation (see Lin, 2010). Thirdly, mobile devices allow both students and teachers to track reading progress, thus addressing one of the main issues of ER: learners' accountability (Chen et al., 2013; Doiron, 2011; Huang, 2013; Lai & Chang, 2011). In addition, the availability of online libraries allows researchers to analyse quantitative reading data (De Lozier, 2019) by downloading statistics from the learners' reading logs, which provide information on the number of books and words read as well as the time spent reading.

Given that ER using printed books is credited with increasing learners' reading motivation (Day & Bamford, 1998; Takase, 2009), a large number of studies on the impacts of electronic ER have focused on learners' attitudes towards reading and e-reading. An increasing number of research studies reveal positive attitudes towards e-books, as well as reduced anxiety and a newly discovered enjoyment of reading (Jeon & Richard Day, 2016; Takase, 2009). Yamashita (2013) investigated the effects of ER on reading attitudes with sixty-one EFL undergraduates and found that ER was effective in reducing learners' anxiety about reading in the L2. De Lozier (2019) offered an intriguing observation by noting that the enjoyment of e-reading varies significantly by ability level. Intermediate and advanced students love reading more because they find it easier and more enjoyable, but lower level students find it more difficult and need to be strongly motivated.

Several studies have explored the attitudes of learners towards various technologies. Comparing reading achievement on tablets and desktop computers in Taiwanese senior high schools, Lin (2014) revealed that mobile devices were the favoured alternative. Cote and Milliner (2015) discovered that, despite some students initially having mixed feelings about reading on PCs or smartphones, their attitudes shifted significantly as they gained experience with these devices, and many of them discovered that they enjoyed reading on electronic devices. In a similar spirit, Dundara and Akcavir (2012) discovered that e-books are favoured over printed books for lengthy reading, even among very young children. However, studies have also revealed that some students experience difficulties with e-reading (Huang, 2013; Huang & Lin, 2011). Some students reported experiencing challenges such as eyestrain, headaches and slower reading speeds, which may be the result of insufficient exposure to reading on electronic devices in the past. Other limitations include the limited screen size of mobile devices and the requirement of a stable, flat-rate internet connection to access the reading materials. In addition, technological devices are tools that include an inherent level of distraction. These difficulties must be considered in a project such as this one that involves EFL students in lower secondary school.

Alongside reading comprehension and reading speed, vocabulary acquisition is one of the three primary topics of ER research (Nakanishi, 2015). Most studies find improvements in incidental vocabulary learning because ER increases the number of meaningful contacts with vocabulary items (see Waring

& Takaki, 2003; Zahar et al., 2006). Studies on language acquisition through e-book reading employ a variety of assessment techniques. Some schools use scores from standardized English language competency examinations that are aligned with the Common European Framework. Milliner (2017), for example, used TOEIC reading comprehension scores to examine increases in reading comprehension. Other research, such as Webb and Chang (2015), utilized ad hoc assessments to measure the retention of certain terms encountered in reading texts. The same study underlines the benefits of audio recording being available. Regarding vocabulary retention through e-reading, Lin and Lin (2019) suggest that receptive knowledge of target words produced the greatest effect compared to mixed and productive word knowledge, which is consistent with previous findings regarding vocabulary acquisition through extensive reading of printed books.

2.2 Technology-mediated TBLT reading

One of the advantages of using technologies in the TBLT classroom is that learners naturally combine the four skills to accomplish a task in the same way that they usually engage with digital communication outside their language classroom (Blake, 2016). In addition, as Godwin-Jones (2015) noted, technology-based communication happens 'within genres that are exclusively or primarily text-based' (p. 11). This means that learners should already be equipped with a variety of different types of reading processes and strategies, such as reading for specific information, reading for gist, scroll reading or reading hyperlinked texts and texts with multimedia glosses. CALL research has always been fascinated by technologies' potential for fostering reading skills. In fact, thanks to *textual persistence,* language learners have more time to understand and internalize linguistic features (Payne, 2004). An early strand of research demonstrated how reading multimedia texts with glosses has a positive impact on learners' vocabulary learning (Chun, 2006). Chun also stressed the importance of providing learners with individual pre-task activities that activate learners' previous lexical knowledge and prepare them for the reading activity. On the other hand, developing reading comprehension skills is a more complex activity that goes beyond vocabulary learning. In this respect, studies began to develop that combined vocabulary acquisition and reading comprehension in technology-mediated contexts (Yanguas, 2009). More recently, a group of studies has investigated the effects of technology-mediated TBLT approaches on EFL learners' reading comprehension skills (Mehri Ghahfarokhi & Tavakoli,

2020; Tavakoli et al., 2017). Using an experimental pre- and post-test design, Tavakoli et al. (2017) investigated the use of technology-mediated TBLT reading tasks to encourage EFL learners' motivation. The study involved eighty-three Iranian university learners divided into two groups (experimental and control). The experimental group received CALL-mediated TBLT instruction on reading while the control group followed the standard language-focused instruction. The pre-task, main task and post-task stages included various reading activities, such as reading for gist or finding detailed information in an online text. Results showed increased student motivation for L2 reading through technology-mediated TBLT tasks compared to the control group. Learners in the experimental group found the reading activities interactive and highly motivating as they could modify the input according to their needs. A similar research design was implemented in a study on the development of learners' autonomy and metacognitive strategies through technology-mediated reading comprehension tasks (Mehri Ghahfarokhi & Tavakoli, 2020). Results showed how traditional reading comprehension instructions are no longer sufficient to engage students and foster their reading skills in digital contexts. Technology-mediated reading instruction contributed to the active involvement of learners as it naturally engaged them in problem-solving activities.

When we consider the importance of developing twenty-first-century reading skills in the digital space, the role of technology-mediated TBLT for reading instruction becomes crucial. Learning L2 vocabulary and developing reading strategies and processes are two essential aspects of EFL teaching, as demonstrated by the studies presented here. A few questions remain open: how can we transfer positive technology-mediated TBLT research practices to secondary school settings? Also, learners in the literature were all intermediate and upper intermediate learners. Would this approach benefit pre-intermediate learners as well?

3. Research questions

The purpose of this study was to illustrate how technology-mediated TBLT reading lessons can be implemented with lower secondary school EFL learners and to investigate the effects of an extensive TBLT e-reading project on students' vocabulary learning. A pilot study was designed and implemented a year before the investigation. It examined students' perceptions and attitudes towards e-reading tasks on mobile devices and served also as a needs analysis for the current study (reported in detail in Morgana & Pavesi, 2021). Based on the results of the pilot study, technology-mediated TBLT reading tasks were designed and implemented within the regular English classes for twenty-five students. Using a pre-/post-test design, the study intended to measure the effects of the ER project on vocabulary learning. A task-based summative writing assessment was also conducted to explore and compare the differences in terms of the learning outcomes of the two groups (experimental and control).

The case study focused on the following research questions:

RQ1: What is the effect of a technology-mediated TBLT Extensive Reading programme on the vocabulary learning of lower secondary school EFL learners?

RQ2: What are the differences between the experimental and control group in terms of vocabulary, grammar and reading comprehension in the summative test?

4. Methodology

4.1 Participants

This study investigated the introduction of an extensive e-reading project using technology-mediated TBLT. It took place in a public lower secondary school in Italy and was conducted with two complete classes of pre-intermediate level EFL learners who were taught by the teacher-researcher. The participants were fifty second-year students (seventh grade). All were aged between eleven and twelve years old at the time of the study. Most of the participants were Italian L1 ($N = 42$); eight learners were bilingual (Italian/Chinese, Italian/Ukrainian, Italian/Bengali, and Italian/Spanish). All participants had had five years of English instruction at primary school, and they were all at an elementary level (CEFR A1-A1+/A2), as confirmed by the Oxford online placement test administered at the beginning of the school year, which focused on grammar and the four language skills (listening, reading, writing and speaking). The two classes were selected (out of five) for the study because of their similar mean values in the placement test (experimental group, $M = 93.2$; control group, $M = 93.6$). Each class was assigned to one of the two different conditions: an experimental technology-mediated TBLT ER group ($N = 25$) and a control group ($N = 25$). Both classes had three one-hour English lessons per week. Students in the experimental group performed technology-mediated reading tasks for one of the three hours and were invited to read eight e-books outside the classroom. The control group followed the standard instruction.

All students used their own mobile devices (smartphones, tablets and new generation laptops) to perform the ER at home and a classroom set of new generation laptops for the classroom reading tasks. Learners' digital literacy was not formally surveyed. However, in view of their age and the fact that the study took place immediately after the period of lockdown and the consequent online education, the students were familiar with the use of mobile applications, instant messaging services and search engines. A letter was sent to students and their families to notify them about the research project, request their permission to collect data and provide basic instructions on how to use the e-library from mobile devices. In this survey, mobile devices comprised smartphones, tablets and latest generation laptops.

4.2 Data collection

The project started in the second half of the school year and was implemented over a period of four months, from February to May. Quantitative data were collected at the beginning and end of the investigation. In order to answer the first research question, students completed a vocabulary test with sixty lexical items taken from the eight e-books selected for the project. The test consisted of a list of words, for which students had to fill in an appropriate translation or an example in context. The students' responses were ranked between 0 (no correct answers) and 60 (all correct answers). Words that learners scored correctly both at the pre- and at the post-test were considered to be *known items*, while words unknown or incorrect at the pre-test and correctly scored at the post-test were considered to be *learned items* (Pujadas & Muñoz, 2019). The number of correct responses and learned items in the pre- and post-programme tests was calculated, and an intra-group analysis of results was conducted (see also Morgana & Pavesi, 2021). To compare the two groups and see if there were any differences in terms of language competence in context (grammar, vocabulary and reading comprehension), students completed a summative TBLT assessment at the end of the experiment. The assessment data were scored by the teacher/researcher and an experienced English teacher from the school, using a set of assessment criteria based on the Common European Framework of Languages (CEFR – level A2+).

4.3 Materials

The graded e-readers

The textbook *Step Up 2* by Philippa Bowen and Denis Delaney published by Oxford University Press (OUP) was used as the English language course book in the two classes involved in the study. The standard English school curriculum followed by all participants was based on this course book and included the same vocabulary, grammar rules and communicative functions for all the students.

The book included access to sixteen graded e-books that students could download on their personal mobile devices and read offline. Students were given a personal code after they had purchased the course book which gave them access to the e-books at no additional cost. The graded e-readers published on the OUP's interactive online platform Oxford Learners' Bookshelf were also used as reading materials. The anthology contained a variety of genres, including adventure tales, fables, crime/mystery tales, comics, nonfiction and classics. The e-books were accessible via a cloud storage service, and students could download them to their devices for offline use. Highlighting, interactive exercises, glossaries of key terms and an audio version of the novel with music/sound effects were provided for the electronic books. The application also automatically logged learners' reading progress and reading time. The e-books in the collection were sorted into two categories: beginner and rapid beginner. Quick starter e-books were shorter than starter e-books (about 1,100 words vs 1,500 words), and also featured more graphics or were in the form of comic books. All of the e-books in the collection were at the A1+/A2 (QCEFR) level and had few headwords and word families (350). Students were awarded virtual certificates upon completion of the e-book reading.

Over the course of the four-month study, students in the experimental group ($N = 25$) were asked to read eight out of the sixteen e-books outside the language classroom. Using the list provided by the teachers, students read at least one e-book every two weeks and had a weekly one-hour TBLT reading lesson. The more motivated students were allowed to read more than one e-book every two weeks (from among the sixteen in the e-library). To measure the learning of specific vocabulary items, all participants took a vocabulary test at the beginning and end of the project. The fact that students read the same e-books made it possible to create a vocabulary test based on the words in the texts rather than using a standardized vocabulary test.

TBLT reading lesson plans

The same English coursebook was used for the two groups. However, task-based lesson plans related to the e-books were developed by the teacher/researcher and implemented weekly with the experimental group. Technology-mediated reading tasks were designed to elicit authentic use of the language and vocabulary met in the stories and to activate learners' previous knowledge and noticing strategies. The TBLT reading lessons followed the same pre-task, main task and post-task procedure throughout the project (see for example Table 6.1). All tasks were performed using a classroom set of Chromebooks and thanks to the technology, students could access and process the input at their own pace. In the pre-task phase learners were provided with a multimodal input that served as a model activator. In the main task phase students performed the task itself, usually in pairs. Finally, in the post-task phase, students either reported on the task with a different partner or in groups, or asked the teacher about specific language features they had noticed or had issues with. To complete their tasks, learners were invited to make use of digital resources and/or presentation tools.

For the control group, the teacher followed the standard lesson procedure, mainly using coursebook activities focused on either grammar or vocabulary (see for example Table 6.2). Learners in the control group only worked on texts and activities individually.

Table 6.1 A sample technology-mediated TBLT lesson focused on reading

TBLT Lesson #A (In the classroom, with Chromebooks)	Witnessing a robbery
Pre-task	Learners look at pictures and read a news article (online) about a robbery that has recently taken place in the UK.
	They can search for extra information about the event and the witness.
Main task	Learners are asked to read a police report with a transcript of the witness interview. In pairs, they must identify key information and compare it to the news article. They are also asked to focus on relevant features of the text type and vocabulary.
Post-task	Each pair of students compares findings with other pairs. Students complete a virtual shared map of findings (tool: Jamboard)
	(Optional – homework) Write a recount.

Table 6.2 A sample EFL lesson activity for the control group (based on the coursebook)

EFL Lesson #B (In the classroom, standard teacher-class lesson)	An event from the past
Warm-up	Learners look at three pictures in the coursebook and guess what the story is about.
Main activity	Learners read the story below the pictures, identify words they do not know and ask the teacher to translate/provide a definition.
	Learners answer two comprehension questions and complete matching exercises (vocabulary). The teacher also explains key linguistic structures (past simple question form).
Review	The teacher provides students with example sentences using question form, and grammar exercises (fill in the gap activities).
	Homework: students read a similar text, underline key words, complete general comprehension + grammar exercises.

4.4 Pre-test, post-test and summative assessment

A vocabulary pre- and post-test was designed to answer the first research question on the effect on learners' lexical knowledge of extensive e-reading combined with technology-mediated TBLT tasks. All students in the experimental group read the same eight e-books, allowing the use of a vocabulary test that was carefully designed around the texts proposed, instead of a standardized test. Each book had about 6,000 words, with 400 to 500 headwords. The researchers selected between five and ten lexical items from each of the eight e-books, based on the keywords provided in the glossary (63 per cent were high frequency words included in the Oxford 3,000 list; 11 per cent were part of the Oxford 5,000 word list; 26 per cent were unclassified words – that is, words not present in frequency wordlists). About half of the lexical items were at A1-A2 level, 24 per cent at B1-B2, 6 per cent at C1 and the remaining 20 per cent were not classified. The same sixty lexical items were covered in the pre- and post- tests. Only nine words were also present in the OUP *Step Up 2* textbook wordlist. None of the words selected from an e-book occurred in the others. The pre-test took place in February. Students from both the experimental and the control group completed the test via Google forms. Learners were required to provide the L1 translation/s or a valid example in context of the words they were familiar with. At the end of the project, in May, the same test was given to learners as a post-test.

The second data collection tool was a general English assessment test, which included different types of activities (e.g. matching, sentence completion, multiple choice questions) on reading comprehension, vocabulary and grammar. The test was designed as a summative assessment to check whether students had reached the planned learning outcomes. The assessment test included eighteen questions and a short text to read. Learners had 45 minutes to complete it. The summative test was administered to both groups (experimental and control) at the end of the project, which corresponded to the end of the school year. Participants' performances in the summative assessment test were scored individually based on the CEFR assessment scales for A2 learners. Teachers compiled an analytical assessment scale with three macro-areas: grammar, vocabulary and reading comprehension. Each area was scored between a minimum of 4 (learning objective not achieved) and a maximum of 10 (learning objective fully achieved).

Both the vocabulary pre- and post-test and the summative test were assessed by two EFL teachers who had extensive experience of this type of test and assessment. This ensured high inter-rater reliability (Pearson's $r = 0.549$ at pre-/post-test; Pearson's $r = 0.627$ at the summative assessment). Where the two teachers did not agree, an average of the marks was calculated to ensure reliability.

5. Analysis

The quantitative data from the pre- and post-tests were analysed using Jasp 0.16.3's descriptive statistical methods. Since students' pre-test knowledge of the target items varied, relative learning gains were also measured using the method [(posttest score – pretest score) / (number of test items – pretest score) × 100], as in Webb and Chang (2015) and Morgana and Pavesi (2021).

For each lexical item, the total, average and percentage scores from the pre-test and post-test were recorded. The lexical data included in the tests were also qualitatively analysed by manually coding items into thematic categories to identify possible explanations for the acquisition of specific words. The researcher coded the data individually before comparing the coded sets.

6. Results

6.1 Pre- and post-test (Vocabulary)

The first research question focused on whether there is a relationship between extensive e-reading combined with technology-mediated TBLT and learners'

Table 6.3 Descriptive statistics of the vocabulary pre- and post-test

	Pre-test experimental ER	Pre-test control	Post-test experimental ER	Post-test control
N of students	25	25	25	25
Mean	26.080	25.520	47.240	38.280
SD	6.157	6.145	7.849	9.809
Minimum score	15.000	15.000	30.000	25.000
Maximum score	35.000	36.000	58.000	58.000

vocabulary acquisition at pre-intermediate level. Table 6.3 compares overall correct answers at the pre-test and at the post-test using descriptive statistics.

Descriptive statistics of the pre- and post-test indicated that the experimental ER group ($M = 26.08$, $SD = 6.15$) and the control group ($M = 25.52$, $SD = 6.14$) had similar mean values at the pre-test, showing that on average and regardless of their group, each student was aware of the meaning of about twenty-five words out of sixty in the vocabulary test. Data in the post-test differed significantly as the experimental ER group ($M = 47,240$, $SD = 7.89$) outperformed the control group ($M = 38.28$, $SD = 9.80$). In fact, students from the experimental ER group showed significant gains in terms of vocabulary knowledge and recognition between the pre-test and the post-test with scores ranging from 15–35 at the pre-test to 38–58 at the post-test. An intra-group analysis of each group identified seven lexical items as *known words (heavy, west, quickly, meteor, gun, copy* and *fight)*, as most of the students identified them correctly in the pre- and post-tests. A substantial improvement was recorded in respect of a group of specific terms, as presented in the following section.

Highest impact lexical items

Further analysis was conducted to examine the acquisition of discrete words and to discover which lexical items had the greatest and least significant effects on students' learning in the experimental ER group. Results were then triangulated to see if the same words had an impact on the control group as well. As in Morgana and Pavesi (2021), researchers established a threshold level to classify the words that the majority of students in the experimental group learnt; hence, lexical items with a percentage increase of 150 per cent or higher were labelled as highest impact words and analysed qualitatively to identify possible explanations. The words *worth* (+1,600 per cent), *evidence* (+1,000 per cent) and *journey* (+700 per cent) registered the highest impact on students' learning at the post-test compared to the pre-test. Twenty out of twenty-five students in the experimental group were able to identify the meaning of the word *worth* at the post-test, while no one had identified it correctly at the pre-test. Similarly, only a small group (8/25 students) gave a correct answer for the word *journey* at the pre-test, while the term *evidence* was almost universally misinterpreted at the pre-test (only one student identifying it correctly). *Evidence* is, in fact, a cognate of the Italian 'evidenza'. A second group of words was revealed to have a very high impact on learners' knowledge at the post-test. These were *pick up* (+ 400 per cent), *suddenly* (+366 per cent), *fall* (+350 per cent) and *turn* (+235 per cent). The terms *fall, suddenly* and *evidence* were also the words that earned the highest scores at the post-test for the control group.

Lowest impact lexical items

As indicated previously, certain lexical elements had an effect on learners' vocabulary knowledge. However, the data revealed that a substantial number of terms had no effect on students' vocabulary recognition. Six out of sixty words, according to statistical analysis, had no discernible effect on students' learning or retention, as their scores on both the pre- and post-tests were zero. These terms were: *holy, nastily, squid, blacksmith, scrolls* and *alley*. Analysis also revealed that there were no words that students had identified correctly at the pre-test that they then proved unable to recall at the post-test. All the words identified as *known words* were confirmed as such by post-test data.

6.2 Summative assessment test

The second research question focused on the differences between the experimental ER TBLT group and the control group in the performance of a summative assessment based on vocabulary, grammar and reading comprehension from the last two units of the coursebook. The final assessment test was used to identify any meaningful difference in learners' performance to see if the implementation of an e-book ER programme supported by TBLT practice had an influence on learning outcomes. The assessment was delivered towards the end of the school year, immediately after the end of the project. The data regarding the potential effects of ER and technology-mediated TBLT on EFL secondary school learners were analysed, comparing learners' scores in the test for each learning area (reading comprehension, vocabulary and grammar) using descriptive statistics. Results showed that the experimental ER group performed better than the control group in all three learning areas. Table 6.4 shows results for the grammar criterion. Although the scores did not differ substantially, learners in the experimental group performed slightly better ($M = 7.84$, $SD = 1.10$) than the control group ($M = 7.08$, $SD = 0.90$).

Results for the vocabulary (Table 6.5) and reading comprehension criteria, however, showed a substantial increase in the ER TBLT group assessment scores compared to the control group. Particularly in the reading comprehension scores, the two groups differed significantly (Table 6.6).

There are several possible explanations for the differences in the performance of the two groups. First, the fact that the experimental and control groups did not differ much on grammar may be due to the control group having received standard form-focused lessons over the four months and consequently, having had more practice at completing grammar tasks and activities. On the other hand, the experimental group slightly outperformed the control group on grammar, demonstrating that a focus on meaning and communication does not impact negatively on noticing and focus on form (Park, 2012). The results for reading comprehension demonstrated how ER combined with technology-mediated TBLT tasks had a significant impact on learners' reading skills. Four months of

Table 6.4 Descriptive statistics for Summative Assessment Test – Grammar

	Experimental ER – grammar	Control – grammar
N of students	25	25
Mean	7.840	7.080
SD	1.106	0.909
Minimum score	6	5
Maximum score	10	9

Table 6.5 Descriptive statistics for Summative Assessment Test – Vocabulary

	Experimental ER – vocabulary	Control – vocabulary
N of students	25	25
Mean	9.040	8.080
SD	0.735	0.812
Minimum score	7	7
Maximum score	10	10

Table 6.6 Descriptive statistics for Summative Assessment Test – Reading Comprehension

	Experimental ER Reading comprehension	Control Reading comprehension
N of students	25	25
Mean	8.880	7.680
SD	0.833	1.030
Minimum score	7	6
Maximum score	10	10

ER TBLT implementation proved to be a sufficient amount of time to improve learners' task performance. Students were, in fact, able to transfer the reading strategies learned during the experiment to a different context (the summative assessment test).

7. Discussion

7.1 Effects of e-reading on students' vocabulary learning

Over the course of eight months, sixteen graded English e-readers were assigned to participants in the experimental group while students in the control group did not receive any ER. The primary goal was to identify the extent to which extensive reading with multimedia functions, supported by a weekly technology-mediated TBLT reading lesson, promotes vocabulary acquisition. As a measure of vocabulary intake, sixty lexical items were chosen from e-book glossaries. The pre-/post-test design contributed to the collection of empirical data, and the analysis of the types of words learned allowed further insights into the vocabulary learning process. Two findings proved to be significant. One relates to the amount of new vocabulary acquired and the other to the types of lexical words recalled. The differences between the pre-test and post-test mean that, on average, students' vocabulary knowledge increased over the course of the study regardless of the group (experimental or control), showing that ER, in this case also supported by well-designed TBLT lessons, contributes to vocabulary acquisition and reading performance, as shown by Pigada and Schmitt (2006) and Webb and Chang (2015). In addition, students appeared to learn and retain vocabulary that was not available in the Oxford frequency wordlists (3,000 and 5,000) and the Cambridge English Vocabulary Profile database, or at CEFR B2 level, because the terms were directly related to the stories (e.g. *journey, evidence*). Although the only control for students' exposure to the English language was their attendance at three one-hour EFL lessons each week, the connection between the acquisition of these specific vocabulary items and the e-reading TBLT project is extremely evident, confirming the findings of Morgana and Pavesi (2021). Alternatively, it appears that the routine of reading e-books also served as a vocabulary scaffolding and recycling exercise.

Analysing the incorrect words, it appears that students of this age approach L2 vocabulary with a strong influence from L1 (e.g. looking for cognates). This may be related to the fact that all participants in this study were pre-intermediate secondary school students, who tend to rely more on their native tongue. Although this study examined ER outside of the language classroom, it took place in a mixed context, as the teacher/researcher planned a weekly TBLT lesson with motivational and meaning-focused activities that always related to topics from the e-books. This is likely to have had a favourable effect on vocabulary acquisition, as research with mixed methodology appears to have greater benefits for vocabulary acquisition (Lin & Lin, 2019).

The second goal of this study was to check whether the combination of ER and technology-mediated TBLT instruction was also relevant to students' overall proficiency in grammar, vocabulary and reading comprehension. The comparison between the experimental and control group results at the final assessment test showed ER and TBLT's positive impact on students' learning. The approach appeared to be particularly significant for the development of reading comprehension strategies. This supports the idea that technology-mediated reading tasks, supported by multimedia functions and interactive glossaries, contribute to the development of learners' overall reading strategies. Despite the text in the final assessment test being neither interactive nor multimodal, students were able to transfer those strategies (from online to offline contexts) to accomplish the task successfully.

7.2 Pedagogical implications

This study has important implications for teaching EFL vocabulary and reading comprehension in secondary schools. ER, combined with a technology-mediated TBLT design, proved to be an effective pedagogical approach to helping young learners develop effective reading skills. The approach is beneficial for teachers as well, as the pre-main-post task design requires learners to be actively involved in their learning, which in turn contributes to a more dynamic and motivated classroom context.

In addition, the multimedia aspects offered by technologies such as audio sounds, listening while reading, digital highlighting, online definitions of keywords and interactive comprehension activities are important benefits for e-reading and classroom work. Technology-mediated tasks allow participants to work with authentic and multimodal inputs, which has impact not only on their reading skills, but also on their pronunciation and listening competence. Furthermore, digital devices (in this study, mobile devices and Chromebooks) mediated students' learning by helping them to be autonomous and self-confident, as confirmed by the most recent studies in the field (Lin & Lin, 2019; Tragant et al., 2019). Finally, the fact that many EFL digital coursebooks for secondary schools provide students and teachers with free access to a digital library, such as the Oxford Learners' Bookshelf, encourages teachers to implement similar projects in their teaching and motivates students towards ER for language learning.

8. Conclusions

ER through technology is an emerging area of study, and this chapter has aimed to contribute to the research by investigating its effects on vocabulary learning and the development of reading comprehension. In this study I attempted to measure learners' vocabulary acquisition of discrete words through an extensive reading programme on mobile devices (smartphones, tablets and Chromebooks), both inside and outside the language classroom. The study also aimed to measure whether the combination of ER with weekly technology-mediated TBLT reading lessons had an impact on the EFL students' learning outcomes in the areas of grammar, vocabulary and reading comprehension.

The results showed significant vocabulary gains of e-book-related lexical items for students in the experimental group. Students particularly retained non-frequent words that were strictly related to the stories, in addition to words that have a meaningful presence in their daily life (e.g. in video games or social networks). The project proved to be successful in terms of motivation, engagement, value for learning and development of competence. The findings confirm that ER facilitates incidental vocabulary learning as it provides learners with important and meaningful encounters (Webb & Chang, 2015). The technology-mediated TBLT reading tasks performed in class complemented this approach by giving learners opportunities to learn and practice online reading strategies and processes. From a methodological point of view, this study used a receptive word measurement as this was found to generate the largest effect (Lin & Lin, 2019; Webb & Chang, 2015) on vocabulary learning, and it complemented receptive measurements with productive measurements (final assessment test), as also suggested by Lin and Lin (2019).

Although the results are promising, the present study has some limitations. Since it is strongly focused on the specific context of lower-secondary education, results cannot be generalized to all EFL learners or other educational contexts. Furthermore, the small number of participants represents an important limitation. Further studies should be implemented at school and curriculum level to test the efficacy of ER and technology-mediated TBLT reading approaches on a larger population of students.

Finally, this study was part of a large project on the implementation of a technology-mediated curriculum for EFL teaching in lower-secondary schools in Italy and it should be used to plan longer longitudinal studies to develop a solid data foundation for the introduction of technology-mediated TBLT practices in the Italian secondary school system.

Appendix 1

Final Summative Assessment Test (extracts)

A. Read the following text and then complete the sentences below

Hi, I'm Olivia. Last Saturday, I went to Manchester with my friends Luca and Camilla. We went to celebrate Luca's fourteenth birthday. Manchester is a fantastic city. It's got a lot of history, and there are some interesting museums and art galleries, too.

We met at the train station at 10 a.m. Luca and Camilla were hungry, so we went to a cafè next to Piccadilly Station. Luca ate eggs and Camilla had a croissant with jam. I wasn't hungry so I only had orange juice. After breakfast, we went shopping in Manchester's Arndale Centre. We love shopping for new clothes! Camilla wanted a new top, and she found one in A&M. It cost 10£ and it looks great! Luca wanted a baseball cap and he bought one from D-Sports. I bought a scarf from Hershop. It's cool!

In the afternoon, we went to the Manchester Art Gallery. Luca loved it there because he likes art and photography. There was a cool exhibition about music in Manchester. We saw lots of photos of famous bands from Manchester. Camilla is mad about music, so she was very happy. We left the gallery at 2 p.m., and we went to my favourite place ... Old Trafford, the home of Manchester United. Manchester United is my and Luca's football team. We took a tour of the stadium. It was amazing. We saw the team's dressing room! Camilla doesn't like football, but she enjoyed the tour. Luca bought a Manchester United shirt from the stadium shop.

After the stadium tour, we went to the city centre again. We were hungry, so we went to a small restaurant. Camilla and I had pizza. Luca doesn't like pizza. He had pasta. Then, we went for a walk. Luca took a photo of me and Camilla. It's really funny!

At 6 p.m., we went to the bus stop because Camilla's bus left at 6.15. Luca went to the shop opposite the train station and he bought some sweets. We ate them on our train home. It was a great day and Manchester is a great city!

1. Olivia and her friends went to Manchester last _____.
2. Olivia says Manchester has got a lot of _____.
3. They went to a _____ next to the train station.
4. Olivia bought a _____ from Hershop.
5. Luca likes_____ and photography.
6. Camilla is mad about _____.
7. Luca bought a _____ from the stadium shop.
8. Luca had_____ in the restaurant.
9. They went to the bus stop at _____.
10. Luca went to a shop_____ the train station.

B. <u>Write a short text including the following information:</u>

the name of the town/city • who you went with • what you did • what you at

C. <u>Complete the text with the correct form of the verbs in brackets.</u>

Example: Last night, I stayed (stay) home.

I 1 (cook) dinner for my family. I think they 2 (enjoy) it. We 3 (finish) our food and my sister 4 (tidy) the kitchen. Then we 5 (relax) in the living room and we 6 (watch) a rugby match on TV.

TBLT, Technology and English Listening Skills

Case study 3 – Using Video-based Tasks in Listening Comprehension

1. Introduction

Listening is probably the skill we practise first from birth and the same process is mirrored in L2 learning. Although it plays a fundamental role in language acquisition, listening in the language classroom has traditionally been less investigated compared to the other language skills (Graham, 2017). However, in the past decade, thanks to the development of video-based platforms such as YouTube or Netflix and the spread of mobile technologies, interest in investigating listening tasks for the language classroom has grown significantly (see for example Chou, 2016; Montero Perez et al., 2014). Learning has become ubiquitous and learners can easily connect with anyone anywhere, accessing multimodal resources in various languages, often for free (Kukulska-Hulme & Viberg, 2018). Technology-mediated learning's capability to connect students and teachers across physical and geographical barriers became a reality in the winter of 2020 when schools went online and the health emergency required students and teachers to study and work from home. Even though digital content has been being developed for years in the field of English as a Foreign Language (EFL), designing technology-mediated TBLT lessons for adolescent learners looked to be fairly difficult (Morgana, 2021). In response to students' demands and preferences for online video and digital content, this chapter reports on a research study investigating the use of multimodal captioned videos to develop listening skills. This case study was part of a larger project on the use and production of multimodal videos for EFL learners. It was conducted during the Covid-19 emergency and involved twenty-four lower-secondary school students in Italy. The chapter describes and evaluates the implementation of two multimodal video pre-listening tasks, drawing attention to the role that technology, in this case captioned multimodal videos and video streaming applications, plays in helping students improve their English listening skills.

Research questions

The following research questions guided the study:

RQ1: What are learners' attitudes towards the use of captioned digital videos to develop listening skills?

RQ2: Does a different focus at the pre-task stage guide learners' attention in the subsequent listening comprehension tasks?

2. Review of the research

According to Warschauer (2000), a school curriculum should include time for students to utilize purposeful digital technology that will help them acquire a foreign language. Since this assertion was made, a large number of studies have been conducted to examine the use of technologies in the learning of second languages in a variety of educational settings (Chun, 2016; Thomas, 2012). Research has also focused on out-of-class learning, considering the opportunity to access authentic information anytime, anywhere, thanks to technology becoming increasing portable (Kukulska-Hulme, 2013; Lai & Zheng, 2018; Wrigglesworth, 2019). Formal and informal practices, on the other hand, have long been seen as distinct, each with their own set of strengths and weaknesses. While the Covid-19 emergency provided a unique opportunity to combine formal and informal learning, it also necessitated the design of a thoughtful pedagogical framework. Using multimodal videos as task input in a technology-mediated TBLT context seemed the perfect circumstances in which to integrate sound pedagogical principles with technology. It was also a response to students' needs, as watching videos and films in a foreign language is one of the most popular activities outside school for young and adolescent learners (see for example Peters, 2018).

2.1 Digital video and stories in EFL

Teaching English language listening skills and a wide range of other literacy skills can be facilitated by the use of multimodal (captioned) digital videos (Montero Perez, 2020; Winke et al., 2010). When it comes to teaching foreign language students how to use multimodal digital videos outside of the classroom, teachers and learners often have very limited knowledge (Godwin-Jones, 2012). Generally, video compositions that integrate digital text, graphics and sound effects have been found to be highly effective for a wide range of educational purposes (Hafner, 2014; Miller et al., 2012; Wagener, 2006). In particular, studies have shown creating digital stories to be a successful method of promoting communicative skills in English language acquisition (Kim, 2014; Miller et al., 2012). Digital narrative projects allow students to narrate or teach a certain topic using video, audio and a soundtrack (Robin & McNeil, 2019). On social media, learners are frequently exposed to a wide range of digital stories of all kinds. Multimodal video projects, as noted by Hafner and Miller (2011), enable users to build a digital output that resembles the stories they watch and share on a regular basis. In addition, because they require a variety of multimodal literacies (including writing, speaking and presenting), they provide an excellent context for developing a variety of linguistic and non-linguistic abilities. Hafner and Miller (2011), in their study of a collaborative video project for English for Science students, drew on lessons learned in informal settings and applied them to formal ones. The same might be done for linguistic objectives and language features, using learners' skills to understand a popular YouTuber or Instagrammer's video, bringing them into the language session. Language aspects, such as vocabulary and collocations, as well as pronunciation issues, could be the focus of teachers' analysis of students in the classroom (Godwin-Jones, 2012).

2.2 Using multimodal captioned videos for listening

Multimodal video input in the form of captioned and non-captioned videos is increasingly used in the second language classroom, mostly because of the ease of accessing authentic videos through live streaming platforms such as YouTube, Netflix or Amazon Prime Video. A growing number of studies have looked at the use of multimodal videos to develop listening comprehension skills (Montero Perez et al., 2014; Winke et al., 2010) with encouraging results. Winke et al. (2010) found that the use of captions with multimodal videos was particularly beneficial for L2 learners as they helped learners focus their attention on vocabulary and language chunks (e.g. collocations). They were also helpful in reducing learners' anxiety, especially with lower-level learners. Similarly, Yeldham's (2018) investigation of multimodal videos in listening comprehension literature found that captioned videos improved learners' listening comprehension, particularly with upper intermediate learners, as they were more skilled in using a series of processing strategies, combining captions, speaking and multimodal video. However, some studies raised concerns that captioned multimodal videos are not beneficial to learners as they risk ending up reading the captions and not listening to the speakers (Vandergrift & Cross, 2014). This is partly true with lower-intermediate learners, although there are a number of variables that could mediate these findings. As recommended in Vanderplank (2016) and Yeldham (2018), it is crucial to select multimodal captioned videos that are at the appropriate level for learners, to reduce cognitive load and increase motivation. Finally, in order to help learners process multimodal videos, it would be beneficial to scaffold their learning by planning suitable tasks and pre-tasks.

2.3 Listening tasks in TBLT

Technology-mediated TBLT seems to possess characteristics that are particularly suitable for this context as it is a student-centred approach; it offers learners autonomous access to authentic materials (e.g. Netflix and YouTube videos) resembling real-world situations (during lockdown students often watched video streaming services); and these features provide motivating and meaningful learning experiences (Kokotsaki et al., 2016). Additionally, in online distance learning, technology-mediated tasks help learners develop digital literacy skills (González-Lloret, 2015).

Input-based tasks play a crucial role in developing learners' receptive skills. Well-designed input tasks prepare the learners to process the input, therefore reducing the chances of learners focusing solely on reading the captions instead of on listening subskills such as assimilation, detection of lexical chunks or intonation. In TBLT, listening tasks are classified into two types: one-way and two-way listening. In one-way listening tasks, learners usually listen to the discourse without interacting with the speaker/s. These types of tasks are commonly used in the language classroom, normally in conjunction with activities that require learners to understand a message, complete specific information etc. (Goh & Vandergrift, 2021). On the other hand, two-way listening tasks involve interaction. The tasks presented in this study are input-based one-way listening tasks. The standard TBLT lesson involves three steps: a pre-listening phase, a during-listening phase and a post-listening phase (Norris, 2009). In the pre-task phase an authentic input is presented to students (e.g. a multimodal video from YouTube). In this phase, the input can also be enhanced to activate language awareness and cognitive learning processes (e.g. by using captioned videos). In this study, the captioned multimodal videos served as input to foster students' listening skills. The main goal was to provide learners with pre-listening tasks with two different foci (vocabulary and language) to see what learners do with the captions (Vanderplank, 2016). Are learners more focused on language structures, vocabulary items or pronunciation?

2.4 Learners and multimodal captioned videos

The literature on the use of captioned multimodal videos in the L2 classroom has generally reported positive attitudes. Learners find the use of captions useful and motivating and they perceive it as an effective strategy for learning the foreign language, particularly because it helps them recognize language chunks and sounds (Montero Perez et al., 2014; Pujadas & Muñoz, 2019; Vanderplank, 2016; Yeldham, 2018). Despite findings on the use of captioned videos being sometimes contradictory with intermediate learners (Vandergrift & Cross, 2014; Wisniewska & Mora, 2020), the use of multimodal videos with captions in the EFL classroom is without doubt an excellent resource that allows teachers to implement tasks relating to videos that lower-secondary school learners would not otherwise be able to use for language learning (Vanderplank, 2016).

3. Methodology

This study follows a mixed method approach, triangulating qualitative data with quantitative results (pre- and post-test) in order to shed light on the learning processes, learners' attitudes and linguistic outcomes of the project. Qualitative data included students' semi-structured interviews ($N = 12$) and classroom observations ($N = 2$). In order to identify similar patterns, interview and observation data were analysed using a standard qualitative coding method. A qualitative interpretive approach (Richards, 2003) proved to be particularly relevant to describe digital environments and behaviours, as such realities are complex and dynamic (Hafner & Miller, 2011; Lier, 1998). Additionally, learners' assessment scores at the pre- and post-test were compared, in an attempt to compare learners' listening comprehension outcomes, and answer the second research question (Does a different focus at the pre-task stage guide learners' attention in the subsequent listening comprehension tasks?). The project started in spring 2020 and was implemented over a period of three weeks. Due to the emergency lockdown imposed by the Italian government, all lessons took place online using Google Meet, a videoconferencing application.

3.1 Research context

The participants were twenty-four students in the third year (eighth grade) of a lower secondary school in Milan, Italy. All students were between thirteen and fourteen years old at the time of the study. The teacher-researcher had known the students for two years and was also familiar with the school environment, thus was able to respond to the need for a rigorous design in interpretive qualitative research (Miles & Huberman, 1994). All lessons took place from home due to the full lockdown imposed by the government. The Italian Ministry of Education requires learners in eighth grade to have three 1-hour English lessons per week, but due to the emergency, the timetable was adapted to two 1-hour slots per week. Students connected from home using the video conference app Meet, part of the GSuite platform for education. Although the learners' digital literacy was not formally examined, all students were able to use the tools and technology required by the study as the teacher-researcher had used them for other language projects in the previous school year. Most learners used a laptop computer to follow the lessons and to perform the tasks; two students used a tablet and one connected via his smartphone. This study looked in particular at the use of two different pre-task activities with multimodal captioned videos, and at the strategies employed by the teachers and learners in response to the scaffolding technique used for the listening tasks. The study was part of a larger project on the implementation of project-based learning and multimodal videos in secondary school EFL classrooms. Table 7.1 shows the outline of the entire project. The case study presented here focuses on week 2.

3.2 Project design and technological tools

According to the school curriculum, by the end of the school year, students were expected to have met a set of English language objectives. The linguistic objectives included the use of countable and uncountable nouns, cookery verb collocations, discourse linkers and organizers and proper pronunciation. As a result, the initial step of the project was to pick a series of linguistic objectives that would serve as a guide for the subsequent processes. In addition, at this stage, students should be able to discuss a personal experience (e.g. a favourite dish) and give a brief presentation on a familiar topic that they have previously chosen. Participants were assisted in designing and performing multimodal video tasks by a variety of multimodal, free internet resources. Specifically, technology tools were employed to: (a) conduct background research; (b) take notes; and (c) view

Table 7.1 Main Project outline – Tasks implemented in the case study are highlighted

Target task	Linguistic objectives, communicative function and/or specific vocabulary	Skills and competences – Digital literacies
Week 1: 'A favorite family dish' – Written text + individual oral presentation	Using food vocabulary (countable/uncountable nouns) Selecting, organizing and sequencing information	Use of search engine (Google) Creating and sharing a Google document Giving an online oral presentation
Week 2: 'Cook with Amber' – Listening to and watching a teen chef's video recipe Compare and contrast	Pre-listening activities, Listening for detailed information Language focus: Cooking verbs	Analyzing the components of a digital video: light, audio/music, shot from above etc. + understanding captions
Week 3: 'The menu' – Reading and watching food recipes for a complete menu Write and present a menu	Reading and listening comprehension. Select and use key vocabulary	Use of Google doc, Google presentations, Jamboard and/or Canva for the virtual menu
Week 4: 'My video recipe' – Plan, rehearse and record a video recipe based on the virtual menu Presentation checklist	Use of key presentation and food vocabulary (how to start, linking words, cooking verb collocations)	Shoot, record and share a digital video recipe using a smartphone or tablet Use of various technological tools and applications (e.g. Canva, Animoto, Movie maker)
Week 5: Project assessment and evaluation	Peer-to-peer comments on video recipe	

Source: Morgana (2021), reproduced with permission of Equinox Publishing.

real digital movies. Due to the health emergency, collaboration among learners or between learners and teachers was not easy. The teacher tried to encourage the class to act as a collaborative group, and any necessary help and scaffolding was always provided for both linguistic and technical challenges and concerns.

3.3 Pre-test

In week 1 all participants took a listening pre-test. The test was based on the Cambridge Preliminary B1 listening paper to assess students' general level of English listening. The activities included in the test consisted of multiple choice items, fill-in-the-gap exercises and completing short notes. The rationale behind the choice of Preliminary B1 listening activities was that they provide learners with the level they are expected to reach by the end of lower-secondary school as well as content that involves familiar everyday topics. The test also included questions that focused on vocabulary items and others that were more focused on language use. The pre-test lasted about 30 minutes and was delivered using Google Form. Scores ranged from a minimum of 1 to a maximum of 5 across three different criteria: general comprehension, vocabulary and language competence. Immediately after the pre-test, learners were divided into two groups: a focus on vocabulary group (FoV) and a focus on language group (FoL). To ensure balance between the groups, students were assigned to their group based on their scores in the Oxford Placement Test they had taken at the beginning of the school year.

3.4 Multimodal video listening pre-tasks

In the first week, both groups of students were introduced to the topic using an inductive content strategy. They were instructed to select and share one of their family's favourite recipes. The purpose of the task was to elicit food-related vocabulary, direct learners towards the structure of the text, and facilitate the transfer of their L1 knowledge into English. Technology served as a mediator throughout the duration of the project. In week 1, students gained the skills necessary to search and select content (on Google), produce a written text synchronously using Google documents and use this as a guide to give their family recipe orally to the class. The shared Google document also enabled teachers and classmates to provide students with synchronous and individualized comments. Activities in week 1 served as preparation for the pre-listening and listening phase.

In week 2, learners in both groups watched a multimodal video recipe with captions, performed by an American teenage chef on her personal YouTube channel. Before watching the video, students were assigned two types of pre-task activities. The FoV group received a digital handout with questions focused on vocabulary, while the FoL group received a similar handout with questions focused on language. As stated in Chou (2016), one-way listening tasks usually include a number of types of activities such as comparison, narrative completion, matching etc. Since this study was conducted with intermediate EFL learners, only less cognitively demanding task types were chosen. Specifically, the pre-listening task included only matching, fill-in-the-gap and reordering sentences activities. Students were given 10 minutes to complete the handout. The digital handout was distributed using Google classroom and the teacher was able to check the status of the task in real time through shared documents. The role of the teacher was to monitor and facilitate the task. After completing the pre-task, students were allowed to watch the first captioned video recipe. They watched it three times: the first in teacher/class mode and the other two individually on their own devices. During the third listening, students could check and revise their answers on the digital worksheet and reflect on their general understanding of the video recipe. The multimodal video task served to provide learners with key vocabulary and language use for the overall project. It was also used as a model for the digital video final project. Learners were able to play parts of the streaming video with captions as many times as they needed and perform the guided tasks at their own pace. As a supporting and recycling activity, students from the FoV and from the FoL group were given a very similar task as homework to perform as an out-of-class task.

3.5 Post-test

In week 3, the participants from both the FoV and the FoL groups took the post-test. As with the pre-test, the post-test content was taken from the Cambridge B1 Preliminary test. In this case the specific test items were related to food, food collocations, imperatives, restaurants and recipes in general. The teacher carefully selected those items from various B1 listening tests.

4. Analysis

The qualitative data for the study included classroom observation notes based on lesson recordings ($N = 2$) and students' interviews ($N = 12$). Observation notes were taken during and immediately after each English lesson, using video recordings (Kahn, 2012). The researcher also wrote detailed notes immediately after each live session, including selected verbatim records of the students' interactions (Vaca Torres & Gómez Rodríguez, 2017). Classroom observation notes included comments on the students' engagement, questions, issues raised, motivation and reflection on language-learning episodes. Each dataset was analysed using a qualitative content analysis of emergent themes approach (Elo & Kyngäs, 2008; Silverman, 2004). This entailed an open coding of the students' and teachers' interviews, lesson plans and classroom observation notes. All the coding units selected were analysed using the qualitative analysis software Nvivo (version 10.8); field notes and the students' comments were coded and grouped into themes and categories.

In order to get a clear picture of the task outcomes and implementation, qualitative data were triangulated with quantitative data from the learners' pre- and post-test scores. The students' listening scores from the pre-test were compared to their scores at the post-test to check if the different focus at the pre-task had an impact on students' listening comprehension skills. The pre-test listening task took place at the beginning of the first week and was performed live during the weekly online English class. Students were aware that the lessons were recorded for research purposes. The post-test listening task took place during week 3, immediately after the multimodal video tasks. The teacher-researcher provided students with an assessment scale adapted from the Cambridge B1 Preliminary, which included the expected listening comprehension and language outcomes. To ensure reliability, all tasks and performances were assessed by the teacher-researcher and by a research assistant. The pre- and post-test scores for each language criterion (language competence, listening comprehension, vocabulary) were entered into JASP 0.16.3 for statistical analysis.

5. Qualitative results

Results from the qualitative analysis helped to answer the first research question on learners' attitudes towards the use of captioned digital videos to develop listening skills. Two main categories emerged most often from the data analysis: language awareness and independent learning. Results from each category are presented in the following sections, evidenced by extracts from live lesson recordings and the students' interviews. In accordance with the ethical rules and regulations for conducting research with secondary school students, proper names have been removed and replaced with numbers (e.g. student 3).

5.1 Language awareness

Extracts from interviews and observation notes show that students frequently asked questions about the correct vocabulary to use when talking about cooking or their favourite recipes. Most of them took notes of vocabulary items they found difficult to decode and cross-checked using Google or online dictionaries, as in the following extract from week 2 of the project:

> Student 5: But … teacher … do you prepare a *pizza base*? Or a **pizza dough**.
> Google says **pizza dough**. I don't know how to say it …

Moreover, as a result of the authentic video comprehension activity from week 2, learners seemed particularly interested in detecting and understanding specific language chunks (e.g. cooking method, home cooking, ready meal, set menu) and expressions related to eating and drinking. Questions on collocations frequently appeared in the data, either spontaneously or prompted by the teacher, and they often led to lively classroom discussions at the post-task stage, as in the example below.

(Learners had just watched the video recipe of Amber's homemade chicken nuggets twice: the first as a group and the second individually, at their own pace)

> Teacher: *Have you noticed any particular verb coming before the name of the food mentioned?*
> Student 1: **Cook** *chicken nuggets*
> Student 2: *No, no ... it's* **do** *real chicken nuggets*
> Student 3: *I don't understand* **season the potatoes.** *Season is ... like summer* (laughing).

The reflection on language learning is also confirmed by the students' comments in the interviews. When asked about the use of captions in listening comprehension, most of the learners reported a perceived improvement in listening skills, particularly in the area of pronunciation and vocabulary. It appears that regardless of the group they belonged to, learners focused their attention on recurring language chunks and difficult sounds (e.g. /ough/ in dough).

> Comment 1: *I think I like it because I understand what she said ... she is fast, but with captions it is easier to understand.*
> Comment 2: *I liked the video from YouTube. In the afternoon I watched the videos again to have the American pronunciation, like Amber.*
> Comment 3: *My English is better now. I like using YouTube in class. Sometimes Amber speaks too fast, but with *sottotitoli (captions) it's ok.*

The multimodal captioned video pre-tasks allowed learners to focus their attention on different subskills (language and vocabulary). According to what students reported, this was only useful in the pre-task stage as in the main listening task performance they directed their attention either to language chunks or to detecting connected speech, regardless of the group they belonged to.

Learners were particularly enthusiastic about captioned videos' supporting role in helping them understand pronunciation subskills, such as intonation and connected speech. Some students from the FoV group also reported perceived improvements in vocabulary understanding. The use of authentic videos on personal devices gave the students the perception of a real-life situation and this supported their engagement in the task. Over the two weeks during which the listening tasks took place, learners gradually became aware of their language competence and skills and it also encouraged them to work on their perceived language weaknesses, as reported by students' comments and observation notes.

5.2 Self-directed learning

The second major category that emerged from the analysis was learner autonomy, as mentioned previously. The framework of remote learning within which this study was conducted naturally encouraged autonomy and self-directed learning, and the scenario required students to assume greater responsibility for their education. Observational notes from lesson recordings revealed that students felt interested and responsible, especially during the research and investigation phases in week 1, when they were asked to find and select a (video) recipe of their favourite family dish (Morgana, in press).

> Student 22: *I am doing my research on the internet. It's [everything is] in English, but it's ok. I try to understand. I like watching videos on You Tube, can I watch more video recipes from Amber's channel? Faccio io! (I'll do it)*
>
> (Partly translated from Italian)

Learners recognized that at times they had experienced moments of frustration due to the demanding level of some of the multimodal videos (particularly in week 1), but they reported that captions and the guided tasks provided by the teachers helped them overcome these issues. Learners from the FoL group recognized the language practice aspect and responded positively to the challenge. In addition, virtual classroom discussions in the post-task phase often focused on what activities they could perform autonomously.

> Student 9: *The best thing is to make the video. Can I try? Copio e incollo le cose più utili [I can cut and paste the most useful things].*

Many of them were worried about recalling key cooking vocabulary and being able to understand it again in future video-based tasks. It appears that learners were particularly willing to keep using captions when watching authentic English videos.

Student 1: *Can I use post-it so I can remember words? Or I write the steps of the recipe. In television they have it.*
Student 15: *How many times can we listen to the video with captions? Can I use them also with films?*

Generally, comments showed a positive attitude towards the tasks as students felt engaged in purposeful, meaningful activities, involving authentic language use (Wisniewska & Mora, 2020).

5.3 Quantitative results from pre- and post-test

In order to answer the second research question and see if a different focus at the pre-task stage guides learners' attention in the subsequent listening comprehension tasks, scores were analysed from the pre- and post-test. An independent-samples t-test was conducted to compare learners' scores at the pre-test for both groups. The t-test showed that there was no significant difference in the listening scores at the pre-test between the FoV group ($M = 3.3$, SD = 0.56) and the FoL group ($M = 3.0$, SD = $0.63 - t = 1.81, p = 0.08$). These results suggest that learners from both groups were at a similar level of proficiency.

The post-test results from the t-test also showed that the two groups were generally balanced. On one hand, no significant difference was found for the 'language competence' criterion (FoV $M = 3.9$, SD = 0.65; FoL $M = 3.6$, SD = 0.63), but on the other hand, the post-test revealed a significant difference in learners' scores for the 'reading comprehension' and 'vocabulary' criteria, with the FoV group outperforming the FoL (see Table 7.2).

Generally, data demonstrated that learners significantly improved their marks over the three weeks and were able to improve their listening comprehension skills. An intra-group analysis of the results showed that students from the two groups obtained very similar scores in 'language competence'. Thus, this result showed that the FoV group was able to reach the same level despite the different focus on pre-task activities. The most significant difference between the two groups was revealed by the scores on vocabulary, including the use of collocations and language chunks and reading comprehension abilities. By comparing the scores between the groups, it became evident that the FoV group significantly enhanced their competences in all three criteria. This means that learners constantly improved their ability to recognize cooking vocabulary in general and were able to retain quite a large range of vocabulary throughout the project. It is interesting to note that one of the teacher's concerns about using exclusively authentic captioned multimodal videos to scaffold students' learning

Table 7.2 Post-test t-test results for the Focus on Vocabulary and Focus on Language groups

FoV group	FoL group	t	df	p
Language competence	Language competence	1.813	23	0.083
Vocabulary	Vocabulary	5.438	23	<.001
Listening comprehension	Listening comprehension	6.261	23	<.001

Note: Student's t-test.

was that learners would get confused and not be able to retain key cooking vocabulary because they would be focusing on too many language aspects at the same time (reading, listening, visuals, lexis etc.). The results demonstrated the opposite.

6. Discussion

Investigating the use of multimodal captioned videos in foreign language learning has been quite a popular area of recent research (Graham, 2017; Montero Perez, 2022; Perez & Rodgers, 2019; Vanderplank, 2016; Wisniewska & Mora, 2020; Yeldham, 2018). However, the implementation of multimodal captioned videos to improve listening skills in a technology-mediated TBLT context with secondary learners has not been investigated.

This study was guided by two main research questions: RQ1 What are learners' attitudes towards the use of captioned digital videos to develop listening skills? RQ2 Does a different focus at the pre-task stage guide learners' attention in the subsequent listening comprehension tasks?

The planning and design of the study were informed by key concepts of sociocultural theory as developed by Lantolf and Thorne (Lantolf & Thorne, 2006). In particular, this study focused on the concepts of mediation and scaffolding (see also Chapter 2). The technology-mediated TBLT cycle allowed for implicit and explicit focus on language features to prepare students for the language demands of the main listening task. The use of multimodal captioned videos mediated, scaffolded and activated the conscious awareness of language features through, for example, noticing as confirmed by results. In particular, although multiple variables could have influenced the development of listening skills over the three weeks (e.g. time spent watching captioned films on Netflix, digital videos or YouTube), there were two main areas that benefited significantly from the task work on captioned multimodal videos. First, the guided pre-task activities fostered spontaneous reflection on various aspects of listening to videos with captions. Secondly, the possibility for learners to access the enhanced input (captioned videos) and process it at their own pace encouraged learner autonomy, not only in terms of learning 'independently', but also in terms of learning 'collaboratively' with teachers and peers (Morgana, 2021), as they could discuss and overcome any issue at the post-task stage, thus confirming the main ideas of a sociocultural classroom. According to Vygotskian principles, the teacher encourages learners to engage with the input, activities and tasks mediate action and interaction, and the way they are designed and presented (e.g. focus on language vs focus on vocabulary at pre-task) can also influence how learners orient themselves (Lantolf & Appel, 1994). During the pre-listening and listening task, students were actively engaged in grasping the correct vocabulary or noticing the most frequent lexical combinations or language chunks. In their comments, they emphasized the importance of understanding multimodal authentic videos with the support of captions and mastering the appropriate vocabulary to perform the various tasks, but also to comprehend the authentic videos and the relative captions, thereby confirming the results in Montero Perez et al. (2014), Winke et al. (2010) and Yeldham (2018).

An assumption often made about task-based language teaching is that it is strongly meaning-oriented, and as a result language focus is often overlooked (Long, 2016). In fact, a TBLT approach has a primary focus on meaning, but it can allow explicit vocabulary and language focus activities, also at the pre-task stage (Ellis et al., 2019). The students' responses from interviews in this study suggest that they found the language- and vocabulary-focused pre-task an important step that supported them in the subsequent listening task performance. They felt strongly driven to reflect on different language features both before and while listening to the multimodal videos. This can be attributed to the fact that the multimodal captioned videos were very recent and authentic, which may have contributed to the students perceiving the classroom work as particularly relevant to their daily lives. Other studies have confirmed the importance of providing meaningful and authentic multimodal captioned video experiences for learners, even if the input was sometimes perceived as particularly complex for intermediate level learners (Hafner & Miller, 2011; Winke et al., 2010).

Behind the design of this case study was the idea that technology mediates and scaffolds our learning and that the online class is a socially constructed environment in which students contribute to each other's advancement in learning (Morgana, 2021). The online digital tools used, particularly Google Meet, effectively mediated online communicative practising by, for example, facilitating turn-taking during conversations and providing a virtual venue for learners to meet (Lenkaitis, 2020). The captions in the multimodal videos also served as scaffolding tools to support and guide students' ability to comprehend authentic listening resources. The present study is part of a large project that led students to produce multimodal videos similar to the most popular YouTube videos of a teenage chef. In this context, the technology-mediated TBLT pre-listening and listening tasks presented here served as scaffolding activities for a more integrated curriculum. Based on this premise, this study argues that a technology-mediated TBLT curriculum should consider relevant opportunities for language learners in a broader sense, not only in terms of technology tools or language needs, but also in terms of authentic pedagogical resources.

7. Conclusion

This chapter reported on the use of authentic multimodal videos to develop secondary school EFL learners' listening skills in an online learning context during the Covid-19 pandemic. The study was part of a larger project that was designed in response to learners' needs, and to investigate project-based learning effects on learners' English language and digital literacy skills.

The unprecedented situation of the pandemic forced teachers and educators to adapt to very unusual learning circumstances. This chapter has illustrated a case study on the use of multimodal captioned videos to improve the listening comprehension of twenty-four lower secondary school students in Italy, using online distance learning. The study's aim was to provide learners with innovative ways to learn language and to keep them involved in their learning, both on their own and within the school community (Morgana, 2021).

Despite the small sample size and the narrow scope of the study, the results demonstrated the positive effects of using captioned multimodal videos on learners' listening skills. Technology-mediated TBLT practices to learn English via online distance learning also contributed to developing autonomous learning and fostering language awareness. The guided pre-tasks were perceived as tools that supported a better understanding of authentic videos with captions and this demonstrated how integrating the use of multimodal videos into the technology-mediated TBLT lesson cycle could benefit both learners and teachers, and help move both research fields forward.

The recent shifts in education have meant that new possibilities for language learning and teaching have arisen. It is imperative that tasks and projects be reworked to incorporate both formal and informal learning, as well as online and face-to-face learning.

The data reported in this chapter are intended to aid comprehension of these novel dynamics.

Although this study can provide a number of valuable insights, it must be acknowledged that there are certain limitations to its findings. The sample of students and teachers was relatively small, and the context where the project took place was also quite particular. For these reasons, it is not easy to generalize the findings. In future research that explores the use of captioned videos in TBLT listening, it would be valuable to implement long-term longitudinal studies as the literature so far has investigated small and experimental contexts. With regard, in particular, to the relevance of TBLT and captioned authentic videos in EFL contexts, it is worth examining the relationship between long-term project work and students' English listening competence in secondary schools.

8

TBLT, Technology and English Speaking Skills

Case study 4 – Using Podcasts in the EFL Classroom: The Impact of Planning and Rehearsal on Learners' Speaking Performance

1. Introduction

It has been more than twenty years since technology started to be a reality in schools, progressing in that time from a form of entertainment to a valuable educational tool. Among other approaches, task-based language teaching (TBLT) has proved to be particularly useful for integrating technologies into English language teaching due to its strong links to 'real language use'.

A few years ago, González-Lloret (2014) argued that a technology-mediated TBLT framework was needed to combine technology and tasks as technology is not neutral. Thus, it needs to be selected and carefully integrated into the design of learning tasks (Chapelle, 2014). Indeed, the application of a technology-mediated task-based language teaching framework has been a broad field of study, especially as regards adults and advanced learners. However, studies on secondary school learners and specific subskills are under-represented in the literature. In order to fill this gap, this chapter argues that a technology-mediated TBLT mediates learning experiences and fosters the development of speaking skills, specifically accuracy, pronunciation and discourse organization features (i.e. the ability to produce well-organized and coherent texts). This mixed-method study, carried out with forty-eight intermediate EFL secondary school learners, concerns the use of mobile devices (smartphones and Chromebooks) and gives a detailed description of how two technology-mediated pedagogic tasks targeted communicative competence (Hymes, 1972). In particular, the study attempted to measure learners' language improvement and investigated students' learning experiences. The tasks and assessment criteria were based on the Cambridge B1 Preliminary Speaking papers as students were taking this formal examination at the end of the semester.

While Italian teachers are particularly concerned with grammar and writing skills, learners appear to be more interested in speaking and pronunciation. In a study I conducted a few years ago on the advantages of mobile technologies for language learning, most of the students in the survey stated that they would like to improve their speaking skills through their device (Morgana & Shrestha, 2018). In this respect, teachers may feel insufficiently prepared to teach pronunciation due to the lack of training and teacher development courses on pronunciation and phonology. Moreover, pronunciation is not usually explicitly cited in the school L2 curriculum and it is quite rare to find specific pronunciation lessons. In their final year of high school, students may sometimes have specific lessons on pronunciation (Ducate & Lomicka, 2009), but this happens very rarely at lower secondary school level.

2. Research questions

The study explored the following research questions:

RQ1: What impact do technology-mediated tasks and podcasting have on EFL secondary school learners' speaking skills?

RQ2: What factors influence secondary students' learning experiences in technology-mediated TBLT, and what are students' perceptions of these?

3. Theoretical underpinnings

The study presented here is founded on a recent application of sociocultural theory (Lantolf et al., 2014) in TBLT that sees the social use of a language, including computer-based interaction, as an activator of cognitive processes that lead to L2 acquisition. Although the theoretical relevance of SCT in TBLT is not always recognized (Long, 2015), tasks are influenced by social dynamics, and the integration of technology in EFL constitutes one of those dynamics.

3.1 Mediation and scaffolding

A central concept of SCT is mediation. In SCT, L2 learning occurs when students interact with social artefacts (such as language or teachers) and physical tools (such as technologies) that act as learning mediators (Lantolf et al., 2018).

Since 'artifacts and tools are not neutral' (Oskoz & Elola, 2014: 118), there are numerous ways students can use them and, therefore, a variety of possibilities for language development. Tasks themselves mediate learning, and task modality (e.g. mobile-based tasks) strongly influences how foreign language learners approach the L2 (Oskoz & Elola, 2014).

Another central concept of SCT is scaffolding. Scaffolding refers to the interaction between the learner and an expert (the teacher, but also a tool) that helps the learner perform a language skill that the learner could not accomplish by themselves (Ellis et al., 2019). In this study, the interaction between students, teachers, tasks and technology mediates, scaffolds and activates the conscious awareness of language features (noticing).

4. Technology mediation in TBLT and CALL research

The mutual opportunities offered by TBLT and CALL have been investigated since the early 1990s. TBLT has been used as a framework for CALL research. Conversely, CALL provided a new environment to benefit specific tasks and compensate for weaknesses in TBLT (Ellis et al., 2019).

The study presented here focused on speaking tasks across a range of technology and their link to certain SLA processes. While several studies focused on the design and perceptions of language speaking tasks (Pellerin, 2014), studies that attempted to measure learners' speaking performances in relation to the task and to SLA processes (Tang, 2019; Winke, 2014) are less frequent in the literature. These areas are the main points addressed in this review.

5. Literature review

5.1 Speaking tasks

Most research has demonstrated a positive impact on learners' development of general speaking skills (Abdous et al., 2009; Stockwell, 2010), discourse management (Thomas & Reinders, 2010) and pragmatics (Sykes, 2005) through synchronous computer-mediated communication (CMC) interaction. However, results on the improvement of speaking skills through technology-mediation are mixed. Nielson (2014) assessed the impact of TBLT on an online Chinese as a foreign language course by looking at students' participation and proficiency rates. Results showed significant gains in speaking proficiency. On the other hand, Tang (2019) has recently looked at the influence of task modality on L2 learners' pragmatics by comparing task-based interaction between two groups of students, one using computer-mediated communication (CMC) and the other using standard face-to-face (FTF) interaction. Although the results of previous research studies on the use of CMC and TBLT were promising (Stockwell, 2010), Tang's (2019) study showed that the FTF group outperformed the CMC group, also using a more significant number of learning strategies such as self-repetitions or self-corrections. Similarly, Sauro (2012) found no significant differences in a study conducted with two groups of university students.

By contrast, Winke (2014) looked at the development and assessment of L2 oral skills supported by technology-mediated tasks. In particular, the study looked at students' self-monitoring of their oral skills after performing a task. Similarly, the study presented here discusses the role of technology in the design and performance of asynchronous speaking tasks and looks at the crucial role of recording capabilities and podcasting in planning and rehearsal.

5.2 Podcast in EFL learning

For over twenty years podcasts have been growing in popularity inside and beyond the language classroom. Podcasts are audio files created using a microphone and an application or software. They can be posted online, published on digital streaming music services (e.g. Spotify) or downloaded as MP3 files. Podcasting has been used in second language research largely because it is an optimal way of focusing on authentic language outputs as it offers the possibility of producing speaking materials for a real audience (Ducate & Lomicka, 2009). Being able to manipulate and modify their own output is a crucial skill for language learners (Swain & Lapkin, 1995). Podcasts allow students to record their audio, listen to it and modify it through self-monitoring or the feedback received from a peer and the teacher, as for example in Lord (2008). Research on the use of podcasting to improve speaking skills has focused on pronunciation (Ducate & Lomicka, 2009; Lord, 2008), listening and speaking combined (Abdous et al., 2009; al Fadda & al Qasim, 2013; Lee, 2016) or on learner perceptions of the podcast-making and their speaking performance (Li, 2010; Yeh et al., 2021). In the study conducted by Ducate and Lomicka (2009) twenty-two university students studying either German or French as L2 recorded five scripted pronunciation podcasts of about 2 to 3 minutes. Results showed that there was no significant improvement of pronunciation in both groups over one semester. The authors suggest that this result might be dependent on students' level, which was probably too high, so that it was difficult to see any relevant improvement in a short period of time. As far as I know, the study by Li (2010) has been the only one to focus on the use of podcasts in secondary education settings. Although this study focused only on the perceptions of six secondary school learners, the study provides interesting insights into the use of podcasts with teenagers. Learners recognized the potential of podcasting in learning English. However, their attitude to learning from this medium depended on the style of podcast selected and the type of activity proposed. Thus, issues with podcasts are more pedagogical than technological. Despite its enormous potential, the area of podcasting in EFL learning in secondary education is still virtually unexplored. This case study aimed to contribute to this field of research by providing insights from secondary education with a mixed-method approach that analyses spoken outputs as well as students' attitudes.

5.3 Students' learning conditions and experiences

This study is based on the assumption that the integration of technology-mediated tasks affects the design and performance of the task itself. This integration changes the standard classroom dynamics, providing students with different learning experiences. Findings from recent classroom-based studies on TBLT and technology have demonstrated how various learning conditions (e.g. the use of digital tools) influence students' learning experiences. In technology-mediated contexts, learners can work at their own pace (Tsai, 2015) as digital tools help them to scaffold learning (Chen, 2012), and provide access to authentic texts (Park, 2012) and multimodal materials (Abrams, 2016). All these factors have often led to reported positive language gains. However, most studies are mainly based on university learners. The question of how and if the integration of technology-mediated tasks into a secondary school EFL curriculum boosts language proficiency remains largely under-researched.

5.4 Pedagogic language tasks (PLTs) and pedagogic technology tasks (PTTs)

The technology-mediated TBLT curriculum includes pedagogic and technology language tasks where language is not only the objective of the task, but also a tool that helps in the performance of the L2 technology task (González-Lloret & Ortega, 2014). A pedagogic language task (PLT) is a classroom activity that requires learners to use, interact and comprehend the target language to convey meaning and focus on form (e.g. identifying essential information at the airport). On the other hand, pedagogic technology tasks (PTTs) focus on the specific tool used to perform the target task (e.g. interactive maps). Usually, it is the pedagogic language task that drives pedagogic technology tasks. As in the model proposed by González-Lloret (2014), pedagogic language tasks (PLTs) and PTTs are always interconnected. PLTs define the PTTs; learners usually need the language performed in PLTs to perform PTTs successfully (González-Lloret & Ortega, 2014). The tasks designed for the present study follow these indications.

6. Methodology

6.1 Participants

The team consisted of a researcher and two EFL teachers. The participants were forty-eight Italian thirteen- to fourteen-year-old secondary students taking part in general English language classes in line with the Italian Ministry of Education requirements. Most students were Italian L1 speakers (seven were Chinese L1 and three Spanish) and all had similar digital skills. Their digital literacy was formally surveyed via Survey Monkey during the pilot study conducted during the previous school year, which also served as a needs analysis for the main study. In technology-mediated TBLT, learners need to develop a complex set of literacies that go beyond the purely digital to include intercultural understanding and a composite communicative competence (e.g. linguistic, sociocultural) (Lai & Li, 2011). This requirement for more than just linguistic competence is partly reflected in the Cambridge B1 Preliminary Speaking assessment criteria, which include, for example, 'the ability to maintain and develop the interaction and negotiation towards an outcome' (from Cambridge B1 Preliminary assessment criteria). Results of the survey showed that students were used to social media (Instagram, TikTok), instant messaging (WhatsApp, WeChat, Telegram), internet searching and video-sharing services (YouTube), but that they only rarely used apps specifically designed for learning English. The students in the study had been provided with a classroom set of Chromebooks for in-class activities.

6.2 The tasks

This study included both language and technology task types organized and sequenced according to complexity (Ellis, 2003; Long, 2015). The tasks designed for this study followed the task principles and characteristics presented in Chapelle (2001) and González-Lloret and Ortega (2014): authenticity, meaning focus, learner fit, language-learning potential and positive impact (see Appendix). In the present study, authenticity refers to the Cambridge B1 Preliminary Speaking tasks which are designed to be similar to authentic tasks that the learners could meet outside the classroom.

6.3 The speaking tasks

For research purposes, students were divided into two groups: the experimental and the control group. Teachers worked to ensure a balance between the two groups in terms of language proficiency, gender and digital literacy. Proficiency was measured with a standard Oxford placement test at the beginning of the school year; digital literacy was evaluated during the pilot study. Any differences related to language levels (e.g. pre-intermediate vs intermediate) or skills (e.g. speaking, reading) were carefully considered when organizing students into the two groups. Students in the control group were not allowed to use any technology to perform the language tasks in the classroom. While both groups received similar materials in terms of content, the experimental group worked on technology-mediated tasks while the control group worked with printed handouts and notebooks. Time on task was the same for the two groups, and all tasks were undertaken in the classroom. It should be acknowledged that the learning experiences of the two groups differed in some dimensions (e.g. personalized feedback, interaction). This issue of comparability will be examined in the Discussion section. The study followed a pre-post and delayed post-test design (Table 8.1).

Table 8.1 Research design

Timing	Stage
Week 0	**Preparation stage** Introduction to B1 Preliminary Speaking tasks
Week 1	**Pre-test** B1 Preliminary Speaking task performance
Week 2	**Speaking task A** Discussion task with visual input: Describe a picture situation
Week 3	**Speaking task B** Interaction task with visual input: Q&A session with picture prompts
Week 4	**Post-test** B1 Preliminary Speaking task performance
One month later	**Delayed post-test** B1 Preliminary Speaking task performance

7. Procedures

A Cambridge 'B1 Preliminary for schools' past paper was used to discuss task procedures and outcomes with the students in the preparation stage. Task 1 (the pre-test) consisted of a standard speaking task without the use of technology. Thanks to the scaffolding lesson in the preparation stage, learners were fully aware of the task structure. Immediately after the pre-test, students were divided into two groups: the experimental ($N = 24$) and the control group ($N = 24$). Two technology-mediated tasks were then designed and implemented. The two tasks were all product-oriented: each task required students to produce an outcome that the teachers assessed. The two tasks targeted speaking skills as presented in the 'B1 Preliminary for schools' paper.

For both tasks, the pre-task stages included receptive skills activities (i.e. reading and listening) to trigger cognitive processes and serve as a model for the production stage. The post-test was delivered at the end of the experiment and consisted of a B1 Preliminary Speaking paper task taken from official Cambridge past papers. The same task was used as a delayed post-test one month after the end of the experiment. Specifically, in Speaking task A the target task was to be able to describe and talk fluently about a situation based on a visual input (video). To get closer to achieving the target task, a series of pedagogic tasks were planned: as a pre-task, students watched a video of a student describing a picture he found on a train. Learners had to think about key points in describing a picture/situation and write down the key strategies used by the student in the video. As the main task they had to plan, rehearse and produce their own picture description. Students in the experimental group used the podcast app Anchor to record, share, edit and discuss their performance, while learners in the control planned their presentation in their notebook, rehearsed it face-to-face with a peer and performed the picture description task in front of the teacher. All tasks were audio recorded. Learners in the experimental group downloaded and shared the final version of their podcast with the teacher using Google classroom. Similarly, in Speaking task B students were asked to interact on a topic based on a visual input (video and pictures). The main task consisted of discussing, planning and agreeing on possible after-school activities. Students followed the same procedure: modelling and noticing activities at the pre-task stage, planning, rehearsing and production in the main task, and open discussion and reflection activities as a post-task.

7.1 Pre-, post- and delayed post-test – B1 Preliminary Speaking task

The B1 Preliminary Speaking paper is divided into two parts. In the first part the examiners show students a photo and learners are required to describe the situation in the photo, while in the second part learners are required to interact with each other about a situation shown in a different picture. All the tests (pre-, post-, and delayed post-test) used official speaking tasks taken from B1 Preliminary past papers. In the pre-test speaking task learners were required to perform two parts. The first was to look at a picture representing students playing different sports at school and describe it for at least 2 minutes. Although students were in pairs, each learner performed the first part of the task individually and each task was audio-recorded. They did not have any time to plan their performance. The second part included a short interaction with a peer based on picture prompts. The pictures from the pre-test were related to sports injuries. Students had to discuss and agree/disagree on which sport was safer. For the post-test and the delayed post-test speaking tasks students were divided into experimental and control groups. The two-part task was very similar to the one used in the pre-test. The learners in the experimental group received the digital pictures and worked on their own individual Chromebook. Learners in the control group were provided with handouts with picture prompts.

7.2 Assessment of tasks

Participants' speaking performances were scored individually, based on the Cambridge B1 Preliminary examination assessment scales. The analytical assessment scale for speaking was divided into four macro-areas: grammar and vocabulary, discourse management, pronunciation and interactive communication. Each criterion was scored between a minimum of 1 and a maximum of 5. The teacher then awarded students a global mark for overall achievement based on the global achievement scale. Each learner received five scores for each test (pre-, post- and delayed post-test): four for each speaking subskill (grammar and vocabulary, discourse management, pronunciation and interactive communication) and one for global achievement.

Each task (pre-, post-, delayed post-test) was assessed by two teachers who had been trained specifically on the grading of Cambridge B1 papers. This ensured high inter-rater reliability (Pearson's $r = 0.658$). Where the two teachers did not agree, an average between the marks was calculated to ensure reliability.

8. Data collection

Quantitative data were collected during the pre-test, post-test and delayed post-test. The pre-test (Week 1) took place at the beginning of the project. Three weeks later, participants performed the post-test in class. Students were allowed 3 minutes to perform the picture-description task and five to perform the interaction task. For the pre-test, all speaking tasks were performed in class and graded directly at the end of each speaking task. For the post-test, the experimental group recorded their performance using Anchor and shared the MP3 files with the teachers via Google classroom. The control group performed their speaking tasks in class. Although they were recorded, the teacher assigned a grade directly at the end of each performance.

The delayed post-tests were delivered one month later, following the same procedures as the post-test. All tasks were assessed and scored by two teachers. Qualitative data were collected from learner and teacher interviews. Notes from teachers' meetings and six lesson observations provided additional data sets for triangulation. Tasks focusing on collaborative work, noticing and personalized feedback, particularly with the help and mediation of technological tools, were observed to collect data on the L2 learning process. Based on one of the SCT fundamental principles that human activity is always mediated activity, this study used SCT concepts to interpret qualitative data and to support and complement statistical analysis.

9. Analysis

Speaking scores from the pre-, post- and delayed post-test were compared, to answer the first research question about the impact of a technology-mediated TBLT design on students' speaking skills. The speaking ratings for grammar and vocabulary, discourse management, pronunciation and interactive communication for the pre-test, post-test, and delayed post-test were entered into JASP 0.16.3 for statistical analysis.

The second research question focused on students' learning experiences and conditions in technology-mediated TBLT. The data for analysis came from three sources: classroom observations (N4), interviews with students (N14) and interviews with teachers (N3). Observation tables were used to collect information on key aspects of each lesson. The tables included information related to the settings, people, behaviours and details on tasks. Each data set was analysed using a qualitative content analysis of emergent themes approach (Elo & Kyngäs, 2008; Silverman, 2004). This entailed an open coding of the students' and teachers' interviews, lesson plans and classroom observation notes. All the coding units selected were analysed using the qualitative analysis software Nvivo (version 12). The qualitative data captured insights into students' learning conditions and experiences and found explanations related to mediation and scaffolding behind the statistical analysis.

10. Results

10.1 The impact of technology-mediated tasks on speaking

The Shapiro–Wilk test showed that the data were normally distributed, so t-tests were conducted to measure between-group differences. The t-test on global achievement scores revealed no significant group difference in the pre-test speaking tasks ($t = 1.813$, $p = 0.083$), indicating that the overall level of the two classes appeared to be quite balanced. As stated above, all students performed the pre-test without any technological mediation. The two groups had a very similar overall achievement score at the pre-test (Experimental group: Mean = 2.62, SD = 0.64; Control group: Mean = 2.5, SD = 0.65), showing that overall participants were at the same level in terms of speaking subskills. However, data from the post-test showed a significant difference in the distribution of rates between the two groups ($t = 5.438$ $p = <.001$). The difference between the groups in their speaking scores increased again at the delayed post-test ($t = 6.261$ $p = <.001$), showing a considerable difference between the two groups after the intervention.

Additionally, descriptive statistics were produced for each group's pre-, post- and delayed post-test detailed speaking scores. The statistical analysis compared the two groups on each macro area of the assessment scale (grammar and vocabulary, discourse management, pronunciation and interactive communication). In the pre-test. no significant difference was found between the two groups in each of the four criteria. Generally, students were less proficient in the areas of discourse management and pronunciation, whilst they performed slightly better against the criteria for grammar and vocabulary and interactive communication. The experimental group outperformed the control group at the post-test and at the delayed post-test in the overall achievement scores (see Table 8.2). Interestingly, data showed no significant difference between the two groups in relation to grammar and vocabulary. With regard to pronunciation and discourse management (Tables 8.3 and 8.4) however, the t-test revealed a significant difference at the post-test ($t = 5.438$, $p = <.001$) and again at the delayed post-test ($t = 6.261$, $p = <.001$). The most significant difference between the two groups was revealed by the scores on pronunciation (Table 8.3), particularly stress and intonation, as also reported by students and teachers in the interviews. By comparing the scores from the post-test and the delayed post-test relating to pronunciation, discourse management and interactive communication, it becomes evident that the experimental group outperformed the control group against these three criteria. Learners in the experimental group constantly improved their scores regardless of their performance in the pre-test, proving to be more fluent and accurate in pronunciation.

Table 8.2 t-test results for Overall Global Achievement score for B1 Preliminary Speaking paper at pre-, post- and delayed post-test

Experimental Group	Control Group	t	df	p
Pre-test Global Achievement Score	Pre-test Global Achievement Score	1.813	23	0.083
Post-test Global Achievement Score	Post-test Global Achievement Score	5.438	23	<.001
Delayed Post-test Global Achievement Score	Delayed Post-test Global Achievement Score	6.261	23	<.001

Table 8.3 Descriptive statistics Speaking Subskills – Pronunciation (Post-test)

	Experimental group	Control group	Experimental group	Control group
	Post-test Pronunciation	Post-test Pronunciation	Delayed Post-test Pronunciation	Delayed Post-test Pronunciation
N of students	24	24	24	24
Mean	3.333	2.583	3.417	2.417
SD	0.637	0.776	0.504	0.776
Minimum	2	2	2	1
Maximum	5	4	5	4

Mean = Average score based on Cambridge B1 Preliminary bands (1 to 5)
SD = Standard Deviation (difference from the mean value of the group)

Table 8.4 Descriptive statistics Speaking Subskills – Discourse Management

	Experimental group	Control group	Experimental group	Control group
	Post-test Discourse management	Post-test Discourse management	Delayed Post-test Discourse management	Delayed Post-test Discourse management
N of students	24	24	24	24
Mean	3.125	2.500	3.125	2.458
SD	0.741	0.590	0.797	0.658
Minimum	2	2	2	1
Maximum	5	4	5	4

Mean = Average score based on Cambridge B1 Preliminary bands (1 to 5)
SD = Standard Deviation (difference from the mean value of the group)

10.2 Students' learning experiences and perceptions

The implementation of the technology-mediated TBLT design has also been analysed in terms of learning experiences and perceptions, triangulating the interview data from teachers and students and the classroom observation notes taken during the planning and delivery of the lessons ($N = 4$). Nine open-ended questions were included in the interviews with teachers and learners. The main focus was on the perceptions and behaviours of students and teachers in relation to self-reported increased language competence in speaking to examine the functions of scaffolding and mediation. The themes that emerged from the content analysis were: 'challenges', 'task type', 'personalization', 'pronunciation', 'collaboration', 'motivation' and 'language proficiency'. In particular, in both observation tables and interviews I found elements related to 'mediation' and 'scaffolding' (e.g. modelling). Generally, it emerged that students from the experimental group and teachers reacted positively to the integration into the EFL curriculum of technology-mediated tasks, specifically the use of the podcast app Anchor on their Chromebooks. In terms of 'challenges', students from the control group also responded positively. However, they were concerned about the technological competence required of teachers, as they felt teachers might not be familiar with the podcasting app.

The theme 'task type' included the sub-themes 'motivation', 'collaboration' and 'personalization'. Personalization refers only to feedback and not to tasks. For both the experimental and the control group, tasks were well-designed and highly motivating, although for different reasons in each case. For the experimental group students, personalization and collaboration were the two aspects that motivated them most. In terms of 'mediation', students mentioned the potential to receive personalized feedback on their recorded speaking performance, the chance to listen to the recordings or part of them as many times as they needed and practise pronunciation, and the ability to edit their podcast easily. The word 'record' was, in fact, the most frequent word used in the interviews with the experimental group students and teachers. On the other hand, students from the control group felt engaged because they perceived the tasks as useful in their real lives.

In relation to 'language proficiency', it emerged that students worked on their language awareness throughout the tasks, although answers from the two groups differed substantially. It appears that students from the experimental group perceived an increase in their English language speaking proficiency, all mentioning that the technology-mediated tasks helped them to become aware of their phonological and intonation mistakes as they were able to listen to their own recordings, compare them with other students' podcasts and therefore notice any differences in various aspects of the language including the range of vocabulary used, discourse organization, rhythm and intonation. By contrast, the control group's perception was that they needed more time on task to improve their language proficiency. They felt they had to put in extra effort to complete similar tasks. They also missed out on the opportunity of having unlimited access to audio and video files and the recording function to practise pronunciation. However, students in the control group felt more focused on the task than the experimental group. This was not confirmed by the observation data, where the researcher noted high engagement from both groups regardless of the type of task and device they were using. None of the students interviewed mentioned the technology they were using but focused on what they were doing with it.

11. Discussion

While various studies have stated the importance of implementing a technology-mediated TBLT in language learning courses (e.g. Solares, 2014) but often missed the link between the use of technology and language acquisition processes, this study aimed to show how technology-mediated tasks can impact on the accuracy, pronunciation and content organization of speaking EFL skills in a secondary school context. Although the co-occurrence of multiple variables could have contributed to the results (motivation, type of feedback etc.) as measured by the pre-test, post-test and delayed post-test, there were specific language acquisition areas where learners in the experimental group outperformed the control group. Additionally, key conditions such as time on task and task type were intentionally left intact for both groups. Thus, it is the combination of specific tasks and conditions that fosters language improvement (Ellis et al., 2019). In particular, it is possible to identify two main findings. First, in performing speaking tasks through a podcast app, learners in the experimental group considerably improved their accuracy and pronunciation, particularly suprasegmental features such as stress and intonation. Second, students in the experimental group produced more complex and well-organized utterances.

With regard to the higher scores in discourse management and pronunciation, this could be explained by the fact that the podcasting app offered students the facility to audio-record the task several times and listen and compare it to the original recording, a practice that was supported by the qualitative data. In fact, the evidence obtained supports the SCT view that through mediation (in this case, an interaction with a technological tool) and scaffolding (e.g. using the audio recording as a model) learners create zones of proximal development (ZPDs) where they 'perform beyond their actual developmental level' (Oskoz & Elola, 2014: 118).

These findings also confirm the important role of pre-task planning, particularly rehearsal, on fluency and speaking performance, as in Ellis (2003, 2009). Moreover, students in the experimental group were observed to work at a different pace. They could identify their weaknesses faster by listening and practising only the parts they perceived as needing improvement. This was also true for language accuracy: learners autonomously looked for alternatives and explanations by accessing web sources and digital books when an error was identified. Thus, technology-mediated tasks may promote the noticing of specific language features or aspects of the learners' interlanguage, as demonstrated in Pellettieri (2010) and Smith (2004). Although there was no control over time on task or motivation, and it is not possible to make a direct link between the higher experimental group performances and the task or the medium (podcasting app and Chromebook computers), the study shows an evident change in learners' experiences and attitudes, leading to more extensive discussion on the role of task-conditions in technology-mediated TBLT. As reported in the qualitative data, all students in the Chromebook group did, in fact, attribute their improvement in language proficiency to the technology-mediated tasks. These findings, in a sense, contradict Tang (2019) as students performing technology-mediated tasks outperformed the other group in speaking performances. A possible explanation could be the different output-based tasks undertaken in the two studies: Tang (2019) focused on interaction, whereas the tasks presented in this study were slightly more oriented towards discussion, discourse management and presentation skills. Nevertheless, this study confirms Winke's (2014) findings, which identified self-assessment and self-regulated learning as enormously beneficial in the development of language learning and self-correction strategies. Further, in this study, technology facilitated personalized feedback on speaking performances and provided learners with multimodal inputs (video, audio, images and animations etc.) that helped students produce high-quality outputs.

The second important finding of this study is related to pronunciation development. It appeared that the podcasting app as a speaking tool helped learners in the planning of their task and the overall performance organization and delivery. This is evident from the statistical analysis and is confirmed by the qualitative data. In the interview, students and teachers recognized the mediation of the tool in mirroring their ideas. This could be explained by the fact that learners often used the recording, modifying (e.g. adding background sounds) and editing functions to reorganize their own performance, as reported by the observation notes and pictures. It also confirmed previous research findings on the role of podcasting in fostering students' reflection on their own product (Ducate & Lomicka, 2009; Lord, 2008; Yeh et al., 2021). The mediation of the technology also encouraged peer collaboration and knowledge sharing, for example, by prompting the students with spoken samples, vocabulary or with certain spoken features (e.g. hesitators, use of linkers), which could explain why learners in the experimental group meaningfully improved their scores on pronunciation and discourse management.

The technology-mediated TBLT approach involving the use of podcasts proved to be a valid alternative as learners were engaged in meaningful, purposeful and goal-directed tasks. The use of the podcasting app Anchor allowed learners to feel directly involved in what they were doing because, for example, they could revisit it and publish real podcast episodes. On the other hand, students in the control group could only access multimedia input when this was provided in the teacher-class mode. The sociocultural concept of putting the learner at the centre of the tasks facilitated interactions between teachers, peers and the tool, which, in turn, served as a scaffolding technique.

12. Implication for teachers

The research findings of this study may have useful implications for language teachers and educators. The impact of technology language tasks on speaking performance in an EFL secondary learning context using podcasts proved to be more focused on pronunciation and discourse features. In particular, the use of podcast-based tasks helped learners notice their strengths and weaknesses in pronunciation and discourse and the TBLT lesson design guided learners towards specific objectives.

A possible misunderstanding of some TBLT approaches is that there is no place for teaching pronunciation in communicative and meaning-based tasks. I argue that teachers who implement a technology-mediated TBLT approach should take advantage of the opportunities offered by this methodology, and that podcasting, as proved by this case study, represents one such opportunity. Intermediate EFL learners in this study created two podcasts to practise speaking, including different spoken features such as pronunciation, discourse management and interaction. The tasks used for this project were based on the Cambridge B1 Preliminary Speaking paper and they served as a useful background to build on practice and learning strategies. Teachers can use those tasks to implement their own projects and work on specific speaking subskills without being burdened with creating new task contents. Additionally, the possibilities offered by podcasting apps such as Anchor (e.g. it is free, works across platforms and operating systems, links with Spotify) allow the teacher to easily integrate its use into classroom practices, offering students more chances to focus on spoken features. Finally, due to the authentic nature of podcasts (real audio performances for real people) learners would feel particularly engaged and motivated to take this type of learning and apply it outside the language classroom.

13. Conclusions

The study presented here investigated the role of mobile devices and podcasting as mediating tools in EFL speaking tasks. Results showed how the planning and rehearsal of technology-mediated tasks significantly influenced the learning process and the subsequent fluency-based speaking performance compared to standard practices. Recent studies on technology-mediated task-based learning have shown the impact of task design and delivery method on English as a foreign language (EFL) learning. However, it is not clear what effect technology-mediated tasks have on learners' English language skills. This chapter illustrated a classroom-based study that showed how the implementation of technology-mediated tasks influenced students' learning experiences and fostered the development of specific speaking subskills in an EFL secondary education context. A qualitative content analysis of lesson observations and student and teacher interviews served as an additional dataset to shed light on learners' experiences and to examine key SCT ideas such as mediation and scaffolding. Descriptive statistics revealed that the experimental group scored higher in pronunciation, and discourse organization features. Tasks involving the active use of the tool for content creation, rehearsing speaking performances and accessing authentic materials were the most popular among students.

Although this study analysed a limited number of outputs by measuring learners' scores, it showed the influence of a new relationship in the classroom: the interaction of teachers and learners with technology-mediated tasks. Two key findings seem to be relevant to this study and for classroom practices. First, although teachers and learners reacted positively to the use of the podcasting app for language learning, the data show mixed results, confirming the assumption that a technology-mediated framework can only work if adapted to specific educational needs and if focused on selected linguistic features. Pronunciation, discourse organization and management appeared to be the areas where technology had a more substantial influence. Teachers expected learners from the experimental group to be more accurate in their spoken performances due to the ease of accessing online grammar references, but this did not happen. Instead, learners from the experimental group produced more complex utterances and more correct oral performances in terms of pronunciation. Second, from a research perspective, this study contributed to identifying the principles to consider when investigating how technologies and digital tools affect tasks and how a task can transform the use of technologies.

There are, nevertheless, a number of considerations to bear in mind. First, there are crucial implications for teachers' development in learning technology-mediated TBLT principles and classroom practices. Second, it would be worth investigating the implementation of a technology-mediated TBLT framework to enhance productive skills over a more extended period of time. Studies investigating this would provide teachers and educators with an overview of the impact of a technology-mediated syllabus rather than of individual tasks.

Appendix 1

Correspondences between the features of the CALL tasks developed by Chapelle (2001) and those of the technology-mediated TBLT framework presented in Gonzales-Lloret (2014) with examples from the studies presented in the volume.

CHAPELLE (2001)	GONZALES-LLORET & ORTEGA (2014)	EXAMPLE OF TASKS FROM THIS VOLUME	
		Writing and reading	Speaking and listening
Authenticity	Holism	Reading a crime story from the BBC website	Listening to a podcast on Anchor or Spotify
Meaning focus	Primary focus on meaning	Focus on key structures in context to convey meaning (use of narrative tenses)	Focus on key expressions for public presentation
Learner fit	Learner centredness		B1 Preliminary modelled speaking task
			Focus on intonation, pronunciation and fluency
Language learning potential	Reflective learning	Use of collaborative writing activities	Interactive tasks: e.g. discuss with your partner key features to include in the presentation
Positive impact	Reflective learning		
Practicality	X		
X	Goal-orientation	Write a crime story	Production of a podcast

Appendix 2

Sample B1 Preliminary Speaking paper

1A <u>Learning a new skill</u>

Interlocutor: Now I'd like each of you to talk on your own about something. I'm going to give each of you a photograph and I'd like you to talk about it. A, here is your photograph. It shows someone learning how to do something. B, you just listen. A, please tell us what you can see in the photograph.

Candidate A Back-up prompts • Talk about the people/person. • Talk about the place. • Talk about other things in the photograph.

Interlocutor: Thank you.

1B <u>At home after school</u>

Interlocutor: B, here is your photograph. It shows someone at home after school.

A, you just listen. B, please tell us what you can see in the photograph.

Candidate A Back-up prompts • Talk about the people/person. • Talk about the place. • Talk about other things in the photograph.

Appendix 3

Teachers' questionnaire

1) Tell me briefly about your experience using technology-mediated tasks to teach English.
2) How do you think technologies are helping your students develop their speaking skills?
3) How do you use mobile devices and technology-enhanced tasks for speaking activities?
4) What differences did you notice between practicing speaking with and without the help of any type of technology or digital tools?

5) What difficulties did you experience and how did you overcome them?
6) Is there any difference in their proficiency?
7) Do you feel students are improving their speaking skills using a technology-mediated TBLT approach?
8) How do you use mobile devices and technologies in general for speaking activities in class with your students?
9) What do you like most about using digital tasks and mobile devices to teach English?

Students' questionnaire

1) Tell me briefly about your experience using technology-mediated tasks to study English.
2) How do you think technologies are helping you develop your speaking skills?
3) How do you use mobile devices and technology-enhanced tasks for your speaking activities?
4) What differences did you notice between practicing speaking with and without the help of any type of technology or digital tools?
5) What difficulties did you experience and how did you overcome them?
6) Do you perceive any difference in your language proficiency?
7) Do you feel you are improving your speaking skills using a technology-mediated TBLT approach?
8) How do you use mobile devices and technologies in general for speaking activities in class with your /teachers?
9) What do you like most about using digital tasks and mobile devices to learn English?

Conclusions: The Future of TBLT and Technology in Secondary Education

1. Introduction

The main motivation for the current volume was that I am an EFL secondary school teacher and a researcher with a longstanding interest in the integration of tasks and technologies into the language classroom. As a teacher and researcher, I have had the chance to talk and work with teachers to understand the challenges they face in their everyday work with the lack of learners' communicative abilities and the integration of technology. According to the Italian curriculum, learners study English for five years at primary school before entering secondary education. However, at the age of eleven, only a few of them can communicate in the foreign language. In this volume, I argued that the TBLT approach integrated with the use of digital technologies can be successfully implemented in the Italian secondary school EFL context. The technology-mediated tasks offered learners opportunities to use English naturally and autonomously. English has been seen as a 'tool' to achieve communication outcomes (Shintani, 2016) based on either input-based or output-based tasks.

The TBLT approach is based on the idea that students learn a language by experiencing it (Norris, 2009), that is by doing things with it (i.e. English in this volume) instead of simply studying it as a set of rules and words. One of the most common misconceptions among secondary school teachers about TBLT is that elementary and pre-intermediate young learners cannot benefit from this approach as they may find tasks too difficult to accomplish. I have shown that using authentic materials and tasks very similar to real-life situations can foster language awareness and incidental acquisition. Teens and pre-teens need to be engaged in authentic tasks and to feel that they can 'make meaning' of existing authentic materials (e.g. Netflix series) by themselves. Within a task-based approach they can start communicating effectively and choose the language they need. Stemming from task-supported language teaching realities, I argued that a full integration of TBLT and technology is possible in the Italian secondary school context.

The book is structured in two main sections. In the first section, I have aimed to provide those interested in implementing TBLT practices at secondary school level with an overview of the basic concepts and principles behind task-based approaches. Chapters 1 and 2 looked at the theory and practice of TBLT focusing on the idea that there are many opportunities and a number of ways to enact it in the language classroom. Provided that the concept of task is clear and well-defined, TBLT can be flexible and adjustable to various classroom situations (East, 2021). In light of the growing interest towards the integration of technology and TBLT practices, in Chapter 3 I have presented the opportunities uncovered by the synergy between digital technologies and TBLT. A technology-mediated TBLT approach, in fact, transforms the EFL classroom from a technology-supported to a technology-integrated context where there is a clear communicative, but also technological outcome (e.g. students learn to produce and publish a podcast). A series of challenges were presented in the first section: what is the role of focus-on-form in the TBLT secondary school classroom? How can we shift from technology-supported to technology-integrated TBLT? Does a TBLT approach respond to learners and teachers' needs for final and formal language examinations? In order to explore these challenges more systematically and contribute to understanding of how EFL secondary school students can benefit from technology-mediated TBLT practices, I designed and developed the case studies presented in the second part of the volume. The studies were concerned with the implementation of technology-mediated tasks to develop reading, writing, listening and speaking skills. The choice of focusing on the different skills was guided by teachers' needs to work on all four skills with lower-intermediate and intermediate learners in view of the requirements of the language certificate examinations (e.g. Cambridge Preliminary test) and the final state exams. However, I acknowledge that keeping the traditional separation of the four skills in the language lesson has become increasingly difficult, if not unreal (East, 2021; González-Lloret & Ortega, 2014). The case studies presented in the volume, therefore, have a primary focus on a specific skill, but often skills are combined. For example, to perform the speaking tasks in Chapter 8 learners need to listen to a podcast first. In this sense, technology-mediated practices opened to a range of integrated language teaching opportunities for the secondary EFL classroom.

The case studies explored challenges and opportunities provided to secondary students and teachers while performing technology-mediated tasks, an area which is still under-researched, particularly from a sociocultural perspective (Viberg & Grönlund, 2012). The theoretical frameworks that underpinned the studies are the Vygotskian sociocultural theory (SCT) of learning and the cognitive interaction hypothesis. SCT and the concepts of mediation and scaffolding informed the case studies on reading and speaking (Chapters 6 and 8), while the case studies on writing and listening are more grounded on cognitive-interaction principles. Generally, interaction in this volume was not intended only as a communicative exchange between two people (e.g. student-teacher, peer-to-peer). More broadly, interaction here refers to the act of interfacing with various resources (e.g. web applications, digital stories) that support learners in the processing of input (East, 2021).

Following mixed method research approaches including pre-/post-test designs, questionnaires and semi-structured interviews the studies investigated the use of technology-mediated tasks as a communicative instructional tool by examining students' strategies and performances in reading, writing, speaking and listening. The case studies were set up to investigate a series of key questions on TBLT and technology implementation. They were:

- How can we design effective technology-mediated pre-tasks to develop learners' writing skills? How does a different focus in the pre-task impact the main writing task performance? (Chapter 5)
- What is the effect of a technology-mediated TBLT Extensive Reading programme on the vocabulary learning of lower secondary school EFL learners? What are the differences between the experimental and control group in terms of vocabulary, grammar and reading comprehension in the summative test? (Chapter 6)
- What are learners' attitudes towards the use of captioned digital videos to develop listening skills? Does a different focus at the pre-task guide learners' attention in the subsequent listening comprehension tasks? (Chapter 7)
- What is the impact of technology-mediated tasks and podcasting on EFL secondary school learners' speaking skills? What factors influence secondary students' learning experiences in technology-mediated TBLT, and what are students' perceptions of them? (Chapter 8)

In this concluding chapter, first, I will present a summary of the key findings in light of the research questions posed in the studies. Then, I will describe the implications of integrating technology and TBLT for EFL teachers, education practitioners, especially those involved in the development and management of mobile devices for language learning, and researchers in the field of second language acquisition. Limitations of the current study will be presented. To conclude, I will suggest areas that would benefit from further research.

2. Summary of key findings

This volume focused on secondary school EFL learners and teachers at a state lower secondary school in Italy, exploring the integration of technology-mediated practices into the EFL classroom. The intent of the case studies was always to use technology-mediated tasks rather than technology-supported tasks. Generally, tasks have been designed following the indications in Ellis (2009): (1) the primary focus should be on meaning, (2) there should be some kind of 'gap', (3) learners should largely have to rely on their own resources to complete the activity, (4) there is a clearly defined outcome other than the use of language. Also, for the technology to be integrated, there must be a clear role and outcome for it as well. However, considering the secondary school context, in some cases, some form of mediation from the teacher or from the technological tool used, as for example language feedback, was allowed (East, 2021; van den Branden et al., 2009). In any case, all lessons were strongly student-centred. The findings of the studies are related to three main areas: (1) the role of focus on form in the TBLT secondary school classroom, (2) the TBLT and secondary school institutional requirements and (3) the move from technology-supported to technology-mediated tasks.

2.1 Focus on form in the TBLT secondary school classroom

Attending to form appeared to be one of the main concerns at secondary school level not only in the Italian context, but also in the Asian and Dutch contexts as presented in Chapter 4. Although, as Ellis et al. (2019) pointed out, it is not a real issue as various studies demonstrated that an explicit focus on grammar does not necessarily lead to a more accurate use of language (Ellis, 2016; Park, 2010; Ryu & Lee, 2018; van de Guchte et al., 2016). The main idea behind the concept of focus on form is that 'when learners begin to notice forms and patterns in the input, they are developmentally ready to acquire those forms' (East, 2021, p. 108). In fact, focus on form facilitates acquisition (Ellis, 2016) and therefore should be embedded in the TBLT lesson cycle. The question whether it is appropriate to introduce it at the pre-task, main-task or post-task stage is still open. According to Long (2000), focus on form should be 'reactive', that is learners drive their attention to form only in response to a problem during the performance of a task. Based on these premises, the post-task stage would be the more appropriate stage to work on form. However, there are various options to introduce some sort of focus on form also at the pre-task stage, for example modelling and planning (van de Guchte et al., 2019). These strategies proved to be particularly relevant for the context of secondary education as they can address teachers' concerns about introducing task-related language before the main task. Two of the case studies presented in this volume aimed at investigating whether a different focus at pre-task leads to greater accuracy. Findings from the study on writing (Chapter 5) showed that there was no relevant difference between the focus on form and focus on content groups in terms of grammar learning. However, the focus on form group was slightly more accurate than the focus on content group in the writing performance. Finally, the quantitative analysis of written texts shows that there was an increasing frequency of the errors and number of sentences for the focus on content group, thereby suggesting that there is a correspondence between text complexity and the increase of errors, confirming the results in Lys (2013) and Larsen-Freeman (2009). Although, no relevant differences were found between the focus on form group and the focus on content group in terms of accuracy, the focus on content group produced slightly more complex texts. Thus, it confirms the results of previous studies (Mochizuki & Ortega, 2008; van de Guchte et al., 2019) and leads us to questioning whether focus on form, in the form of explicit grammar teaching before task performance is useful as its impact in the subsequent task performance may not be relevant at all. The case study on listening (Chapter 7) also led to very similar results. Findings revealed that a different focus at the pre-task (vocabulary vs language) did not have any relevance in students' performance at the post-test. These are promising results for the implementation of TBLT in traditional secondary school contexts as they demonstrated that a main focus on meaning leads to foreign language proficiency, in terms of fluency, vocabulary and linguistic structures.

2.2 TBLT and secondary school requirements

A second important concern of EFL teachers and school administrators of secondary education in Italy is that learners must reach the Ministry of Education requirements to pass the final state exams, at the end of the lower secondary school and at the end of the upper secondary school. In addition, it is a common practice for schools to offer learners the possibility to get an official English language certification from external organizations such as Cambridge Assessment English. Both examinations have an important impact on how English teachers plan their lessons and these circumstances have often prevented teachers to implement TBLT practices in their own teaching. The studies presented in this volume demonstrated that it is possible to integrate a technology-mediated TBLT approach with official language exam preparation. The tasks and assessment criteria of the studies on listening (Chapter 7) and speaking (Chapter 8) were based on the Cambridge B1 Preliminary papers. Since students were taking the formal examination at the end of the school year, the teachers were invited to adapt the Cambridge language speaking and listening tasks to the purpose of the studies. In particular, based on the B1 Preliminary task they wanted to focus on, a technology-mediated TBLT lesson plan was developed to provide practice for learners and reach the required outcomes.

The speaking tasks required students to practice a particular meaningful task (e.g. comparing ideas, giving opinions on recent news events) and to produce a podcast using mobile devices (new generation laptops and smartphones) as described in Chapter 8. This procedure is consistent with the study of Leis et al. (2015) on the use of smartphones to develop language learning autonomy. Following the technology-mediated TBLT approach combined with the two key concepts of mediation and personalization of SCT (Lantolf & Appel, 1994), I observed and recorded students' speaking task practices. The teachers analysed all students' performances providing them with synchronous feedback. Their overall comments on students speaking performances also informed my analysis as a researcher. Findings revealed that technology-mediated language tasks had a particular impact on pronunciation and discourse management features. Two areas that are usually quite critical for Italian secondary school learners as they do not have much time to practise them. Both areas are also particularly relevant for the Cambridge B1 examination according to the assessment criteria. The study also addressed teachers' concerns on the risk of an excessive workload when implementing technology-mediated TBLT. In fact, it demonstrated that there is no extra work required for teachers when adapting Cambridge B1 Preliminary tasks to the TBLT context and that technology-mediated tasks scaffolded and supported students learning of specific listening and speaking subskills. Based on these results, the integration of official exam preparation and technology-mediated TBLT practices is not only suggested, but also recommended.

2.3 Technology-supported vs technology-mediated tasks

The third important finding of the studies presented in this volume is that technology-mediated TBLT practices are clearly more beneficial for language acquisition than technology-supported tasks and it is worth to implement them in the language classroom. In technology-mediated TBLT digital technologies are part of the task outcome and learners are engaged in meaningful, purposeful and goal-directed tasks. Technology-supported tasks are basic tasks simply transferred to the technological medium (e.g. writing a text on word instead of writing it on the notebook). Teachers and learners in the studies presented here used mobile devices and new-generation laptops (e.g. Chromebooks) to perform the tasks.

First, to have an overall picture of the use of such devices in the EFL classroom, the case studies looked at the characteristics of technological-mediated TBLT tasks in secondary education. The activities and tasks used throughout the project were selected and divided according to this main goal. Four groups of tasks were created: tasks targeting writing, reading, listening and speaking skills. The tasks were designed using the technology-mediated TBLT framework as in González-Lloret (2015). The tasks selected proved to be successful for learners, as students reported in the interviews. Activities involving the active use of the tool for creating, practicing speaking performances and accessing authentic materials were the most successful among students and teachers; this is possibly due to the specific needs analysis conducted before the projects. Overall, findings showed a clear change both in practice for teachers and learners and also in learners' performances of tasks. This is consistent with the results of other studies (Lin, 2014; Lys, 2013).

Overall, my results suggest that these devices are appropriate tools to develop English skills proficiency at intermediate levels with secondary school students. The technology-mediated TBLT approach proved to be a valid alternative to technology-supported practices as the concept of putting the learner at the centre of the tasks facilitated interactions with the teachers, peers and with the tool. It also provided more opportunities for scaffolding, thus confirming the results in Lys (2013).

The analysis of the use of mobile devices and multimodal digital applications to perform speaking, reading and listening tasks provided insights into the role of potential mediator of the mobile device as reported in Chapters 5, 7 and 8. The qualitative analysis of the mediational uses suggests that the students benefited from the use of the different features of technology to facilitate language production. Technology allowed learners to find successful time-management strategies and simplify their tasks (e.g. the recording function, the access to authentic samples on YouTube). Students all reported that the integration of digital tools and mobile devices changed their standard school day habit, making them almost paperless. Applications such as Classroom and Google Drive reduced the need for external data storage (Eichenlaub et al., 2011), and different recording and note taking options were available (e.g. Podcast, Anchor). The qualitative results of the learners' speaking performances perceptions indicate that the learners became more independent in the performance of technology-mediated tasks overtime. This may have been a result of the mediation they experienced exploring different speaking tasks. The findings also show the changes in students' behaviours from novice users to more expert users as in Bird and Edwards (2015). For example, one approach involved synchronizing students' written notes and texts with Google docs to simplify notes, timetable, assignments etc., and another involved the use of an annotating application to annotate and personalize course materials and texts. Throughout the project students noted the importance of the synchronous use of different apps, such as Classroom, GoogleDrive, Anchor and Haiku Deck for content creation. As in Eichenlaub et al. (2011), students recommended various applications to enhance note taking without a keyboard and to improve the organization and layout of written texts and virtual notebooks (i.e. TinyPdf, Penultimate etc.).

Likewise, the results coming from the triangulation with the interviews with teachers and learners support the idea that technology-mediated tasks had an important influence on students' self-regulated learning. The same questionnaire was delivered to teachers and learners at the end of the case study on speaking. The responses (mainly in English) help to understand in more depth students' and teachers' perceptions about the usefulness of technology to develop speaking skills in the English as a foreign language classroom. From the answers to the first open-ended question (tell me briefly about your experience using technology-mediated tasks to teach/learn English) both teachers and learners seemed to have received many benefits from the use of technology integrated tasks in their teaching/learning. The learners in particular did not mention any challenges unless requested. This interpretation is based on the fact that only 5 percent of these students mentioned some issues on the use of technology-mediated tasks to improve their English. Moreover, all of them mentioned positive reasons why technology-mediated tasks were particularly useful in their language-learning practices.

In sum, the results show that through the implementation of TBLT principles and its integration with technology, it is possible to gain insights into learners' developing writing, reading, listening and speaking abilities and use them further to help learners and teachers adopt a technology-mediated TBLT approach in the future. It also indicates that the process of integration of mobile devices and digital technologies into the language learning secondary classroom takes a long time and requires motivation and strong methodology from teachers and engagement from learners.

The findings presented here cannot be generalized due to the particular context where it was implemented (Italian secondary EFL classroom) and the specific mobile devices used (Chromebooks and smartphones). However, it reveals several possible implications for EFL teachers, policy makers and researchers in the field that would like to integrate TBLT and technologies into the secondary language classroom.

3. Implications for practice: EFL teachers

Mobile devices and digital technologies allow individuals to engage in powerful learning experiences inside and outside the classroom, and their use is expanding and evolving considerably (Lys, 2013). Teachers, SLA researchers and educators cannot ignore these changes, as future learners will expect them to deliver new ways of learning to improve motivation and to provide innovative learning tools. This study showed how digital technologies can be used with effective TBLT approaches to provide alternative and innovative learning opportunities to the traditional secondary language classroom.

This study has a number of implications for EFL teachers and educators. As mentioned throughout the volume, the use of technology to access authentic material in English is changing the way students and teachers approach language learning. This study aimed at providing possible and affordable practices to be integrated in a well-formulated curriculum. It is not the technology in itself that will solve pedagogic challenges in the EFL secondary school classroom, but rather the way these technologies are used and perceived by teachers and learners (Warschauer & Healey, 1998) and the way they are integrated into strong methodological practices such as TBLT. Therefore, the findings from this study may provide EFL teachers with insights into how the use of mobile devices and digital technologies in general could be combined with TBLT principles to develop receptive (listening and reading) and productive (speaking and writing) skills and subskills (e.g. inferring meaning from context).

The studies identified a group of technology-mediated tasks and mobile apps that worked effectively not only in developing learners' proficiency in the four skills, but also in enhancing participants' motivation and engagement. Although these activities were identified in the context of secondary school language education, the context of this volume, they could be explored in other language learning contexts. For example, there were a few technology-mediated tasks that were frequently used and mentioned in the studies presented here: recording speaking performances to focus on task repetition, sharing written notes and texts assignments for planning and providing synchronous and personalized feedback on speaking and writing performances. Together with other effective TBLT techniques, an EFL teacher could use these activities in different second language teaching contexts (i.e. young learners, one-to-one teaching, distance language courses etc.). Additionally, rather than focusing on a specific skill such as speaking or writing, teachers could concentrate on integrated skills using the same strategies.

Another crucial implication for teachers is that, as demonstrated in the case studies, the move from the standard presentation-practice-production to a more integrated TBLT approach with pre-intermediate learners is possible and advocated. The concerns related to low proficiency learners not being able to perform a task because they need to study the language first can be overcome as teens and pre-teens are willing to communicate and can easily find their strategies to accomplish the task. The discussion on linguistic structures and explicit focus on form activities can be moved to the last part of the TBLT cycle, if needed. Also, teachers should not be concerned about leaving some students behind because the technology-mediated TBLT approach proved to foster collaborative work (online and offline) and inclusive practices.

Another important finding that has a more general pedagogical implication is the development of learners' motivation and self-regulated learning. All the participants involved in the study showed a growing independence in the use of technology for the performance of the task, the processing of the multimodal input and their own language development. Overall, the findings support the SCT view that learners' interaction with a learning tool, a physical tool (digital technologies, in this study) can mediate and scaffold the developing of different language skills and digital literacies. In fact, another important implication of the studies presented in the volume is the power of technology in helping learners to overcome some difficulties related to language production (e.g. public speaking).

Due to the nature of the medium, it was not possible to measure the amount of tool-learner mediation in these studies, although, for example, data showed an increasing length of speech recordings, or a fast organization of tasks overtime from the beginning to the end of the projects.

Although the study presents encouraging results in the integration of the technology-mediated approach into the EFL classroom, there are, nevertheless, a number of considerations to bear in mind. For example, an inexperienced young teacher may find it apparently easy to teach with technologies, considering the usual self-confidence in using smartphones and tablets, and could ignore the importance of having a strong TBLT methodology background on second language teaching and on technology-mediated curriculum design. An experienced teacher, on the other hand, may find it challenging to identify key features of technology-mediated tasks for ELT. In this respect, the implications for teachers' development are crucial in order to support the learners methodologically and technically as observed also in several studies (Bird and Edwards, 2015; Liu et al., 2014).

4. Implications for policy makers and institutions

The studies in this volume have important implications for institutions and policy makers. As presented in previous chapters, the distribution of technologies in schools is rapidly increasing and institutions are looking for new directions to integrate these technologies into a well-designed curriculum, particularly for language learning.

Although limited to the specific Italian EFL contexts, this volume offers general indications for institutions and policy makers on how to integrate technology and TBLT practices into the secondary language sector. The school involved in the project initially implemented the projects only as a classroom set, as students were not allowed to bring the device home. This was mainly due to the fact that the school did not have a specific policy on the use of mobile devices for educational purposes. It took almost one school year to agree on a policy to propose to students and families that could allow the use of personal mobile devices to perform technology-mediated tasks in the classroom. The experience of the studies presented in the volume indicates that, in order to have a successful implementation of technology-mediated TBLT in education, institutions are required to provide teachers with appropriate teachers' development methodological courses on TBLT together with proper basic skills on the management of technological devices and participants (learners, teachers, families etc.) with an appropriate policy of use where rules and regulations are clearly stated and signed from people involved. The key point relevant to the policy about the current study was whether to allow students to take the device home and/or use their own devices, because that would imply additional regulations to be set and agreed at management level. The school involved in this study made this decision after the Covid-19 emergency, and learners were allowed to take the devices home after school. Findings showed how the possibility to use the device also outside the school offered students more opportunities to engage in technology-mediated tasks with no boundaries of place and time. It would be beneficial to further investigate this aspect in future studies.

5. Contributions

The primary aim of this study was to investigate the implementation of technology-mediated TBLT practices in the EFL secondary school classroom in order to understand: (1) what the characteristics of technological-mediated language reading, writing, speaking and listening tasks are and (2) how technology-mediated tasks impact the development of the four language skills. As presented above, findings show how well-designed and goal-directed technology-mediated tasks contribute to the performance of effective language tasks. Also, technology proved to have positive influence, mainly acting as a scaffolding tool, on learners' task performance.

This study contributes to the broad area of second language acquisition research, specifically it adds knowledge to technology-mediated TBLT research and SCT-based research. One of the most significant contributions of this study is the implementation of the technology-mediated TBLT framework as conceptualized by Gonzales-Lloret (2014) to design and support EFL tasks to develop reading, writing, listening and speaking skills with pre-teens and teens. This research applied and evaluated the technological-mediated TBLT framework in an EFL secondary mobile-learning context following mixed-method approaches collecting both quantitative and qualitative data. In particular, it showed how the use of technology affects the complexity of a task. Unfortunately, it was not possible to measure how they affected tasks generally, and answers are not straightforward. For example, adding notes to a text, as students did, using the interactive e-book functions, may reduce the complexity of a reading task, but it adds new features as web searching and digital literacy. This study aimed at contributing to identify what principles researchers need to consider when they look at how mobile technologies affect tasks and how a task can transform mobile technologies use. More research is needed in this area.

This volume also contributes to the growing body of SCT-oriented technology-mediated and MALL research. In SCT, technology is seen as a tool that can mediate the learning experience. This means that mobile devices are seen as mediational tools that contribute to students' learning and development. Moreover, they facilitate (1) 'personalization' in terms of content creation, feedback received by the teacher through mobile devices (in the case of this volume), and (2) 'scaffolding' developed from the interaction and collaboration through the device while performing tasks.

This study also contributes to the area of EFL teacher professional development and practice by providing professionals with a group of effective technology mediated tasks and mobile apps that could be of immediate use in the classroom through collaborative action research, specifically in the secondary language classroom or at intermediate level.

6. Limitations of the study

This study has had a number of limitations that must be noted. They are mainly related to the context of the research and to the data collection and analysis. The sample of students and teachers was relatively small and the context was quite specific (i.e. Italian state secondary education). In particular, this study took place in the context of a sate lower secondary school in the north of Italy, many of the students involved owned already various technological devices at home, so they were quite familiar with them, and probably came from affluent families which could afford this type of devices. It is crucial to consider that a study carried out in a public state school, in a different area of the city or the country could have different impact and present different challenges. Future research should include large-scale participants and over a longer period of time. The four case studies were carried out over a period of two years overall. One of them was carried out in blended learning modality due to the Covid-19 health emergency. The participants were students and teachers of the school, but some of them changed over the two school years. For example, one teacher moved to another school, and two students who participated in the needs analysis and pilot studies moved to another city in the second year. Obviously, these unforeseen circumstances had an impact on the data collection and on the implementation of the various case studies.

Moreover, I have collected and analysed samples of written tasks performed by students, but due to time constraints, I did not analyse sample of speaking recordings overtime. This resulted in two different approaches to the data: qualitative on speaking, quantitative and qualitative for writing. Having speech samples could have contributed to analyse both productive skills (speaking and writing) using the same analytical tools. Finally, effective tasks and activities were selected based only on interviews and teachers' meeting data; I am aware that different choices would have provided richer insights into the mediating role of technologies.

7. Future directions for technology-mediated TBLT in secondary education

There are a number of directions that future studies in this area can take. Technology-mediated TBLT is still a relatively innovative area of research particularly in secondary school settings. Considering that technology should and can support language learning, and the large distribution of mobile devices among teenagers, it would be beneficial to have more studies investigating the implementation of mobile devices and TBLT at secondary school levels in different countries. Many studies have concentrated on methods using mobile devices as content distributor (e.g. vocabulary studies) rather than focusing on the interaction of the tool with learners, teachers and its role in the collaborative tasks. Studies on this area would give important contributions to the fields of MALL and TBLT.

Another important area to explore is the use of multimodal input with pre-intermediate learners and its impact on TBLT and language learning (González-Lloret & Ortega, 2014; Sauro, 2009). The role of input-based tasks with low proficiency and elementary learners in schools proved to be effective in promoting language learning (Shintani, 2016). In particular, an interesting question to pose would be whether technology-mediated multimodal input tasks have the same impact on learners' language skills. In terms of research methodology, larger scale studies that carry out a more comprehensive analysis of the development of integrated skills rather than specific skills, is thus needed in future research by using qualitative and quantitative data collection procedures. Finally, mobile technologies are essentially social in nature and teenagers make large use of social media and instant messaging tools to stay connected. Yet another area for future research with young teenage learner pertains to the use of technology-mediated tasks to develop learner's pragmatic and intercultural competence (Canto et al., 2014; Sykes & González-Lloret, 2020).

The main aim of future studies in the field should be to explore classroom practices that will exploit the technological affordances of TBLT learning so as to turn challenges into opportunities. Research suggests that the adoption of TBLT is hindered by teachers' comfort levels and expertise in TBLT, as well as by students' attitudes to language learning and their learning abilities. Studies have shown that these two problems could be turned into advantages. To maximise student learning results, Song (2009) recommends psychological preparation and strategy training for learners on China's mainland. Prior to any course, the literature recommends that learners should be familiarized with the philosophy, pedagogical approaches and assessment principles of TBLT, with specific metacognitive knowledge and cognitive and socio-affective strategies that students can use to help them perform better on individual tasks also being highlighted, as also stated in Lai (2015).

For TBLT to work, teachers must be properly trained, and research has revealed a few key characteristics of effective teacher training programmes. Teachers, first and foremost, must be given a sense of ownership and they should feel comfortable with designing and implementing tasks in their lessons (van den Branden, 2006). In this respect, research studies have shown that when students receive specific training on how to complete a task, this can enhance their task performance (see, for example, Kim, 2013).

I believe that the task-based approach combined with technology-enhanced practices can help the unique context of Italian secondary schools to move from traditional and often unsuccessful practices to innovative ways to foster English language acquisition. Young and teenage learners in Italy increasingly feel the need to fill the gap in language proficiency that separates them from their colleagues in other European countries (e.g. Sweden, the Netherlands). TBLT can provide them with tools for communicating and communication brings opportunities.

References

Abdous, M., Camarena, M. M., & Facer, B. R. (2009). MALL Technology: Use of Academic Podcasting in the Foreign Language Classroom. *ReCALL*, 21(1), 76–95. https://doi.org/10.1017/S0958344009000020

Abrams, Z. I. (2016). Possibilities and Challenges of Learning German in a Multimodal Environment: A Case Study. *ReCALL*, 28(3), 343–63. https://doi.org/10.1017/S0958344016000082

Adams, R., Amani, S., Newton, J., & Alwi, N. (2014). Planning and Production in Computer-Mediated Communication (CMC) Writing. In H. Byrnes & R. M. Manchòn (Eds.), *Task-Based Language Learning: Insights from and for L2 Writing* (pp. 137–59). Amsterdam/Philadelphia: John Benjamins Publishing.

Al Fadda, H. & Al Qasim, N. (2013). From Call to Mall: The Effectiveness of Podcast on EFL Higher Education Students' Listening Comprehension. *English Language Teaching*, 6(9), 30. http://www.ccsenet.org/journal/index.php/elt/article/view/29635

Aljaafreh, A. & Lantolf, J. P. (1994). Negative Feedback as Regulation and Second Language Learning in the Zone of Proximal Development. *The Modern Language Journal*, 78(4), 465. https://doi.org/10.2307/328585

Bachman, L. F. (2002). Some Reflections on Task-Based Language Performance Assessment. *Language Testing*, 19(4), 453–76.

Bailey, D. R. & Lee, A. R. (2020). Learning from Experience in the Midst of COVID-19: Benefits, Challenges, and Strategies in Online Teaching. *Computer-Assisted Language Learning Electronic Journal*, 21(2), 176–96.

Bax, S. (2003). The End of CLT: A Context Approach to Language Teaching. *ELT Journal*, 57(3), 278–87.

Beglar, D. & Hunt, J. A. (2014). Pleasure Reading and Reading Rate Gains. *Reading in a Foreign Language*, 26(1). http://nflrc.hawaii.edu/rfl

Bird, J. & Edwards, S. (2015). Children Learning to Use Technologies through Play: A Digital Play Framework. *British Journal of Educational Technology*, 46(6), 1149–60. https://doi.org/10.1111/bjet.12191

Blake, R. (2016). Technology and the Four Skills. *Language Learning & Technology*, 20(2), 129–42. http://llt.msu.edu/issues/june2016/blake.pdf, http://llt.msu.edu/issues/june2016/blake.pdf

Blake, R. J. (2013). *Brave New Digital Classroom: Technology and Foreign Language Learning*. Washington, DC: Georgetown University Press.

Bowen, P. & Delaney, D. (2019). *Step Up 2* (Student's book). Oxford, UK: Oxford University Press.

Bower, M. (2019). Technology-Mediated Learning Theory. *British Journal of Educational Technology*, 50(3), 1035–48. https://doi.org/10.1111/BJET.12771

Brooks, J. J. G. & Brooks, M. G. (1999). In Search of Understanding: The Case for Constructivist Classrooms. In *Association for Supervision and Curriculum Development*.

Brown, J. D. & Hudson, T. (1998). The Alternatives in Language Assessment. *Source: TESOL Quarterly*, 32(4), 653–75.

Brown, R., Waring, R., & Sangrawee Donkaewbua, J. (2008). Incidental Vocabulary Acquisition from Reading, Reading-While-Listening, and Listening to Stories. *Reading in a Foreign Language*, 20(2), 136–63. http://nflrc.hawaii.edu/rfl

Bruton, A. (2005). Task-Based Language Teaching: For the State Secondary FL Classroom? *Language Learning Journal*, 31(1), 55–68. https://doi.org/10.1080/09571730585200091

Buckingham, D. (2006). Defining Digital Literacy – What Do Young People Need to Know about Digital Media? *Nordic Journal of Digital Literacy*, 1(4), 263–77. https://doi.org/10.18261/ISSN1891-943X-2006-04-03

Burns, A. C. (2009). *Doing Action Research in English Language Teaching: A Guide for Practitioners*. New York: Routledge.

Butler, Y. G. (2019). Assessment of Young English Learners in Instructional Settings. In X. Gao (Ed.), *Second Handbook of English Language Teaching. Springer International Handbooks of Education* (pp. 477–96). Cham: Springer. https://doi.org/10.1007/978-3-030-02899-2_24

Byrnes, H., Crane, C., Maxim, H. H., & Sprang, K. A. (2006). Taking Text to Task: Issues and Choices in Curriculum Construction1. *ITL – International Journal of Applied Linguistics*, 152(1), 85–109. https://doi.org/10.2143/ITL.152.0.2017864

Cameron, L. (2001). *Teaching Languages to Young Learners*. Cambridge: Cambridge University Press.

Canale, M. & Swain, M. (1981). A Theoretical Framework for Communicative Competence. In A. S. Palmer, P. J. M. Groot, & G. A. Trosper (Eds.), *The Construct Validation of Tests of Communicative Competence, Including Proceedings of a Colloquium at TESOL'79* (pp. 31–6). Boston: Teachers of English to Speakers of Other Languages.

Canto, S., de Graaff, R., & Jauregi, K. (2014). Collaborative Tasks for Negotiation of Intercultural Meaning in Virtual Worlds and Video-Web Communication. In *Technology-Mediated TBLT* (pp. 183–212). Amsterdam: John Benjamins. https://doi.org/10.1075/tblt.6.07can

Carless, D. (2007). The Suitability of Task-Based Approaches for Secondary Schools: Perspectives from Hong Kong. *System*, 35, 595–608. https://doi.org/10.1016/j.system.2007.09.003

Carless, D. R. (2015). Teachers' Adaptations of TBLT: The Hong Kong Story. In M. Thomas & H. Reinders (Eds.), *Contemporary Task-Based Language Teaching in Asia* (pp. 366–80). New York/London: Bloomsbury.

Chapelle, C. (1998). Multimedia CALL: Lessons to be Learned from Research on Instructed SLA. *Language Learning and Technology*, 2(1), 21–39. http://llt.msu.edu/vol2num1/article1/

Chapelle, C. A. (2001). *Computer Applications in Second Language Acquisition: Foundations for Teaching, Testing, and Research*. Cambridge: Cambridge University Press. https://doi.org/10.1093/elt/57.1.82

Chapelle, C. A. (2003). *English Language Learning and Technology: Lectures on Applied Linguistics in the Age of Information and Communication Technology*. Amsterdam/Philadelphia: John Benjamins Publishing. https://doi.org/10.1177/136216880601000209

Chapelle, C. A. (2009). The Relationship between Second Language Acquisition Theory and Computer-Assisted Language Learning. *The Modern Language Journal*, 93(SUPPL. 1), 741–53. https://doi.org/10.1111/J.1540-4781.2009.00970.X

Chapelle, C. A. (2014). Afterword: Technology-Mediated TBLT and the Evolving Role of the Innovator. In M. Gonzàlez-Lloret & L. Ortega (Eds.), *Technology-Mediated TBLT* (pp. 323–34). Amsterdam/Philadelphia: John Benjamins Publishing.

Chen, C. M. & Chung, C. J. (2008). Personalized Mobile English Vocabulary Learning System Based on Item Response Theory and Learning Memory Cycle. *Computers & Education*, 51, 624–45. https://doi.org/10.1016/j.compedu.2007.06.011

Chen, C. N., Chen, S. C., & Eileen Chen, S. H. (2013). The Effects of Extensive Reading Via e-books on Tertiary Level EFL Students' Reading Attitude, Reading Comprehension and Vocabulary. *Turkish Online Journal of Educational Technology-TOJET*, 12(2), 303–12.

Chen, J. C. C. (2012). Designing a Computer-Mediated, Task-Based Syllabus: A Case Study in a Taiwanese EFL Tertiary Class. *The Asian EFL Journal Quarterly*, 14(3), 63.

Chih-Kai and Hsu, C. K. C. (2011). A Mobile-Assisted Synchronously Collaborative Translation – Annotation System for English as a Foreign Language (EFL) Reading Comprehension. *Computer Assisted Language Learning*, 24(2), 155–80.

Chinnery, G. M. (2006). Going to the MALL: Mobile Assisted Language Learning. *Language Learning & Technology*, 10, 9–16.

Chou, M. H. (2016). A Task-Based Language Teaching Approach to Developing Metacognitive Strategies for Listening Comprehension. *International Journal of Listening*, 31(1), 51–70. https://doi.org/10.1080/10904018.2015.1098542

Chun, D. (2006). CALL Technologies for L2 Reading. In Ducate, L. & Arnold, N. (Eds.), *Calling on CALL: From Theory and Research to New Directions in Foreign Language Teaching* (pp. 81–98). CALICO Monograph Series (Vol. 5). San Marcos, TX: CALICO.

Chun, D. M. (2016). The Role of Technology in SLA Research. *Language Learning and Technology*, 20(2).

Colpaert, J. (2004). Editorial: From Courseware to Coursewear? *Computer Assisted Language Learning*, 21(1), 261–6. https://doi.org/10.1080/0958822042000319575

Corder, S. P. (1967). The Significance of Learner's Errors. *IRAL – International Review of Applied Linguistics in Language Teaching*, 5(1–4), 161–70.

Cote, T. & Milliner, B. (2015). Implementing and Managing Online Extensive Reading: Student Performance and Perceptions. *The IALLT Journal*, 45(1), 71–90. www.xreading.com

Council of Europe. (2001). *Common European Framework of Reference for Languages: Learning, Teaching, Assessment*. Cambridge, UK: Cambridge University Press. www.coe.int/lang-cefr

Council of Europe (2020). *Common European Framework of Reference for Languages: Learning, Teaching, Assessment. Companion Volume*. Strasbourg: Council of Europe.

Davis, C. (1995). Extensive Reading: An Expensive Extravagance? *ELT Journal*, 49(4), 329–36. https://doi.org/10.1093/ELT/49.4.329

Day, R. R., Bamford, J., Renandya, W. A., Jacobs, G. M., & Yu, V. W. S. (1998). Extensive Reading in the Second Language Classroom. *RELC Journal*, 29(2), 187–91.

de Lozier, C. D. M. (2019). Motivation, Proficiency and Performance in Extensive Reading. *International Journal of Innovation and Research in Educational Sciences*, 6(3), 2349–5219.

Dingli, A. & Seychell, D. (2015). Who Are the Digital Natives? *The New Digital Natives*, 9–22. https://doi.org/10.1007/978-3-662-46590-5_2

Doiron, R. (2011). Using E-Books and E-Readers to Promote Reading in School Libraries: Lessons from the Field. *IFLA General Conference Proceedings*, 13–18. http://conference.ifla.org/ifla77

Doughty, C. J. & Long, M. H. (2003). Optimal Psycholinguistic Environments for Distance Foreign Language Learning. *Language Learning & Technology*, 7(3), 50–80. https://doi.org/10.18999/forids.23.35

Ducate, L. & Lomicka, L. (2009). Podcasting: An Effective Tool for Honing Language Students' Pronunciation? *Language Learning & Technology*, 13(3), 66–86.

Dundar, H. & Akcayir, M. (2012). Tablet vs. Paper: The Effect on Learners' Reading Performance. *International Electronic Journal of Elementary Education*, 4(3), 441–50. www.iejee.com

Duran, G. (1994). Wegen en omwegen naar een grotere taalvaardigheid Nederlands. Een praktijkbeschrijving uit het secundair onderwijs in Vlaanderen. In S. Kroon & T. Vallen (Eds.), *Nederlands als tweede taal in het onderwijs. Praktijkbeschrijvingen uit Nederland en Vlaanderen* (pp. 161–96). 's-Gravenhage: Nederlandse Taalunie Voorzetten 46.

East, M. (2008). *Dictionary Use in Foreign Language Writing Exams: Impact and Implications* (Vol. 22). Amsterdam/Philadelphia: John Benjamins Publishing.

East, M. (2012). *Task-Based Language Teaching from the Teachers' Perspective: Insights from New Zealand* (Vol. 3). Amsterdam/Philadelphia: John Benjamins Publishing.

East, M. (2014). Encouraging Innovation in a Modern Foreign Language Initial Teacher Education Programme: What Do Beginning Teachers Make of Task-Based Language Teaching? *Language Learning Journal*, 42(3), 261–74. https://doi.org/10.1080/09571736.2013.856455

East, M. (2021). *Foundational Principles of Task-based Language Teaching* (1st ed.). New York: Routledge.

Eichenlaub, N., Gabel, L., Jakubek, D., McCarthy, G., & Wang, W. (2011). Project iPad: Investigating Tablet Integration in Learning and Libraries at Ryerson University. *Computers in Libraries*, 31(7), 17–21.

Ellis, R. (2000). Task-Based Research and Language Pedagogy. *Language Teaching Research*, 4(3), 193–220. https://doi.org/10.1177/136216880000400302

Ellis, R. (2003). *Task-Based Language Learning and Teaching*. Oxford: Oxford University Press.

Ellis, R. (2009). The Differential Effects of Three Types of Task Planning on the Fluency, Complexity, and Accuracy in L2 Oral Production. *Applied Linguistics*, 30, 474–509. https://doi.org/10.1093/applin/amp042

Ellis, R. (2015). The Importance of Focus on Form in Communicative Language Teaching. *Eurasian Journal of Applied Linguistics*, 1(2), 1–12.

Ellis, R. (2016). Focus on Form: A Critical Review. *Language Teaching Research*, 20(3), 405–28. https://doi.org/10.1177/1362168816628627

Ellis, R. (2017). Task-Based Language Teaching. In *The Routledge Handbook of Instructed Second Language Acquisition* (pp. 108–25). New York: Routledge. https://doi.org/10.4324/9781315676968

Ellis, R. (2021). The Effects of Pre-Task Planning on Second Language Writing: A Systematic Review of Experimental Studies. *Chinese Journal of Applied*, 44(2), 131–65.

Ellis, R. (Ed.), (2005). *Planning and Task Performance in a Second Language* (Vol.11). Amsterdam/Philadelphia: John Benjamins Publishing.

Ellis, R. & Ellis, R. R. (2000). *The Study of Second Language Acquisition* (2nd ed.). Oxford: Oxford University Press.

Ellis, R. & Shintani, N. (2014). *Exploring Language Pedagogy through Second Language Acquisition Research*. New York: Routledge.

Ellis, R. & Yuan, F. (2004). The Effects of Planning on Fluency, Complexity, and Accuracy in Second Language Narrative Writing. *Studies in Second Language Acquisition*, 26(1), 59–84. https://doi.org/10.1017/S0272263104026130

Ellis, R., Li, S., & Zhu, Y. (2018). *The Effects of Pre-Task Explicit Instruction on the Performance of a Focused Task*. https://doi.org/10.1016/j.system.2018.10.004

Ellis, R., Skehan, P., Li, S., Shintani, N., & Lambert, C. (2019). *Task-Based Language Teaching*. Cambridge, UK: Cambridge University Press. https://doi.org/10.1017/9781108643689

Elo, S. & Kyngäs, H. (2008). The Qualitative Content Analysis Process. *Journal of Advanced Nursing*, 62(1), 107–15.

Erlam, R. & Tolosa, C. (2022). *Pedagogical Realities of Implementing Task-Based Language Teaching*. Amsterdam: John Benjamins Publishing Company.

Erstad, O. (2010). Educating the Digital Generation. *Nordic Journal of Digital Literacy*, 5(1), 56–71. https://doi.org/10.18261/ISSN1891-943X-2010-01-05

Estaire, S. & Zanon, J. (1994). *Planning Classwork: A Task-Based Approach*. Portsmouth, New Hampshire: Heinemann.

Foster, P. & Skehan, P. (1996). The Influence of Planning and Task Type on Second Language Performance. *Studies in Second Language Acquisition*, 18(3), 299–323. https://doi.org/10.1017/S0272263100015047

Foster, P. & Skehan, P. (1999). The Influence of Source of Planning and Focus of Planning on Task-Based Performance. *Language Teaching Research*, 3(3), 215–47. https://doi.org/10.1177/136216889900300303

Foster, P. & Skehan, P. (2013). Anticipating a Post-Task Activity: The Effects on Accuracy, Complexity, and Fluency of Second Language Performance. *Canadian Modern Language Review*, 69(3), 249–73. https://doi.org/10.3138/CMLR.69.3.249

Gabarre, C., Gabarre, S., Din, R., Shah, P. M., & Karim, A. A. (2014). IPads in the Foreign Language Classroom: A Learner's Perspective. *3L: Language, Linguistics, Literature*, 20(1), 115–28.

Gaies, S. J. (1980). T-Unit Analysis in Second Language Research: Applications, Problems and Limitations. *TESOL Quarterly*, 14(1), 53. https://doi.org/10.2307/3586808

Godwin-Jones, R. (2012). Emerging Technologies Digital Video Revisited: Storytelling, Conferencing, Remixing. *Language, Learning and Technology*, 16(1), 1–9.

Godwin-Jones, R. (2015). Emerging Technologies Contributing, Creating, Curating: Digital Literacies for Language Learners. *Language Learning & Technology*, 19(3), 8–20. http://llt.msu.edu/issues/october2015/emerging.pdfhttp://llt.msu.edu/issues/october2015/emerging.pdf

Godwin-Jones, R. (2017). Smartphones and Language Learning. *Language Learning & Technology*, 21(2), 3–17.

Goh, C. C. M. & Vandergrift, L. (2021). Teaching and Learning Second Language Listening: Metacognition in Action. *Teaching and Learning Second Language Listening: Metacognition in Action*, 1–361.

González-Lloret, M. (2003). Designing Task-Based Call to Promote Interaction: En Busca de Esmeraldas. *Language Learning and Technology*, 7(1), 86–104.

González-Lloret, M. (2014). The Need for Needs Analysis in Technology-Mediated TBLT. *Technology-Mediated TBLT: Researching Technology and Tasks*, 6, 23–50.

González-Lloret, M. (2015). *A Practical Guide to Integrating Technology Into Task-Based Language Teaching*. Georgetown University Press.

González-Lloret, M. (2017). Technology for Task-Based Language Teaching. *The Handbook of Technology and Second Language Teaching and Learning*, 234–47.

González-Lloret, M. & Nielson, K. B. (2015). Evaluating TBLT: The Case of a Task-Based Spanish Program. *Language Teaching Research*, 19(5), 525–49. https://doi.org/10.1177/1362168814541745

González-Lloret, M. (2014). The Need for Needs Analysis in Technology-Mediated TBLT. In *Technology-Mediated TBLT: Researching Technology and Tasks*, 6 (pp. 23–50). Amsterdam/Philadelphia: John Benjamins Publishing Company.

González-Lloret, M. & Ortega, L. (2014). Towards Technology-Mediated TBLT. In *Technology-Mediated TBLT: Researching Technology and Tasks*, 6 (pp. 1–22). Amsterdam/Philadelphia: John Benjamins Publishing Company.

Graham, S. (2017). Research into Practice: Listening Strategies in an Instructed Classroom Setting. *Language Teaching*, 50(1), 107–19. https://doi.org/10.1017/S0261444816000306

Gurzynski-Weiss, L. & Baralt, M. (2014). Exploring Learner Perception and Use of Task-Based Interactional Feedback in FTF and CMC Modes. *Studies in Second Language Acquisition*, 36(1), 1–37. https://doi.org/10.1017/S0272263113000363

Gurzynski-Weiss, L. & Baralt, M. (2015). Does Type of Modified Output Correspond to Learner Noticing of Feedback? A Closer Look in Face-to-Face and Computer-Mediated Task-Based Interaction. *Applied Psycholinguistics*, 36(6), 1393–420. https://doi.org/10.1017/S0142716414000320

Hafner, C. A. (2014). Embedding Digital Literacies in English Language Teaching: Students' Digital Video Projects as Multimodal Ensembles. *TESOL Quarterly*, 48(4), 655–85. https://doi.org/10.1002/tesq.138

Hafner, C. A. & Miller, L. (2011). Fostering learner Autonomy in English for Science: A Collaborative Digital Video Project in a Technological learning Environment. *Language Learning and Technology*, 15(3), 68–86. http://llt.msu.edu/issues/october2011/hafnermiller.pdf

Hampel, R. & Hauck, M. (2006). Computer-Mediated Language Learning: Making Meaning in Multimodal Virtual learning Spaces. *JALT CALL Journal*, 2(2), 3–18.

Hassanzadeh-Taleshi, M., Yaqubi, B., & Bozorgian, H. (2021). The Effects of Combining Task Repetition with Immediate Post-Task Transcribing on L2 learners' Oral Narratives. *The Language Learning Journal*, 4, 1–12.

Hernández-Martín, A., Martín-del-pozo, M., & Iglesias-Rodríguez, A. (2021). Pre-adolescents' Digital Competences in the Area of Safety. Does Frequency of Social Media Use Mean Safer and More Knowledgeable Digital Usage? *Education and Information Technologies*, 26(1), 1043–67. https://doi.org/10.1007/S10639-020-10302-4

Hiep, P. H. (2007). Communicative Language Teaching: Unity within Diversity. *ELT Journal*, 61(3), 193–201.

Hinkel, E. (Ed.), (2011). *Handbook of Research in Second Language Teaching and Learning*. New York: Routledge.

Holliday, A. (1997). Six lessons: Cultural Continuity in Communicative language Teaching. *Language Teaching Research*, 1(3), 212–38.

Housen, A. & Kuiken, F. (2009). Complexity, Accuracy, and Fluency in Second Language Acquisition. *Applied Linguistics*, 30(4), 461–73. https://doi.org/10.1093/applin/amp048

Hsu, H. C. (2012). Investigating the Effects of Planning on L2 Text Chat Performance. *CALICO Journal*, 29, 619–38. https://www.jstor.org/stable/calicojournal.29.4.619

Hsu, H. C. (2017a). The Combined Effect of Task Repetition and Post-Task Transcribing on L2 Speaking Complexity, Accuracy, and Fluency. Https://Doi.Org/10.1080/09571 736.2016.1255773, 47(2), 172–87. https://doi.org/10.1080/09571736.2016.1255773

Hsu, H. C. (2017b). The Effect of Task Planning on L2 Performance and L2 Development in Text-Based Synchronous Computer-Mediated Communication. *Applied Linguistics*, 38(3), 359–85. https://doi.org/10.1093/APPLIN/AMV032 https://doi.org/10.1177/0033688213488466

Hu, G. (2005). 'CLT Is Best for China'— an Untenable Absolutist Claim. *ELT Journal*, 59(1), 65–8. https://doi.org/10.1093/ELT/CCI009

Huang, H. chou. (2013). E-reading and E-discussion: EFL Learners' Perceptions of an E-book Reading Program. *Computer Assisted Language Learning*, 26(3), 258–81. https://doi.org/10.1080/09588221.2012.656313

Huang, L. L. & Lin, C. C. (2011). Forum EFL learners' Reading on Mobile Phones. *The JALT CALL Journal*, 7(1), 61–78.

Huang, Y. M., Huang, Y. M., Huang, S. H., & Lin, Y. T. (2012). A Ubiquitous English Vocabulary Learning System: Evidence of Active/Passive Attitudes vs. Usefulness/Ease-of-Use. *Computers and Education*, 58, 273–82.

Hubbard, P. (2008). CALL and the Future of Language Teacher Education. *CALICO Journal*, 25(2), 175–88. https://www.jstor.org/stable/calicojournal.25.2.175

Hubbard, P. & Levy, M. (2016). *Theory in Computer-Assisted Language Learning Research and Practice*. https://doi.org/10.4324/9781315657899.ch2

Huberman, A. M. & Miles, M. B. (1994). An Expanded Sourcebook: Qualitative Data Analysis. USA: Sage Publications, 300, 13–25.

Hunt, K. W. (1965). A Synopsis of Clause-to-Sentence Length Factors. *The English Journal*, 54(4), 300. https://doi.org/10.2307/811114

Hymes, D. (1972). On Communicative Competence. *Sociolinguistics*, 269–93.

Ishikawa, S. (1995). Objective Measurement of Low-Proficiency EFL Narrative Writing. *Journal of Second Language Writing*, 4(1), 51–69. https://doi.org/10.1016/1060-3743(95)90023-3.

Izumi, S. (2002). Output, Input Enhancement, and the Noticing Hypothesis: An Experimental Study on ESL Relativization. *Studies in Second Language Acquisition*, 24(4), 541–77. https://doi.org/10.1017/S0272263102004023

Jeon, E. Y. & Richard Day, K. R. (2016). The Effectiveness of ER on Reading Proficiency: A Meta-Analysis. *Reading in a Foreign Language*, 28(2). http://nflrc.hawaii.edu/rfl

Jepson, K. (2005). Conversations—and Negotiated Interaction—in Text and Voice Chat Rooms. *Language Learning & Technology*, 9(3), 79–98. http://dx.doi.org/10125/44033

Jiang, J., Bi, P., & Liu, H. (2019). Syntactic Complexity Development in the Writings of EFL Learners: Insights from a Dependency Syntactically-Annotated Corpus. *Journal of Second Language Writing*, 46, 100666. https://doi.org/10.1016/J.JSLW.2019.100666

Johnson, M. D., Mercado, L., & Acevedo, A. (2012). The Effect of Planning Sub-processes on L2 Writing Fluency, Grammatical Complexity, and Lexical Complexity.

Journal of Second Language Writing, 21(3), 264–82. https://doi.org/10.1016/J. JSLW.2012.05.011

Kahn, G. (2012). Open-Ended Tasks and the Qualitative Investigation of Second Language Classroom Discourse. *Journal of Ethnographic & Qualitative Research*, 6, 90–107.

Kim, Y. J. (2012). Task Complexity, Learning Opportunities, and Korean EFL Learners' Question Development. *Studies in Second Language Acquisition*, Cambridge, UK: Cambridge University Press, 34(4), 627–58.

Kim, S. (2014). Developing Autonomous Learning for Oral Proficiency Using Digital Storytelling. *Language Learning and Technology*, 18(2), 20–35.

Kim, Y. (2013). Effects of Pretask Modeling on Attention to Form and Question Development. *Tesol Quarterly*, 47(1), 8–35. https://doi.org/10.1002/tesq.52

Kim, Y. & Taguchi, N. (2015). Promoting Task-Based Pragmatics Instruction in EFL Classroom Contexts: The Role of Task. *Source: The Modern Language Journal*, 99(4), 656–77. https://doi.org/10.1111/modi

Kokotsaki, D., Menzies, V., & Wiggins, A. (2016). Project-Based Learning: A Review of the Literature. *Improving Schools*, 19(3), 267–77. https://doi.org/10.1177/1365480216659733

Kozulin, A., Gindis, B., Ageyev, V. S., & Miller, S. M. (2003). Vygotsky's Educational Theory in Cultural Context. *Educational Research*.

Krashen, S. (1985). *The Input Hypothesis: Issues and Implications*. New York: Longman.

Kukulska-Hulme, A. (2006). Mobile Language Learning Now and in the Future. In P. Svensson (Ed.), *From Vision to Practice: Language Learning and IT* (pp. 295–310). Sweden: Swedish Net University.

Kukulska-Hulme, A. (2012). Language Learning Defined by Time and Place: A Framework for Next Generation Designs. In J. E. Díaz-Vera (Ed.), *Left to My Own Devices: Learner Autonomy and Mobile Assisted Language Learning* (pp. 1–13). Bingley, UK: Emerald Group Publishing Limited.

Kukulska-Hulme, A. (2013). *Re-skilling Language Learners for a Mobile World*. Monterey, USA: The International Research Foundation for English Language Education (TIRF) (pp. 1–16).

Kukulska-Hulme, A. & Viberg, O. (2018). Mobile Collaborative Language Learning: State of the Art. *British Journal of Educational Technology*, 49(2), 207–18. https://doi.org/10.1111/bjet.12580

Lai, C. (2015). Task-Based Language Teaching in the Asian Context: Where Are We Now and Where Are We Going? In M. Thomas & H. Reinders (Eds.), *Contemporary Task-Based Language Teaching in Asia* (pp. 12–24). New York/London: Bloomsbury.

Lai, C. & Li, G. (2011). Technology and Task-Based Language Teaching: A Critical Review. *CALICO Journal*, 28(2), 498–521. Equinox Publishing Ltd. https://doi.org/10.11139/cj.28.2.498-521

Lai, C. & Lin, X. (2015). Strategy Training in a Task-Based Language Classroom. *The Language Learning Journal*, 43(1), 20–40.

Lai, C. & Zhao, Y. (2006). Noticing and Text-Based Chat. *Language Learning & Technology*, 10(3), 102–20. http://llt.msu.edu/vol10num3/laizhao/

Lai, C. & Zheng, D. (2018). Self-Directed Use of Mobile Devices for Language Learning beyond the Classroom. *ReCALL*, 30(3), 299–318. https://doi.org/10.1017/S0958344017000258

Lai, J. Y. & Chang, C. Y. (2011). User Attitudes toward Dedicated E-book Readers for Reading: The Effects of Convenience, Compatibility and Media Richness. *Online Information Review*, 35(4), 558–80. https://doi.org/10.1108/14684521111161936/FULL/XML

Lantolf, J. P. & Appel, G. (1994). Theoretical Framework: An Introduction to Vygotskian Approaches to Second Language Research. In *Vygotskian Approaches to Second Language Research* (pp. 1–32).

Lantolf, J. P. & Thorne, S. L. (2006). *Sociocultural Theory and Genesis of Second Language Development*. Oxford: Oxford University Press, 2006.

Lantolf, J. P., Poehner, M. E., & Swain, M. (Eds.). (2018). *The Routledge Handbook of Sociocultural Theory and Second Language Development* (pp. 1–594). New York, NY: Routledge.

Lantolf, J. P., Thorne, S. L., & Poehner, M. E. (2014). Sociocultural Theory and Second Language Development. In *Theories in Second Language Acquisition: An Introduction*. https://doi.org/10.4324/9780203628942-16

Larsen-Freeman, D. (1978). An ESL Index of Development. *TESOL Quarterly*, 12(4), 439. https://doi.org/10.2307/3586142

Larsen-Freeman, D. (2009). Adjusting Expectations: The Study of Complexity, Accuracy, and Fluency in Second Language Acquisition. *Applied Linguistics*, 30(4), 579–89. https://doi.org/10.1093/applin/amp043

Larson, L. C. (2009). E-Reading and E-Responding: New Tools for the Next Generation of Readers. *Journal of Adolescent & Adult Literacy*, 53(3), 255–8. https://doi.org/10.1598/JAAL.53.3.7

Lee, J. (2020). Task Closure and Task Complexity Effects on L2 Written Performance. *Journal of Second Language Writing*, 50. https://doi.org/10.1016/j.jslw.2020.100777

Lee, L. (2016). Autonomous Learning through Task-Based Instruction in Fully Online Language Courses. *Language Learning & Technology*, 20(2), 81–97. http://llt.msu.edu/issues/june2016/lee.html

Lee, S. K. & Huang, H. T. (2008). Visual Input Enhancement and Grammar Learning: A Meta-Analytic Review. *Studies in Second Language Acquisition*, 30(3), 307–31. https://doi.org/10.1017/S0272263108080479

Leis, A., Tohei, A., & Cooke, S. D. (2015). Smartphone Assisted Language Learning and Autonomy. *International Journal of Computer-Assisted Language Learning and Teaching*, 5(3), 75. https://doi.org/10.4018/IJCALLT.2015070105

Lenkaitis, C. A. (2020). Teacher Candidate Reflection: Benefits of Using a Synchronous Computer-Mediated Communication-Based Virtual Exchange. *Teaching and Teacher Education*, 92, 103041.

Levy, M. & Stockwell, M. (2006). Effective Use of CALL Technologies: Finding the Right Balance. R. P. Donaldson & M. A. Haggstrom (Eds.), *Changing Language Education through CALL,* 1(18), 301–20.

Li, H. C. (2010). Using Podcasts for Learning English: Perceptions of Hong Kong Secondary 6 ESL Students. *Début: The Undergraduate Journal of Languages, Linguistics and Area Studies,* 1(2), 78–91. www.llas.ac.uk/debutwww.llas.ac.uk/debut

Liao, X. (2004). The Need for Communicative Language Teaching in China. *Elt,* 58(3), 270–3.

Lier, L. Van. (1998). All Hooked Up: An Ecological Look at Computers in the Classroom. *Studia Anglica Posnaniensia: International Review of English Studies,* 281–302.

Lin, C. C. (2014). Learning English Reading in a Mobile-Assisted Extensive Reading Program. *Computers and Education,* 78, 48–59. https://doi.org/10.1016/j.compedu.2014.05.004

Lin, C. C. (2010). 'E-Book Flood' for Changing EFL Learners' Reading Attitudes. *US-China Education Review,* 7(11), 36–43. http://www.icce2009.ied.edu.hk

Lin, J. J. & Lin, H. (2019). Mobile-Assisted ESL/EFL Vocabulary Learning: A Systematic Review and Meta-Analysis. *Computer Assisted Language Learning,* 32(8), 878–919. https://doi.org/10.1080/09588221.2018.1541359

Littlewood, W. (2004). The Task-Based Approach: Some Questions and Suggestions. *ELT Journal,* 58(4), 319–26.

Littlewood, W. (2007). Communicative and Task-Based Language Teaching in East Asian Classrooms. *Language Teaching,* 40(3), 243–9. https://doi.org/10.1017/S0261444807004363

Littlewood, W. (2014). Communication-Oriented Language Teaching: Where Are We Now? Where do we go from Here? *Language Teaching,* 47(03), 349–62. https://doi.org/10.1017/S0261444812000134

Liu, G. Z., Lu, H. C., & Lai, C. T. (2016). Towards the Construction of a Field: The Developments and Implications of Mobile Assisted Language Learning (MALL). *Digital Scholarship in the Humanities,* 31(1), 164–80.

Long, M. H. (1983). Native Speaker/Non-native Speaker Conversation and the Negotiation of Comprehensible Input. *Applied Linguistics,* 4(2), 126–41. https://doi.org/10.1093/APPLIN/4.2.126

Long, M. H. (1991). Focus on form in Task Based Language Teaching. In R. Lambert & E. Shohamy (Eds.), *Language Policy and Pedagogy: Essays in Honour of A. Ronald Walton* (pp. 179–92). Amsterdam: John Benjamins Publishing Company.

Long, M. H. (2000). Focus on form in Task-Based Language Teaching. *Language Policy and Pedagogy: Essays in Honor of A. Ronald Walton,* 179–92. https://doi.org/10.1075/z.96.11lon

Long, M. H. (2015). *Second Language Acquisition and Task-Based Language Teaching.* New York: John Wiley & Sons, Incorporated. https://doi.org/10.6018/ijes.4.1.48261

Long, M. H. (2016). In Defense of Tasks and TBLT: Nonissues and Real Issues. *Annual Review of Applied Linguistics,* 36, 5–33. https://doi.org/10.1017/S0267190515000057

Long, M. H. (2017). Problems in Second Language Acquisition. *Problems in Second Language Acquisition*, 1–201. https://doi.org/10.4324/9781315089447/PROBLEMS-SLA-MICHAEL-LONG

Long, M. H. & Doughty, C. J. (2009). The Handbook of Language Teaching. In *The Handbook of Language Teaching*. New York: Wiley Blackwell. https://doi.org/10.1002/9781444315783

Long, M. H. & Porter, P. A. (1985). Group Work, Interlanguage Talk, and Second Language Acquisition. *TESOL Quarterly*, 19(2), 207–28. https://doi.org/10.2307/3586827

Lopes, A. (2016). PETALL: A European Project on Technology-Mediated TBLT. *CALL Communities and Culture. Short Papers from EUROCALL 2016*, 290–4.

Lord, G. (2008). Podcasting Communities and Second Language Pronunciation. *Foreign Language Annals*, 41(2), 364–79.

Lys, F. (2013). The Development of Advanced Learner Oral Proficiency Using iPads. *Language Learning & Technology*, 17, 94–116.

Mackey, A. (2006). Feedback, Noticing and Instructed Second Language Learning. *Applied Linguistics*, 27(3), 405–30. https://doi.org/10.1093/APPLIN/AMI051

Mackey, A., Gass, S., & McDonough, K. (2000). How do Learners Perceive Interactional Feedback? *Studies in Second Language Acquisition*, 22(4), 471–97. https://doi.org/10.1017/S0272263100004010

Mehri Ghahfarokhi, M. & Tavakoli, M. (2020). The Effect of Technology-Mediated Reading Comprehension Tasks on Autonomy and Metacognitive Strategy Use by Iranian EFL Intermediate Learners. *Journal of Modern Research in English Language Studies*, 7(3), 45–69. https://doi.org/10.30479/jmrels.2020.11739.1459

Miller, L., Hafner, C. A., & Fun, C. N. K. (2012). Project-Based Learning in a Technologically Enhanced Learning Environment for Second Language Learners: Students' Perceptions. *E-Learning and Digital Media*, 9(2), 183–95. https://doi.org/10.2304/elea.2012.9.2.183

Milliner, B. (2017). One Year of Extensive Reading on Smartphones: A Report. *JALT Call Journal*, 13(1), 49–58.

Milton, J. (2002). Literature Review in Languages, Technology and Learning Literature Review in Languages, Technology and Learning. In *Futurelab*.

Mochizuki, N. & Ortega, L. (2008). Balancing Communication and Grammar in Beginning-Level Foreign Language Classrooms: A Study of Guided Planning and Relativization. *Language Teaching Research*, 12, 11–37. https://doi.org/10.1177/1362168807084492

Montero Perez, M. (2020). Multimodal Input in SLA Research. *Studies in Second Language Acquisition*, 42(3), 653–63. https://doi.org/10.1017/S0272263120000145

Montero Perez, M. (2022). Second or Foreign Language Learning through Watching Audio-Visual Input and the Role of On-Screen Text. *Language Teaching*, 55(2), 163–92. https://doi.org/10.1017/S0261444821000501

Montero Perez, M., Peters, E., & Desmet, P. (2014). Is Less More? Effectiveness and Perceived Usefulness of Keyword and Full Captioned Video for L2

Listening Comprehension. *ReCALL*, 26(1), 21–43. https://doi.org/10.1017/S0958344013000256

Moorhouse, B. L. & Kohnke, L. (2021). Responses of the English-Language-Teaching Community to the COVID-19 Pandemic. https://Doi-Org.Ezproxy.Unicatt.It/10.1177/00336882211053052, 52(3), 359–78. https://doi.org/10.1177/00336882211053052

Morgana, V. (2018). The iPad as Mediating Tool to Support EFL Speaking Skills. *International Journal of English and Education,* 7(4), 189–98.

Morgana, V. (2021). Project-Based English Language Learning through Multimodal Videos: An Online Learning Case Study. In M. Thomas & K. Yamazaki (Eds.), *Project-Based Language Learning and CALL - from Virtual Exchange to Social Justice.* Sheffield, UK: Equinox eBooks Publishing.

Morgana, V. & Pavesi, C. (2021). Effects of an Extensive E-Book Reading Programme on Middle School EFL Students. *Mobile Assisted Language Learning across Educational Contexts,* 61–80. https://doi.org/10.4324/9781003087984-4

Morgana, V. & Shrestha, P. N. (2018). Investigating Students' and Teachers' Perceptions of Using the iPad in an Italian English as a Foreign Language Classroom. *International Journal of Computer-Assisted Language Learning and Teaching,* 8(3). https://doi.org/10.4018/IJCALLT.2018070102

Morgana, V. & Thomas, M. (2023). Technology-Mediated Writing Tasks in the Online English Classroom: Focus on Form via Synchronous Videoconferencing. In Sadeghi, K., M. Thomas & F. Gadheri (Eds.), *Technology-Enhanced Language Teaching and Learning: Lessons from the Covid-19 Pandemic.* Bloomsbury. London.

Motteram, G. (2013). *Innovations in Learning Technologies for English Language Teaching.* London: British Council. http://man.ac.uk/04Y6Bo

Motteram, G. & Thomas, M. (2010). Afterword: Future Directions for Technology-mediated Tasks. In *Task-Based Language Learning and Teaching with Technology* (pp. 218–37).

Naismith, L., Lonsdale, P., Vavoula, G., & Sharples, M. (2004). Literature Review in Mobile Technologies and Learning. *Educational Technology*, 11, 1–25. http://citeseerx.ist.psu.edu/viewdoc/download?doi=10.1.1.136.2203&rep=rep1&type=pdf

Nakanishi, T. (2015). A Meta-Analysis of Extensive Reading Research. *TESOL Quarterly*, 49(1), 6–37. https://doi.org/10.1002/TESQ.157

Neumann, M. M. & Neumann, D. L. (2014). Touch Screen Tablets and Emergent Literacy. *Early Childhood Education Journal*, 42, 231–39.

Nielson, K. B. (2014). Evaluation of an Online, Task-Based Chinese Course. In *Technology-Mediated TBLT* (pp. 295–322). Amsterdam: John Benjamins.

Norris, J. M. (2009). Task-Based Teaching and Testing. In M.H. Long & C.J. Doughty (Eds.) *The Handbook of Language Teaching* (pp. 578–94). New York: Blackwell Publishing.

Norris, J. M. (2016). Current Uses for Task-Based Language Assessment. *Annual Review of Applied Linguistics*, 36, 230–44. https://doi.org/10.1017/S0267190516000027

Nunan, D. (1988). The Learner-Centred Curriculum: A Study in Second language Teaching. In *booksgooglecom*. Cambridge, UK: Cambridge University Press.

Nunan, D. (1991). Communicative Tasks and the Language Curriculum. *TESOL Quarterly*, 25, 279. https://doi.org/10.2307/3587464

Nunan, D. (2004). *Task-Based Language Teaching*. Cambridge, UK: Cambridge University Press. https://doi.org/10.1017/CBO9780511667336

Ogilvie, G. & Dunn, W. (2010). Taking Teacher Education to Task: Exploring the Role of Teacher Education in Promoting the Utilisation of Task-Based Language Teaching. *Language Teaching Research*, 14(2), 161–81. https://doi.org/10.1177/1362168809353875

Olofsson, A. D., Ola Lindberg, J., Fransson, G., & Hauge, T. E. (2015). Uptake and Use of Digital Technologies in Primary and Secondary Schools – A Thematic Review of Research. *Nordic Journal of Digital Literacy*, 2015, (4), 103–21. https://doi.org/10.18261/ISSN1891-943X-2015-JUBILEUMSNUMMER-08

Ortega, L. (1999). Planning and Focus on Form in L2 Oral Performance. *Studies in Second Language Acquisition*, 21(1), 109–48. https://doi.org/10.1017/s0272263199001047

Oskoz, A. & Elola, I. (2014). Promoting Foreign Language Collaborative Writing through the Use of Web 2.0 Tools and Tasks. In M. González-Lloret & L. Ortega (Eds.), *Technology-Mediated TBLT* (pp. 115–48). Amsterdam: John Benjamins Publishing Company.

Oskoz, A. & Elola, I. (2016). Digital Stories: Bringing Multimodal Texts to the Spanish Writing Classroom. *ReCALL*, 28(3), 326–42. https://doi.org/10.1017/S0958344016000094

Park, M. (2012). Implementing Computer-Assisted Task-Based Language Teaching in the Korean Secondary EFL Context. In C. A. Shehadeh, A. & Coombe (Ed.), *Task-based Language Teaching in Foreign Language Contexts: Research and Implementation* (Vol. 4) (pp. 215–40). Amsterdam: John Benjamins Publishing Company. https://doi.org/10.1075/tblt.4.14par

Park, M. (2015). Development and Validation of Virtual Interactive Tasks for An Aviation English Assessment.

Park, S. (2010). The Influence of Pretask Instructions and Pretask Planning on Focus on Form during Korean EFL Task-Based Interaction. *Language Teaching Research*, 14(1). https://doi.org/10.1177/1362168809346491

Payne, J. S. (2004). Making the Most of Synchronous and Asynchronous Discussion in Foreign Language Instruction. *Teaching with Technology*, 171–9.

Pegrum, M., Oakley, G., & Faulkner, R. (2013). Schools Going Mobile: A Study of the Adoption of Mobile Handheld Technologies in Western Australian Independent Schools. *Australasian Journal of Educational Technology*, 29(1). https://doi.org/10.14742/ajet.64

Pellerin, M. (2014). Language Tasks Using Touch Screen and Mobile Technologies: Reconceptualizing Task-Based CALL for Young Language Learners. *Canadian Journal of Learning & Technology*, 40(1), 1–23.

Pellettieri, J. (2010). Online Chat in the Foreign Language Classroom: From Research to Pedagogy. *Mextesol Journal*, 34(1), 41–57.

Perez, M. M. & Rodgers, M. P. (2019). Video and Language Learning. *The Language Learning Journal*, 47(4), 403–6. https://doi.org/10.1080/09571736.2019.1629099

Peters, E. (2018). The Effect of Out-of-Class Exposure to English Language Media on Learners' Vocabulary Knowledge. *ITL - International Journal of Applied Linguistics*, 169(1), 142–68. https://doi.org/10.1075/ITL.00010.PET

Pigada, M. (2006). R. in a F. L. 18 (1), 1–28., & Schmitt, N. (2006). Vocabulary Acquisition from Extensive Reading: A Case Study. *Reading in a Foreign Language*, 18(1), 1–28.

Plonsky, L. & Kim, Y. (2016). Task-Based Learner Production: A Substantive and Methodological Review. *Annual Review of Applied Linguistics*, 36, 73–97. https://doi.org/10.1017/S0267190516000015

Power, Tom & Shrestha, P. (2009). Is There a Role for Mobile Technologies in Open and Distance Language Learning? An Exploration in the Context of Bangladesh. In *8th International Language and Development Conference*, 23–25 June 2009, Dhaka, Bangladesh.

Prensky, M. (2001). Digital Natives, Digital Immigrants Part 1. *On the Horizon*, 9(5), 1–6. https://doi.org/10.1108/10748120110424816/FULL/XML

Pujadas, G. & Muñoz, C. (2019). Extensive Viewing of Captioned and Subtitled TV Series: A Study of L2 Vocabulary Learning by Adolescents. *The Language Learning Journal*, 47(4), 479–96. https://doi.org/10.1080/09571736.2019.1616806

Richards, J. C. (2006). Communicative Language Teaching Today. In *Language Teaching*, 25. https://doi.org/10.2307/3587463

Richards, J. C. & Rodgers, T. S. (2001). Approaches and Methods in Language Teaching. *ELT Journal*, Vol. 57, 305–8).

Richards, K. (2003). *Qualitative Inquiry in TESOL*. Palgrave, Basingstoke: Palgrave Macmillan.

Robin, B. R. & McNeil, S. G. (2019). Digital Storytelling. In *The International Encyclopedia of Media Literacy* (pp. 1–8). New York: Wiley. https://doi.org/10.1002/9781118978238.ieml0056

Ryu, J. & Lee, B. (2018). Effects of Task Complexity and Planning on L2 Speaking Performances and Focus on Form. *Korean Journal of Applied Linguistics*, 34(4). https://doi.org/10.17154/kjal.2018.12.34.4.255

Samuda, V. & Bygate, M. (2008). *Tasks in Second Language Learning*. UK: Palgrave Macmillan. https://doi.org/10.1057/9780230596429

Sandberg, J., Maris, M., & De Geus, K. (2011). Mobile English Learning: An Evidence-Based Study with Fifth Graders. *Computers and Education*, 57, 1334–47.

Sarani, A. & Sahebi, L. F. (2012). The Impact of Task-Based Approach on Vocabulary Learning in ESP Courses. *English Language Teaching*, 5(10), 118–28. https://doi.org/10.5539/elt.v5n10p118

Sasaki, M. & Hirose, K. (1996). Explanatory Variables for EFL Students' Expository Writing. *Language Learning*, 46(1), 137–68. https://doi.org/10.1111/j.1467-1770.1996.tb00643.x

Sato, R. (2010). Perspectives Reconsidering the Effectiveness and Suitability of PPP and TBLT in the Japanese EFL Classroom. *JALT Journal*, 32(2).

Sauro, S. (2009). Computer-Mediated Corrective Feedback and the Development of L2 Grammar. *Language Learning and Technology*, 13(1), 96–120.

Sauro, S. (2012). L2 Performance in Text-Chat and Spoken Discourse. *System*, 40(3), 335–48.

Sauro, S. J. (2014). Lessons from the Fandom: Technology-Mediated Tasks for Language Learning. In M. González-Lloret & L. Ortega (Eds.), *Technology-Mediated TBLT* (pp. 239–62). Amsterdam: John Benjamins Publishing Company.

Seiz Ortiz, R. (2017). New Perspectives on Teaching and Working with Languages in the Digital Era. *The EuroCALL Review*, 24(2), 65. https://doi.org/10.4995/eurocall.2016.6516

Sekiguchi, S. (2011). Investigating Effects of the iPad on Japanese EFL Students' Self-Regulated Study. *International Conference 'ICT for Language Learning'*, 4–7.

Sharafi-Nejad, M., Raftari, S., Ismail, S. A. M. M., & Eng, L. S. (2016). The Effects of Pre-Task Planning on Iranian EFL Learners' Accuracy of Writing Performance. *Journal of Studies in Education*, 6(4). https://doi.org/10.5296/jse.v6i4.10228

Shintani, N. (2012). Repeating Input-Based Tasks with Young Beginner Learners. *RELC Journal*, 43(1), 39–51. https://doi.org/10.1177/0033688212439322

Shintani, N. (2015). The Incidental Grammar Acquisition in Focus on Form and Focus on Forms Instruction for Young Beginner Learners. *Tesol Quarterly*, 49(1), 115–40.

Shintani, N. (2016a). *Input-Based Tasks in Foreign Language Instruction for Young Learners* (Vol. 9). Amsterdam: John Benjamins Publishing Company.

Shintani, N. (2016b). The Effects of Computer-Mediated Synchronous and Asynchronous Direct Corrective Feedback on Writing: A Case Study. *Computer Assisted Language Learning*, 29(3), 517–38. https://doi.org/10.1080/09588221.2014.993400

Shintani, N. & Ellis, R. (2014). Tracking 'Learning Behaviours' in the Incidental Acquisition of Two Dimensional Adjectives by Japanese Beginner Learners of L2 English. *Language Teaching Research*, 18(4), 521–42. https://doi.org/10.1177/1362168813519885

Shintani, N., Aubrey, S., & Donnellan, M. (2016). The Effects of Pre-Task and Post-Task Metalinguistic Explanations on Accuracy in Second Language Writing. *TESOL Quarterly*, 50(4), 945–54.

Shrestha, P. N. (2013). English Language Classroom Practices: Bangladeshi Primary School Children's Perceptions. *RELC Journal*, 44(2), 147–62.

Silverman, D. (2004). Qualitative Research: Theory, Method and Practice. In *Qualitative Research*. https://doi.org/10.1073/pnas.0703993104

Skehan, P. (1998). Task-Based Instruction. *Annual Review of Applied Linguistics*. https://doi.org/10.1017/s0267190500003585

Skehan, P. (2003). Task-Based Instruction. *Language Teaching*, 36(1), 1–14.

Skehan, P. (2022). Tasks Versus Conditions: Two Perspectives on Task Research and their Implications for Pedagogy. *Annual Review of Applied Linguistics*, 36, 34–49. https://doi.org/10.1017/S0267190515000100

Smith, B. (2003). The Use of Communication Strategies in Computer-Mediated Communication. *System*, 31(1), 29–53.

Smith, B. (2004). Computer-Mediated Negotiated Interaction and Lexical Acquisition. *Studies in Second Language Acquisition*, 26(03), 365–98. https://doi.org/10.1017/s027226310426301x

Smith, B. & González-Lloret, M. (2020). Technology-Mediated Task-Based Language Teaching: A Research Agenda. *Language Teaching*, 1–17. https://doi.org/10.1017/S0261444820000233

Solares, M. (2014). Textbooks, Tasks, and Technology: An Action Research Study in a Textbook-bound EFL Context. In *Technology-Mediated TBLT: Researching Technology and Tasks* (pp. 79–114). Amsterdam: John Benjamins Publishing Company. https://doi.org/10.1017/CBO9781107415324.004

Song, Y. (2009). How Can Chinese English Teachers Meet the Challenge of Creating a Learner-Centered, Communicative, Intercultural Classroom to Achieve Optimal Student Learning Outcomes? *Canadian Social Science*, 5(6), 81–91.

Steinberg, L. D. (2014). *Age of Opportunity: Lessons from the New Science of Adolescence*. Boston: Houghton Mifflin Harcourt.

Stockwell, G. (2010). Using Mobile Phones for Vocabulary Activities: Examining the Effect of the Platform. *Language Learning & Technology*, 14(2), 95–110.

Sung, K. Y. (2010). Promoting Communicative Language Learning through Communicative Tasks. *Journal of Language Teaching and Research*, 1(5), 704.

Swain, M. & Lapkin, S. (1995). Problems in Output and the Cognitive Processes They Generate: A Step towards Second Language Learning. *Applied Linguistics*, 16(3), 371–91. https://doi.org/10.1093/APPLIN/16.3.371

Swain, M., Kinnear, P., & Steinman, L. (2011). *Sociocultural Theory in Second Language Education*. Bristol: Multilingual matters.

Swain, M., Skehan, P., & Bygate, M. (2001). Researching Pedagogic Tasks: Second Language Learning, Teaching, and Testing. *Applied Linguistics and Language Study.*, *1982*, x, 258.

Swan, M. (2005). Legislation by Hypothesis: The Case of Task-Based Instruction. *Applied Linguistics*, 26(3), 376–401. https://doi.org/10.1093/APPLIN/AMI013

Sykes, J. M. (2005). Synchronous CMC and Pragmatic Development: Effects of Oral and Written Chat. *CALICO Journal*, 399–431.

Sykes, J. M. & González-Lloret, M. (2020). Exploring the Interface of Interlanguage (L2) Pragmatics and Digital Spaces. *CALICO Journal*, 37(1), I–XV. https://doi.org/10.1558/cj.40433

Takase, A. (2009). *The Effects of Different Types of Extensive Reading Materials on Reading Amount, Attitude, and Motivation*. Japan: Kinki University.

Tang, X. (2019). The Effects of Task Modality on L2 Chinese Learners' Pragmatic Development: Computer-Mediated Written Chat vs. Face-to-Face Oral Chat. *System*, 80, 48–59. https://doi.org/10.1016/j.system.2018.10.011

Tavakoli, H., Lotfi, A. R., & Biria, R. (2017). Effects of CALL-Mediated TBLT on Motivation for L2 Reading. *Cogent Education*, 6(1). https://doi.org/10.1080/2331186X.2019.1580916

Terrell, T. D. & Krashen, S. (1983). *The Natural Approach: Language Acquisition in the Classroom*. Oxford: Pergamon Press.

Thomas, M. (2012). Task-Based Language Teaching and CALL. *Contemporary Computer-Assisted Language Learning*, 341–58.

Thomas, M. & Reinders, H. (Eds.). (2010). *Task-Based Language Learning and Teaching with Technology*. London, UK: Continuum.

Thomas, M. & Reinders, H. (2015). *Contemporary Task-Based Language Teaching in Asia*. New York/London: Bloomsbury.

Thorne, S. (2003). Artifacts and Cultures-of-Use in Intercultural Communication. *Language Learning & Technology*, 7(2), 38–67.

Tragant Mestres, E., Llanes Baró, À., & Pinyana Garriga, À. (2019). Linguistic and Non-Linguistic Outcomes of a Reading-While-Listening Program for Young Learners of English. *Reading and Writing*, 32, 819–38.

Tsai, S. C. (2015). Implementing Courseware as the Primary Mode of Task-Based ESP Instruction: A Case Study of EFL Students, 28(2), 171–86. https://doi.org/10.1080/09588221.2013.818554

Vaca Torres, A. M. & Gómez Rodríguez, L. F. (2017). Increasing EFL Learners' Oral Production at a Public School through Project-Based Learning. *Profile Issues in Teachers' Professional Development*, 19(2), 57–71. https://doi.org/10.15446/profile.v19n2.59889

Van De Guchte, M., Braaksma, M., Rijlaarsdam, G., & Bimmel, P. (2015). Learning New Grammatical Structures in Task-Based Language Learning: The Effects of Recasts and Prompts. *The Modern Language Journal*, 99(2), 246–62.

Van de Guchte, M., Braaksma, M., Rijlaarsdam, G., & Bimmel, P. (2016). Focus on Form through Task Repetition in TBLT. *Language Teaching Research*, 20(3), 300–20.

Van de Guchte, M., Rijlaarsdam, G., Braaksma, M., & Bimmel, P. (2019). Focus on Language Versus Content in the Pre-Task: Effects of Guided Peer-Video Model Observations on Task Performance. *Language Teaching Research*, 23(3), 310–29.

Van den Branden, K. (Ed.). (2006). *Task-Based Language Education: From Theory to Practice*. Ernst Klett Sprachen.

van den Branden, K. & van Gorp, K. (2021). Implementing Task-Based Language Education in Primary Education. Lessons Learnt from the Flemish Experience. *Language Teaching for Young Learners*, 3(1), 3–27. https://doi.org/10.1075/ltyl.20013.bra

van den Branden, K., van Gorp, K., & Verhelst, M. (2009). *Tasks in Action: Task-Based Language Education from a Classroom-Based Perspective*. Cambridge, UK: Cambridge Scholars Publishing.

van Gorp, K. & Bogaert, N. (2006). Developing Language Tasks for Primary and Secondary Education. In *Task-Based Language Education: From Theory to Practice* (pp. 76–105).

van Gorp, K. & Deygers, B. (2013). Task-Based Language Assessment. In A. J. Kunnan (Ed.), *The Companion to Language Assessment: Vol.II. Approaches and Development: Vol. 2*. (pp. 578–93). New York: Wiley. https://doi.org/10.1002/9781118411360.wbcla058

Vandergrift, L. & Cross, J. (2014). Captioned Video: How Much Listening Is Really Going On. *Contact*, 40(3), 31–3.

Vanderplank, R. (2016). Captioned Media in Foreign Language Learning and Teaching. *Captioned Media in Foreign Language Learning and Teaching*. https://doi.org/10.1057/978-1-137-50045-8

Viberg, O. & Grönlund, Å. (2012). Mobile Assisted Language Learning: A Literature Review. *In Proceedings of the 11th International Conference on Mobile and Contextual Learning*, 1–8.

Vygotsky, L. S. (1978). Mind in Society: The Development of Higher Psychological Processes. In *Mind in Society The Development of Higher Psychological Processes: Vol. Mind in So*.

Wagener, D. (2006). Promoting Independent Learning Skills Using Video on Digital Language Laboratories. *Computer Assisted Language Learning*, 19(4–5), 279–86. https://doi.org/10.1080/09588220601043180

Waring, R. & Takaki, M. (2003). At What Rate Do Learners Learn and Retain New Vocabulary from Reading a Graded Reader? *Reading in a Foreign Language*, 15, 130–63.

Warschauer, M. (1997). Computer-Mediated Collaborative Learning: Theory and Practice. *The Modern Language Journal*, 81(4), 470–81. https://doi.org/10.1111/j.1540-4781.1997.tb05514.x

Warschauer, M. (2000). The Changing Global Economy and the Future of English Teaching. *TESOL Quarterly*. https://doi.org/10.2307/3587741

Warschauer, M. (2004). *Technology and Social Inclusion: Rethinking the Digital Divide*. Boston, MA: MIT press.

Warschauer, M. & Healey, D. (1998). Computers and Language Learning: An Overview. *Language Teaching*, 31, 57. https://doi.org/10.1017/S0261444800012970

Webb, S. & Chang, A. C. S. (2015). Second Language Vocabulary Learning through Extensive Reading with Audio Support: How Do Frequency and Distribution of Occurrence Affect Learning? *Language Teaching Research*, 19(6), 667–86. https://doi.org/10.1177/1362168814559800

Wilkins, D. A. (1976). *Notional Syllabuses: A Taxonomy and Its Relevance to Foreign Language Curriculum Development*. Oxford: Oxford University Press.

Williams, C. & Beam, S. (2019). Technology and Writing: Review of Research. *Computers & Education*, 128, 227–42. https://doi.org/10.1016/J.COMPEDU.2018.09.024

Willis, J. (1996). *A Flexible Framework for Task-Based Learning*. New York: Longman.

Willis, J. & Willis, D. (2013). *Doing Task-Based Teaching*. Oxford: Oxford University Press.

Winke, P. M. (2014). Formative, Task-Based Oral Assessments in an Advanced Chinese-language Class. In *Technology-Mediated TBLT* (pp. 263–94). Amsterdam: John Benjamins Publishing Company.

Winke, P., Gass, S., & Sydorenko, T. (2010). The Effects of Captioning Videos Used for Foreign Language Listening Activities. *Language Learning and Technology*, 14(1), 65–86.

Wisniewska, N. & Mora, J. C. (2020). Can Captioned Video Benefit Second Language Pronunciation? *Studies in Second Language Acquisition*, 42(3), 599–624. https://doi.org/10.1017/S0272263120000029

Wood, D., Bruner, J. S., & Ross, G. (1976). The Role of Tutoring in Problem Solving. *Journal of Child Psychology and Psychiatry, and Allied Disciplines*, 17, 89–100.

Woollard John, P. A. (2010). Constructivism and Social Learning. In *Zhurnal Eksperimental'noi i Teoreticheskoi Fiziki*. New York: Routledge.

Wrigglesworth, J. (2019). Using Smartphones to Extend Interaction beyond the EFL Classroom. *Computer Assisted Language Learning*. https://doi.org/10.1080/09588221.2019.1569067

Yamashita, J. (2013). *Effects of Extensive Reading on Reading Attitudes in a Foreign Language*. 25(2). http://nflrc.hawaii.edu/rfl

Yanguas, I. (2009). *Multimedia Glosses and Their Effect on L2 Text Comprehension and Vocabulary Learning*. 13(2), 48–67.

Yeh, H. C., Chang, W. Y., Chen, H. Y., & Heng, L. (2021). Effects of Podcast-making on College Students' English-Speaking Skills in Higher Education. *Educational Technology Research and Development*, 69, 2845–67. https://doi.org/10.1007/s11423-021-10026-3.

Yeldham, M. (2018). Viewing L2 Captioned Videos: What's in It for the Listener? *Computer Assisted Language Learning*, 31(4), 367–89. https://doi.org/10.1080/09588221.2017.1406956

Zahar, R., Cobb, T., & Spada, N. (2006). Acquiring Vocabulary through Reading: Effects of Frequency and Contextual Richness. *The Canadian Modern Language Review*, 57(4), 541–65. https://doi.org/10.3138/CMLR.57.4.541

Zheng, X. & Borg, S. (2014). Task-Based Learning and Teaching in China: Secondary School Teachers' Beliefs and Practices. *Language Teaching Research*, 18(2), 205–21. https://doi.org/10.1177/1362168813505941

Ziegler, N. (2016). Taking Technology to Task: Technology-Mediated TBLT, Performance, and Production. *Annual Review of Applied Linguistics*. https://doi.org/10.1017/S0267190516000039

Ziegler, N. (2018). Pre-Task Planning in L2 Text-Chat: Examining Learners' Process and Performance. *Language Learning and Technology*, 22(3), 193–213.

Ziegler, N. & González-Lloret, M. (2022). The Routledge Handbook of Second Language Acquisition and Technology. *The Routledge Handbook of Second Language Acquisition and Technology*. https://doi.org/10.4324/9781351117586

Index

accuracy 15, 21, 30, 43, 51, 55, 65–6, 76–8, 80–3, 85–8, 131, 144–5, 157
assessment 9, 20, 24–6, 47–9, 54, 73, 96, 98–9, 102–3, 105–8, 110, 117, 122, 131, 134, 136, 139, 141, 146, 158, 167
authenticity 25, 136

cognitive-interaction 9, 27, 34, 36, 38–9, 155
collaboration 35, 38, 52, 119, 143, 146, 165
Common European Framework of Reference for Languages 6, 26, 82
communication 1, 3, 5, 14–16, 23–5, 28–31, 38, 47, 49, 52–3, 96, 106, 133, 139–40, 153, 167
communicative approach 14, 24, 76
communicative task 22, 47
completion of a task 4
complexity 32–3, 42–4, 51, 55, 66, 76–8, 80–3, 85–8, 136, 157, 164
computer-assisted language learning (CALL) 1, 9, 19, 22, 27, 41–2, 49–52, 55, 59, 76, 96, 133, 149
computer language teaching (CLT) 13–15, 24
curriculum 3, 5, 10, 20–2, 25–6, 39, 43–4, 48–9, 52, 54–5, 66, 71–2, 82, 91, 100, 110, 114, 118, 128, 132, 135, 143, 153, 161, 163

descriptive analysis 7
digital and blended settings 2
digital literacy 8, 19, 44–6, 51–2, 99, 116, 118, 128, 136–7, 165

e-books 8–9, 94–6, 99–102, 108
English as a foreign language (EFL) 1–2, 5, 7–8, 10, 14, 18–19, 21, 24–5, 29, 37, 39, 42, 45–7, 49, 51, 54, 56, 60, 63, 66, 71, 73, 76–82, 85, 88–91, 93–8, 102–3, 105, 108–110, 113–15, 117–18, 120, 128–9, 131–2, 134–6, 143–4, 147, 153–7, 159, 161–5
examination 6, 64–6, 68, 72, 132, 139, 158
explicit grammar teaching 3, 157
explicit learning 30–1

feedback 7, 21, 25, 28, 30, 32, 46, 48, 67, 85, 90, 134, 137, 140, 143, 145–6, 156, 158, 162, 165
fluency 9, 15, 31, 43, 59, 77–8, 80, 86, 88, 145, 147, 149, 157
focus-on-form 22–4
focus on meaning 127
formal language learning 2

grammatical awareness 3

implicit learning 30–1, 34
innovative practices 3, 70
input 5, 17, 20–1, 28–31, 33–4, 39, 46, 60, 65, 67, 77, 84, 89–91, 97, 101, 114–16, 127, 138, 146, 153, 155–6, 162, 166
integration 2–3, 8, 14, 20, 22, 43, 48–51, 53–5, 70–1, 75, 91, 132, 135, 143, 153–4, 156, 158, 160–1, 163
interaction 6, 26, 28–34, 39, 44, 47, 52, 116, 127, 132–3, 136–7, 139–40, 145–8, 155, 162, 165–6
issues 2–3, 5, 9, 13, 24–5, 29, 35, 37, 42, 54, 64, 68, 70, 94, 101, 115, 121, 124, 135, 160

language awareness 3–4, 90, 116, 122, 128, 144, 153
language awareness activities 3
language competence 99, 120, 122, 124–5, 143
language education 1–2, 7, 24, 55, 63, 72–3, 75, 162
language forms 3, 21–2

language learning 1, 3, 5–6, 13–16, 18–19, 22, 24, 26–9, 33–4, 36–9, 41–2, 46, 49–50, 52–4, 56, 64, 70, 76, 91, 109, 117, 121, 123, 126, 129, 132, 137, 144, 146, 148, 156, 158, 160–3, 166–7
language skills 44, 55
language teacher 1
learning processes 8, 32, 116–17
linguistic competence 23, 51, 70, 136
listening 4–9, 19, 21, 29, 36, 39, 44, 49, 54, 60, 64, 82, 84, 89, 93, 98, 109, 113–29, 134, 138, 145, 154–5, 157–9, 161–2, 164
lower-intermediate learners 65, 116
L2 development 28, 32

main task 21
meaning 1, 5, 13, 15–20, 23–4, 28, 31, 33–4, 37, 43, 53, 59–60, 76–7, 89, 91, 104–6, 108, 127, 135–6, 147, 149, 153, 156–7, 162
mobile-assisted language learning (MALL) 6–7, 22, 42, 47, 49–52, 55, 71, 165–6
mobile devices 2, 4, 6–7, 9, 22, 36–7, 50, 55, 94–5, 97, 99–100, 109, 131, 147, 150–1, 156, 158–9, 161, 163, 165–6
multimodal approach 8

needs 3, 18–20, 25–6, 28, 30, 43, 45–6, 48–9, 51–2, 54, 63, 91, 94, 97–8, 114, 128, 131, 136, 148, 154, 159, 165
noticing 21, 24, 30–2, 34, 77, 82, 101, 106, 126, 133, 138, 140, 145

output 17, 19, 28, 32, 53, 115, 134, 146, 148, 153

pedagogic tasks 18, 24
personalization 36, 143
planning 4, 9, 21, 23, 35, 43, 45–9, 54, 65, 69, 76, 78–85, 89–91, 116, 126, 134, 138, 143, 145–7, 157, 162
post-task 21, 23, 26, 48, 76–7, 97, 101, 123–4, 127, 138, 157
presentation-practice-production (PPP) 3
pre-task 9, 21, 23, 29, 65, 69, 75–86, 89–91, 96, 101, 114, 116–18, 120, 122–3, 125–7, 138, 145, 155, 157

principles of TBLT 3, 28, 69, 167
productive skills 6

reading 5–9, 18, 21, 36, 39, 49, 54–5, 60, 64, 82, 84, 89, 93–103, 105–10, 116, 125, 137–8, 154–5, 159, 161–2, 164
research areas 4

scaffolding 5, 9, 36–9, 50, 108, 118–19, 126, 128, 132–3, 138, 141, 143, 145–6, 148, 155, 159, 164
secondary schools 1, 24, 39, 63–6, 69, 71, 73, 94, 108–10, 129, 167
second language acquisition (SLA) 1, 8, 13, 15, 18, 23, 27–8, 30, 32–3, 38, 41–2, 46, 76, 81, 133, 156, 161, 164
skills 5–9, 17, 19, 25–6, 35–7, 44, 51–4, 60, 66, 68, 75, 81, 93, 96–8, 106, 108–9, 113–16, 120, 122–6, 128, 131–4, 136–8, 140, 144, 146, 148, 150–1, 154–5, 159–60, 162, 164, 166
sociocultural theories 9, 37
speaking 5–9, 19, 35–6, 39, 43, 47–9, 54–5, 59, 64, 93, 98, 115–16, 131–4, 136–47, 149–51, 154–5, 158–62, 164, 166
speaking skills 7, 132–3, 151
state school 2, 165
structural approach 4
student-centred 3, 13, 52, 116, 156
synchronous 82

task-as-process 17
task-as-workplan 16–17, 23
task-based language teaching (TBLT) 1–9, 13–39, 41–55, 59–60, 63–71, 73, 75–7, 86, 90–1, 94, 96–103, 105–10, 113–14, 116–17, 126–9, 131–3, 135–6, 140, 143–8, 151, 153–9, 161–4, 166–7
task design 8, 17, 22, 39, 45–6, 51, 70, 91, 108, 148
task performance 21, 26, 29, 31–2, 53, 60, 75, 77–81, 85, 107, 123, 127, 155, 157, 164, 167
TBLT approach 3, 8, 13–16, 20, 24, 36, 46, 51, 53, 64–6, 68–9, 73, 127, 146–7, 151, 153–4, 158–9, 161–2
TBLT methodology 1, 67, 163
teacher-learner 7

teachers 1–4, 6–9, 13, 18–21, 24–5, 27, 29, 34, 37–9, 41–3, 47–9, 54–6, 60, 63–73, 75–6, 79, 84–5, 90–1, 94, 100, 103, 108–9, 113, 115, 118–21, 124, 127–9, 132–3, 136, 138–40, 142–4, 146–8, 151, 153–63, 165–7
technology-mediated TBLT practices 2, 7, 9, 70, 110, 154, 158, 164
theories 8–9, 27–8, 31–8
t-unit 83, 85, 86–7, 88

vocabulary 6, 9, 29–30, 45, 48, 60, 84, 93–109, 115, 117, 120, 122–5, 127, 139–41, 144, 146, 155, 157, 166

writing 5–8, 19, 25, 30, 33, 35–9, 45, 47, 49, 51, 54–5, 59, 64, 68, 70, 75, 79–81, 83–4, 86, 90, 93, 98, 115, 132, 149, 154–5, 157, 159, 161–2, 164, 166
writing tasks 6–7, 38, 81
written accuracy 9, 82, 89

www.ingramcontent.com/pod-product-compliance
Lightning Source LLC
Chambersburg PA
CBHW052119300426
44116CB00010B/1715